THE D.
OF COMN

MW00986420

THE DAILY BOOK OF
COMMON PRAYER

READINGS AND PRAYERS
THROUGH THE YEAR

Compiled by Owen Collins

WILLIAM B. EERDMANS PUBLISHING COMPANY
GRAND RAPIDS, MICHIGAN / CAMBRIDGE, U.K.

Compilation © 1999 Owen Collins

First published in Great Britain in 1999 by Fount
an imprint of HarperCollins*Religious*
Part of HarperCollins*Publishers*

This edition published in 2000 by
Wm. B. Eerdmans Publishing Co.
255 Jefferson Ave. S.E., Grand Rapids, Michigan 49503 /
P.O. Box 163, Cambridge CB3 9PU U.K.

07 06 05 04 03 02 01 00   7 6 5 4 3 2

Library of Congress Cataloging-in-Publication Data

Church of England.
[Book of common prayer]
The daily book of common prayer : readings and prayers
through the year / compiled by Owen Collins.
p.   cm.
ISBN 0-8028-4711-0 (pbk. : alk. paper)
1. Spiritual life — Church of England — Prayer-books and devotions —
English.   2. Church of England — Prayer-books and devotions —
English.   3. Devotional calendars.   I. Collins, Owens.   II. Title.
BV4501.2.C516 2000
242′.803 — dc21   99-088804

INTRODUCTION

Thomas Cranmer discovered the biblical doctrine of justification by faith alone when he was a student at Cambridge University. When he became Archbishop of Canterbury he used his considerable liturgical talents to ensure that this doctrine was incorporated into the official forms of worship of the reformed Church of England.

The Book of Common Prayer (first published in 1662) is the title given to the traditional service book used in the Church of England and in other churches of the Anglican Communion. It is based largely on the work of Thomas Cranmer, who was the primary author of the Prayer Book of 1549 (revised in 1552). From the many books of medieval worship and prayers Cranmer created a single-volume Prayer Book that contained all the services needed for daily, Sunday and occasional use and also included the Psalms and a lectionary for the whole year.

Using the material in the 1662 Prayer Book, *The Daily Book of Common Prayer* provides a page of readings for every day of the year. No material from outside *The Book of Common Prayer* has been introduced. So all the Bible readings, except the Psalms, use the Authorized Version of the Bible. The Psalms in *The Book of Common Prayer* are not from the Authorized Version, but come from Miles Coverdale's Bible (1535), which was the first whole Bible published in English. It is also known as 'The Great Bible' or 'The Great English Bible'. Coverdale's capacity for beautiful rhythm and phrasing is still widely appreciated today.

Most of the Christian festivals and other special days which are earmarked for special remembrance in *The Book of Common Prayer* are included in *The Daily Book of Common Prayer*. It has been compiled with Easter Day falling on 23 April, which is correct for the year 2000. When the book is used in other years this needs to be borne in mind if you wish to keep your readings in step with the Church calendar.

In addition to readings linked to Easter, Christmas and other parts of the Christian year, *The Daily Book of Common Prayer* has a number of other themes running through it, including 'In Deep Trouble', 'Contrition', 'The Messiah in the Psalms', 'Psalms of Praise and Thanksgiving' and 'Luke's Account of Christ's Passion'.

The Book of Common Prayer states that 'The Psalter shall be read through once every month, as it is there appointed, both for Morning and Evening Prayer.' *The Daily Book of Common Prayer* devotes many days of readings to a psalm or part of a psalm, and also incorporates sections of psalms on other days.

The Book of Common Prayer contains many inspiring prayers in services which are rarely used today. The most helpful of these are included in the present book and are drawn from such quaint-sounding services as 'A Commination', 'The Churching of Women' and 'The Accession Service'.

The apostle Peter told his readers, 'Grow in the grace and knowledge of our Lord and Saviour Jesus Christ' (2 Peter 3:18). The readings in *The Daily Book of Common Prayer* provide a straightforward way to do this. It faithfully reflects the belief of the compilers of *The Book of Common Prayer* that 'Holy Scripture containeth all things necessary to salvation: so that whatsoever is not read therein, nor may be proved thereby, is not to be required of any man, that it should be believed as an article of the Faith, or be thought requisite or necessary to salvation' (the 'Articles of Religion', Article VI).

Owen Collins

THE CIRCUMCISION OF CHRIST

...his name was called Jesus. St. Luke 2. 21

The Collect
From 'The Circumcision of Christ'

ALMIGHTY God, who madest thy blessed Son to be circumcised, and obedient to the law for man: Grant us the true circumcision of the Spirit; that, our hearts, and all our members, being mortified from all worldly and carnal lusts, we may in all things obey thy blessed will; through the same thy Son Jesus Christ our Lord. Amen.

Psalm 98. *Cantate Domino*

O SING unto the Lord a new song : for he hath done marvellous things.

2. With his own right hand, and with his holy arm : hath he gotten himself the victory.

3. The Lord declared his salvation : his righteousness hath he openly showed in the sight of the heathen.

4. He hath remembered his mercy and truth toward the house of Israel : and all the ends of the world have seen the salvation of our God.

Meditation
But Mary kept all these things, and pondered them in her heart. St. Luke 2. 19

INNER CIRCUMCISION

Circumcision is nothing, and uncircumcision is nothing, but the keeping of the commandments of God. 1 Corinthians 7. 19

The Epistle. Romans 4. 8
From 'The Circumcision of Christ'

BLESSED is the man to whom the Lord will not impute sin. Cometh this blessedness then upon the circumcision only, or upon the uncircumcision also? For we say, that faith was reckoned to Abraham for righteousness. How was it then reckoned? when he was in circumcision, or in uncircumcision? Not in circumcision, but in uncircumcision. And he received the sign of circumcision, a seal of the righteousness of the faith which he had yet being uncircumcised; that he might be the father of all them that believe, though they be not circumcised; that righteousness might be imputed unto them also: And the father of circumcision to them who are not of the circumcision only, but who also walk in the steps of that faith of our father Abraham, which he had being yet uncircumcised. For the promise, that he should be the heir of the world, was not to Abraham, or to his seed, through the law, but through the righteousness of faith. For if they which are of the law be heirs, faith is made void, and the promise made of none effect.

Meditation
Circumcise therefore the foreskin of your heart, and be no more stiff-necked.
Deuteronomy 10. 16

SAVING YOUR SOUL

When the wicked man turneth away from his wickedness that he hath committed, and doeth that which is lawful and right, he shall save his soul alive.
Ezekiel 18. 27

A General Confession
From 'Morning Prayer'

ALMIGHTY and most merciful Father; We have erred, and strayed from thy ways like lost sheep. We have followed too much the devices and desires of our own hearts. We have offended against thy holy laws. We have left undone those things which we ought to have done; And we have done those things which we ought not to have done; And there is no health in us. But thou, O Lord, have mercy upon us, miserable offenders. Spare thou them, O God, who confess their faults. Restore thou them that are penitent; According to thy promises declared unto mankind in Christ Jesu our Lord. And grant, O most merciful Father, for his sake; That we may hereafter live a godly, righteous, and sober life, To the glory of thy holy Name. Amen.

Meditation
If we say that we have no sin, we deceive ourselves, and the truth is not in us. If we confess our sins, he is faithful and just to forgive us our sins, and to cleanse us from all unrighteousness. 1 St. John 1. 8–9

WORSHIP

Rejoice in his holy Name : let the heart of them rejoice that seek the Lord.
Psalm 105. 3

Psalm 105. *Confitemini Domino*

O GIVE thanks unto the Lord, and call upon his Name : tell the people what things he hath done.

2. O let your songs be of him, and praise him : and let your talking be of all his wondrous works.

3. Rejoice in his holy Name : let the heart of them rejoice that seek the Lord.

4. Seek the Lord and his strength : seek his face evermore.

5. Remember the marvellous works that he hath done : his wonders, and the judgements of his mouth,

6. O ye seed of Abraham his servant : ye children of Jacob his chosen.

7. He is the Lord our God : his judgements are in all the world.

FROM 'HOLY COMMUNION'

I T is very meet, right, and our bounden duty, that we should at all times, and in all places, give thanks unto thee, O Lord, Holy Father, Almighty, Everlasting God.

Therefore with Angels and Archangels, and with all the company of heaven, we laud and magnify thy glorious Name; evermore praising thee, and saying, Holy, holy, holy, Lord God of hosts, heaven and earth are full of thy glory : Glory be to thee, O Lord most High. Amen.

THE LORD'S PRAYER

When ye pray, use not vain repetitions, as the heathen do : for they think that they shall be heard for their much speaking. St. Matthew 6. 7

From 'A Catechism'

MY good Child, know this, that thou art not able to do these things of thyself, nor to walk in the Commandments of God, and to serve him, without his special grace; which thou must learn at all times to call for by diligent prayer. Let me hear therefore, if thou canst say the Lord's Prayer.

Answer. Our Father, which art in heaven, Hallowed be thy Name. Thy kingdom come. Thy will be done, in earth as it is in heaven. Give us this day our daily bread. And forgive us our trespasses, As we forgive them that trespass against us. And lead us not into temptation; But deliver us from evil. Amen.

Question. What desirest thou of God in this Prayer?

Answer. I desire my Lord God our heavenly Father, who is the giver of all goodness, to send his grace unto me, and to all people; that we may worship him, serve him, and obey him, as we ought to do. And I pray unto God, that he will send us all things that be needful both for our souls and bodies; and that he will be merciful unto us, and forgive us our sins; and that it will please him to save and defend us in all dangers ghostly and bodily; and that he will keep us from all sin and wickedness, and from our ghostly enemy, and from everlasting death.

THE EPIPHANY

Unto me, who am less than the least of all saints, is this grace given, that I should preach among the Gentiles the unsearchable riches of Christ. Ephesians 3. 8

The Gospel. St. Matthew 2. 1
From 'The Epiphany'

WHEN Jesus was born in Bethlehem of Judaea, in the days of Herod the king, behold, there came wise men from the east to Jerusalem, saying, Where is he that is born King of the Jews? for we have seen his star in the east, and are come to worship him. When Herod the king had heard these things, he was troubled, and all Jerusalem with him ... Then Herod, when he had privily called the wise men, inquired of them diligently what time the star appeared. And he sent them to Bethlehem, and said, Go, and search diligently for the young child, and when ye have found him, bring me word again, that I may come and worship him also. When they had heard the king, they departed; and lo, the star which they saw in the east went before them, till it came and stood over where the young child was. When they saw the star, they rejoiced with exceeding great joy. And when they were come into the house, they saw the young child with Mary his mother, and fell down and worshipped him: and when they had opened their treasures, they presented unto him gifts; gold, and frankincense, and myrrh. And being warned of God in a dream that they should not return to Herod, they departed into their own country another way.

ACKNOWLEDGING SIN

I acknowledge my faults : and my sin is ever before me. Psalm 51. 3

Psalm 51. *Miserere mei, Deus*

HAVE mercy upon me, O God, after thy great goodness : according to the multitude of thy mercies do away mine offences.

2. Wash me throughly from my wickedness : and cleanse me from my sin.

3. For I acknowledge my faults : and my sin is ever before me.

4. Against thee only have I sinned, and done this evil in thy sight : that thou mightest be justified in thy saying, and clear when thou art judged.

5. Behold, I was shapen in wickedness : and in sin hath my mother conceived me.

6. But lo, thou requirest truth in the inward parts : and shalt make me to understand wisdom secretly.

7. Thou shalt purge me with hyssop, and I shall be clean : thou shalt wash me, and I shall be whiter than snow.

8. Thou shalt make me hear of joy and gladness : that the bones which thou hast broken may rejoice.

9. Turn thy face from my sins : and put out all my misdeeds.

10. Make me a clean heart, O God : and renew a right spirit within me.

11. Cast me not away from thy presence : and take not thy holy Spirit from me.

12. O give me the comfort of thy help again : and stablish me with thy free Spirit.

WAITING ON GOD

I am weary of crying; my throat is dry : my sight faileth me for waiting so long upon my God. Psalm 69. 3

Psalm 69. *Salvum me fac*

SAVE me, O God : for the waters are come in, even unto my soul.
2. I stick fast in the deep mire, where no ground is : I am come into deep waters, so that the floods run over me.
3. I am weary of crying; my throat is dry : my sight faileth me for waiting so long upon my God.
4. They that hate me without a cause are more than the hairs of my head : they that are mine enemies, and would destroy me guiltless, are mighty.
5. I paid them the things that I never took : God, thou knowest my simpleness, and my faults are not hid from thee.
6. Let not them that trust in thee, O Lord God of hosts, be ashamed for my cause : let not those that seek thee be confounded through me, O Lord God of Israel.
7. And why? for thy sake have I suffered reproof : shame hath covered my face.

Meditation
The humble shall consider this, and be glad: seek ye after God, and your soul shall live. St. Matthew 6. 8

GRACE TO DO GOD'S WILL

I beseech you therefore, brethren, by the mercies of God, that ye present your bodies a living sacrifice, holy, acceptable unto God, which is your reasonable service.
Romans 12. 1

The Gospel. St. Luke 2. 41
From 'The First Sunday After the Epiphany'

NOW his parents went to Jerusalem every year at the feast of the passover. And when he was twelve years old, they went up to Jerusalem, after the custom of the feast. And when they had fulfilled the days, as they returned, the child Jesus tarried behind in Jerusalem; and Joseph and his mother knew not of it. But they, supposing him to have been in the company, went a day's journey, and they sought him among their kinsfolk and acquaintance. And when they found him not, they turned back again to Jerusalem, seeking him. And it came to pass, that after three days they found him in the temple, sitting in the midst of the doctors, both hearing them, and asking them questions. And all that heard him were astonished at his understanding and answers. And when they saw him, they were amazed: and his mother said unto him, Son, why hast thou thus dealt with us? behold, thy father and I have sought thee sorrowing. And he said unto them, How is it that ye sought me? wist ye not that I must be about my Father's business? And they understood not the saying which he spake unto them. And he went down with them, and came to Nazareth, and was subject unto them: but his mother kept all these sayings in her heart. And Jesus increased in wisdom, and stature, and in favour with God and man.

MORNING PRAYER (1)

Turn thy face from my sins : and put out all my misdeeds. Psalm 51. 9

PSALM 95. *Venite, exultemus*

O COME, let us sing unto the Lord : let us heartily rejoice in the strength of our salvation.

2. Let us come before his presence with thanksgiving : and shew ourselves glad in him with psalms.

3. For the Lord is a great God : and a great King above all gods.

4. In his hand are all the corners of the earth : and the strength of the hills is his also.

5. The sea is his, and he made it : and his hands prepared the dry land.

6. O come, let us worship and fall down : and kneel before the Lord our Maker.

7. For he is the Lord our God : and we are the people of his pasture, and the sheep of his hand.

8. To-day if ye will hear his voice, harden not your hearts : as in the provocation, and as in the day of temptation in the wilderness;

9. When your fathers tempted me : proved me, and saw my works.

10. Forty years long was I grieved with this generation, and said : It is a people that do err in their heart, and they have not known my ways;

11. Unto whom I sware in my wrath that they should not enter into my rest.

PRAISE THE LORD

Praise the Lord, O my soul; while I live will I praise the Lord : yea, as long as I have any being, I will sing praises unto my God. Psalm 146. 1

Te Deum Laudamus
From 'Morning Prayer'

WE praise thee, O God: we acknowledge thee to be the Lord.

All the earth doth worship thee: the Father everlasting.
To thee all Angels cry aloud: the Heavens, and all the Powers therein.
To thee Cherubim, and Seraphim: continually do cry,
Holy, Holy, Holy: Lord God of Sabaoth;
Heaven and earth are full of the Majesty: of thy Glory.
The glorious company of the Apostles: praise thee.
The goodly fellowship of the Prophets: praise thee.
The noble army of Martyrs: praise thee.
The holy Church throughout all the world: doth acknowledge thee;
The Father: of an infinite Majesty;
Thine honourable, true: and only Son;
Also the Holy Ghost: the Comforter.
Thou art the King of Glory: O Christ.
Thou art the everlasting Son: of the Father.

HELP US, LORD

Day by day: we magnify thee. From 'Te Deum Laudamus'

Te Deum Laudamus
From 'Morning Prayer'

WE therefore pray thee, help thy servants: whom thou hast redeemed with thy precious blood.

Make them to be numbered with thy Saints: in glory everlasting.

O Lord, save thy people: and bless thine heritage.

Govern them: and lift them up for ever.

Day by day: we magnify thee;

And we worship thy Name: ever world without end.

Vouchsafe, O Lord: to keep us this day without sin.

O Lord, have mercy upon us: have mercy upon us.

O Lord, let thy mercy lighten upon us: as our trust is in thee.

O Lord, in thee have I trusted: let me never be confounded.

The Lord's Prayer
From 'Morning Prayer'

OUR Father, which art in heaven, Hallowed be thy Name. Thy kingdom come. Thy will be done, in earth as it is in heaven. Give us this day our daily bread. And forgive us our trespasses, As we forgive them that trespass against us. And lead us not into temptation; But deliver us from evil: For thine is the kingdom, The power, and the glory, For ever and ever. Amen.

THE UNITY OF THE CHURCH

O pray for the peace of Jerusalem : they shall prosper that love thee. Psalm 122. 6

A Prayer for Unity
From 'The Accession Service'

O GOD, the Father of our Lord Jesus Christ, our only Saviour, the Prince of Peace; Give us grace seriously to lay to heart the great dangers we are in by our unhappy divisions. Take away all hatred and prejudice, and whatsoever else may hinder us from godly Union and Concord: that, as there is but one Body, and one Spirit, and one Hope of our Calling, one Lord, one Faith, one Baptism, one God and Father of us all, so we may henceforth be all of one heart, and of one soul, united in one holy bond of Truth and Peace, of Faith and Charity, and may with one mind and one mouth glorify thee; through Jesus Christ our Lord. Amen.

Psalm 122. *Laetatus sum*

I WAS glad when they said unto me : We will go into the house of the Lord.

2. Our feet shall stand in thy gates : O Jerusalem.

3. Jerusalem is built as a city : that is at unity in itself.

4. For thither the tribes go up, even the tribes of the Lord : to testify unto Israel, to give thanks unto the Name of the Lord.

5. For there is the seat of judgement : even the seat of the house of David.

6. O pray for the peace of Jerusalem : they shall prosper that love thee.

MISSIONARY WORK

*Confounded be all they that worship carved images, and that delight in vain gods :
worship him, all ye gods.* Psalm 97. 7

Psalm 97. *Dominus regnavit*

THE Lord is King, the earth may be glad thereof : yea, the multitude of
the isles may be glad thereof.

2. Clouds and darkness are round about him : righteousness and judgement
are the habitation of his seat.

3. There shall go a fire before him : and burn up his enemies on every side.

4. His lightnings gave shine unto the world : the earth saw it, and was afraid.

5. The hills melted like wax at the presence of the Lord : at the presence of
the Lord of the whole earth.

6. The heavens have declared his righteousness : and all the peoples have
seen his glory.

7. Confounded be all they that worship carved images, and that delight in
vain gods : worship him, all ye gods.

8. Sion heard of it, and rejoiced : and the daughters of Judah were glad,
because of thy judgements, O Lord.

9. For thou, Lord, art higher than all that are in the earth : thou art exalted
far above all gods.

10. O ye that love the Lord, see that ye hate the thing which is evil : the
Lord preserveth the souls of his saints; he shall deliver them from the hand
of the ungodly.

PRAYING FOR OTHERS

I thank my God upon every remembrance of you. Philippians 1. 3

A Collect or Prayer For All Conditions of Men
From 'Prayers and Thanksgivings, upon Several Occasions'

O GOD, the Creator and Preserver of all mankind, we humbly beseech thee for all sorts and conditions of men; that thou wouldest be pleased to make thy ways known unto them, thy saving health unto all nations. More especially, we pray for the good estate of the Catholick Church; that it may be so guided and governed by thy good Spirit, that all who profess and call themselves Christians may be led into the way of truth, and hold the faith in unity of spirit, in the bond of peace, and in righteousness of life. Finally, we commend to thy fatherly goodness all those, who are any ways afflicted, or distressed, in mind, body, or estate; that it may please thee to comfort and relieve them, according to their several necessities, giving them patience under their sufferings, and a happy issue out of all their afflictions. And this we beg for Jesus Christ his sake. Amen.

THE WEDDING AT CANA

And both Jesus was called, and his disciples, to the marriage. St. John 2. 2

The Gospel. St. John 2. 1
From 'The Second Sunday After the Epiphany'

AND the third day there was a marriage in Cana of Galilee, and the mother of Jesus was there. And both Jesus was called, and his disciples, to the marriage. And when they wanted wine, the mother of Jesus saith unto him, They have no wine. Jesus saith unto her, Woman, what have I to do with thee? mine hour is not yet come. His mother saith unto the servants, Whatsoever he saith unto you, do it. And there were set there six water-pots of stone, after the manner of the purifying of the Jews, containing two or three firkins apiece. Jesus saith unto them, Fill the water-pots with water. And they filled them up to the brim. And he saith unto them, Draw out now, and bear unto the governor of the feast. And they bare it. When the ruler of the feast had tasted the water that was made wine, and knew not whence it was, (but the servants which drew the water knew,) the governor of the feast called the bridegroom, and saith unto him, Every man at the beginning doth set forth good wine, and when men have well drunk, then that which is worse: but thou hast kept the good wine until now. This beginning of miracles did Jesus in Cana of Galilee, and manifested forth his glory, and his disciples believed on him.

USING GOD'S GIFTS

Distributing to the necessity of saints; given to hospitality. Romans 12. 13

The Epistle. Romans 12. 6
From 'The Second Sunday After the Epiphany'

HAVING then gifts differing according to the grace that is given to us, whether prophecy, let us prophesy according to the proportion of faith; or ministry, let us wait on our ministering; or he that teacheth, on teaching; or he that exhorteth, on exhortation: he that giveth, let him do it with simplicity; he that ruleth, with diligence; he that sheweth mercy, with cheerfulness. Let love be without dissimulation. Abhor that which is evil, cleave to that which is good. Be kindly affectioned one to another with brotherly love, in honour preferring one another: not slothful in business; fervent in spirit; serving the Lord; rejoicing in hope; patient in tribulation; continuing instant in prayer; distributing to the necessity of saints; given to hospitality. Bless them which persecute you; bless, and curse not. Rejoice with them that do rejoice, and weep with them that weep. Be of the same mind one towards another. Mind not high things, but condescend to men of low estate.

From 'The Ordering of Deacons'

PREVENT us, O Lord, in all our doings with thy most gracious favour, and further us with thy continual help; that in all our works begun, continued, and ended in thee, we may glorify thy holy Name, and finally by thy mercy obtain everlasting life; through Jesus Christ our Lord. Amen.

THE SHEPHERD OF ISRAEL

Turn us again, thou God of hosts : shew the light of thy countenance, and we shall be whole. Psalm 80. 7

Psalm 80. *Qui regis Israel*

HEAR, O thou Shepherd of Israel, thou that leadest Joseph like a sheep : shew thyself also, thou that sittest upon the cherubims.

2. Before Ephraim, Benjamin, and Manasses : stir up thy strength, and come, and help us.

3. Turn us again, O God : shew the light of thy countenance, and we shall be whole.

4. O Lord God of hosts : how long wilt thou be angry with thy people that prayeth?

5. Thou feedest them with the bread of tears : and givest them plenteousness of tears to drink.

6. Thou hast made us a very strife unto our neighbours : and our enemies laugh us to scorn.

7. Turn us again, thou God of hosts : shew the light of thy countenance, and we shall be whole.

8. Thou hast brought a vine out of Egypt : thou hast cast out the heathen, and planted it.

Lead me forth in thy truth, and learn me : for thou art the God of my salvation; in thee hath been my hope all the day long. Psalm 25. 4

THE HOLY SPIRIT'S GUIDANCE

Psalm 25. *Ad te, Domine, levavi*

UNTO thee, O Lord, will I lift up my soul; my God, I have put my trust in thee : O let me not be confounded, neither let mine enemies triumph over me.

2. For all they that hope in thee shall not be ashamed : but such as transgress without a cause shall be put to confusion.

3. Shew me thy ways, O Lord : and teach me thy paths.

4. Lead me forth in thy truth, and learn me : for thou art the God of my salvation; in thee hath been my hope all the day long.

5. Call to remembrance, O Lord, thy tender mercies : and thy loving-kindnesses, which have been ever of old.

6. O remember not the sins and offences of my youth : but according to thy mercy think thou upon me, O Lord, for thy goodness.

7. Gracious and righteous is the Lord : therefore will he teach sinners in the way.

Meditation

The secret of the Lord is among them that fear him : and he will shew them his covenant. Psalm 25. 13

PRAYING FOR WORLD PEACE

Then shall he judge thy people according unto right : and defend the poor.
Psalm 72. 2

Psalm 72. *Deus, judicium*

GIVE the King thy judgements, O God : and thy righteousness unto the King's son.

2. Then shall he judge thy people according unto right : and defend the poor.

3. The mountains also shall bring peace : and the little hills righteousness unto the people.

4. He shall keep the simple folk by their right : defend the children of the poor, and punish the wrong doer.

5. They shall fear thee, as long as the sun and moon endureth : from one generation to another.

6. He shall come down like the rain into a fleece of wool: even as the drops that water the earth.

7. In his time shall the righteous flourish : yea, and abundance of peace, so long as the moon endureth.

8. His dominion shall be also from the one sea to the other : and from the flood unto the world's end.

9. They that dwell in the wilderness shall kneel before him : his enemies shall lick the dust.

IN TIMES OF TROUBLE

For I reckon that the sufferings of this present time are not worthy to be compared with the glory which shall be revealed in us. Romans 8. 18

Psalm 86. *Inclina, Domine*

BOW down thine ear, O Lord, and hear me : for I am poor, and in misery.

2. Preserve thou my soul, for I am holy : my God, save thy servant that putteth his trust in thee.

3. Be merciful unto me, O Lord : for I will call daily upon thee.

4. Comfort the soul of thy servant : for unto thee, O Lord, do I lift up my soul.

5. For thou, Lord, art good and gracious : and of great mercy unto all them that call upon thee.

6. Give ear, Lord, unto my prayer : and ponder the voice of my humble desires.

7. In the time of my trouble I will call upon thee : for thou hearest me.

Meditation
Comfort the soul of thy servant : for unto thee, O Lord, do I lift up my soul.
Psalm 86. 4

A CONTRITE HEART

Eschew evil, and do good : seek peace, and ensue it. Psalm 34. 14

Psalm 34. *Benedicam Domino*

I WILL alway give thanks unto the Lord : his praise shall ever be in my mouth.

2. My soul shall make her boast in the Lord : the humble shall hear thereof, and be glad.

3. O praise the Lord with me : and let us magnify his Name together.

4. I sought the Lord, and he heard me : yea, he delivered me out of all my fear.

5. They had an eye unto him, and were lightened : and their faces were not ashamed.

6. Lo, the poor crieth, and the Lord heareth him : yea, and saveth him out of all his troubles.

7. The angel of the Lord tarrieth round about them that fear him : and delivereth them.

8. O taste, and see, how gracious the Lord is : blessed is the man that trusteth in him.

9. O fear the Lord, ye that are his saints : for they that fear him lack nothing.

10. The lions do lack, and suffer hunger : but they who seek the Lord shall want no manner of thing that is good.

11. Come, ye children, and hearken unto me : I will teach you the fear of the Lord.

LOOKING TO GOD IN TIMES OF ILLNESS

Lord, I am not worthy that thou shouldest come under my roof: but speak the word only, and my servant shall be healed. St. Matthew 8. 8

The Gospel. St. Matthew 8. 1
From 'The Third Sunday After the Epiphany'

WHEN he was come down from the mountain, great multitudes followed him. And behold, there came a leper and worshipped him, saying, Lord, if thou wilt, thou canst make me clean. And Jesus put forth his hand, and touched him, saying, I will; be thou clean. And immediately his leprosy was cleansed. And Jesus saith unto him, See thou tell no man, but go thy way, shew thyself to the priest, and offer the gift that Moses commanded, for a testimony unto them. And when Jesus was entered into Capernaum, there came unto him a centurion beseeching him, and saying, Lord, my servant lieth at home sick of the palsy, grievously tormented. And Jesus saith unto him, I will come and heal him. The centurion answered and said, Lord, I am not worthy that thou shouldest come under my roof; but speak the word only, and my servant shall be healed. For I am a man under authority, having soldiers under me: and I say to this man, Go, and he goeth; and to another, Come, and he cometh; and to my servant, Do this, and he doeth it. When Jesus heard it, he marvelled, and said to them that followed, Verily I say unto you, I have not found so great faith, no not in Israel.

PRAYING FOR THE TERMINALLY ILL

Is any sick among you? let him call for the elders of the church; and let them pray over him, anointing him with oil in the name of the Lord. St. James 5. 14

A Prayer for a sick person, when there appeareth small hope of recovery
From 'The Visitation of the Sick'

O FATHER of mercies, and God of all comfort, our only help in time of need; We fly unto thee for succour in behalf of this thy servant, here lying under thy hand in great weakness of body. Look graciously upon him, O Lord; and the more the outward man decayeth, strengthen him, we beseech thee, so much the more continually with thy grace and holy Spirit in the inner man. Give him unfeigned repentance for all the errors of his life past, and stedfast faith in thy Son Jesus; that his sins may be done away by thy mercy, and his pardon sealed in heaven, before he go hence, and be no more seen. We know, O Lord, that there is no word impossible with thee; and that, if thou wilt, thou canst even yet raise him up, and grant him a longer continuance amongst us: Yet, forasmuch as in all appearance the time of his dissolution draweth near, so fit and prepare him, we beseech thee, against the hour of death, that after his departure hence in peace, and in thy favour, his soul may be received into thine everlasting kingdom, through the merits and mediation of Jesus Christ, thine only Son, our Lord and Saviour. Amen.

THE CONVERSION OF SAINT PAUL (1)

Suddenly there shined round about him a light from heaven. Acts 9. 3

For The Epistle. Acts 9. 1
From 'The Conversion of Saint Paul'

AND Saul, yet breathing out threatenings and slaughter against the dis-ciples of the Lord, went unto the high priest, and desired of him letters to Damascus to the synagogues, that, if he found any of this way, whether they were men or women, he might bring them bound unto Jerusalem. And, as he journeyed, he came near Damascus, and suddenly there shined round about him a light from heaven. And he fell to the earth, and heard a voice saying unto him, Saul, Saul, why persecutest thou me? And he said, Who art thou, Lord? And the Lord said, I am Jesus whom thou persecutest: it is hard for thee to kick against the pricks. And he, trembling and aston-ished, said, Lord, what wilt thou have me to do? And the Lord said unto him, Arise, and go into the city, and it shall be told thee what thou must do. And the men which journeyed with him stood speechless, hearing a voice, but seeing no man. And Saul arose from the earth, and when his eyes were opened he saw no man; but they led him by the hand, and brought him into Damascus. And he was three days without sight, and nei-ther did eat nor drink.

Meditation
Woe is unto me, if I preach not the gospel! 1 Corinthians 9. 16

THE CONVERSION OF SAINT PAUL (2)

He is a chosen vessel unto me, to bear my name before the Gentiles, and kings, and the children of Israel. Acts 9. 15

For The Epistle. Acts 9. 10
From 'The Conversion of Saint Paul'

AND there was a certain disciple at Damascus, named Ananias, and to him said the Lord in a vision, Ananias. And he said, Behold, I am here, Lord. And the Lord said unto him, Arise, and go into the street which is called Straight, and enquire in the house of Judas for one called Saul, of Tarsus: for behold, he prayeth, and hath seen in a vision a man named Ananias, coming in, and putting his hand on him, that he might receive his sight. Then Ananias answered, Lord, I have heard by many of this man, how much evil he hath done to thy saints at Jerusalem; and here he hath authority from the chief priests to bind all that call on thy Name. But the Lord said unto him, Go thy way; for he is a chosen vessel unto me, to bear my name before the Gentiles, and kings, and the children of Israel: for I will shew him how great things he must suffer for my Name's sake. And Ananias went his way, and entered into the house; and, putting his hands on him, said, Brother Saul, the Lord, (even Jesus that appeared unto thee in the way as thou camest,) hath sent me, that thou mightest receive thy sight, and be filled with the holy Ghost. And immediately there fell from his eyes as it had been scales; and he received sight forthwith, and arose, and was baptized.

OUR SOUL IS ESCAPED

Our soul is escaped even as a bird out of the snare of the fowler : the snare is broken, and we are delivered. Psalm 124. 6

Psalm 124. *Nisi quia Dominus*

IF the Lord himself had not been on our side, now may Israel say: if the Lord himself had not been on our side, when men rose up against us;

2. They had swallowed us up quick: when they were so wrathfully displeased at us.

3. Yea, the waters had drowned us : and the stream had gone over our soul.

4. The deep waters of the proud : had gone even over our soul.

5. But praised be the Lord : who hath not given us over for a prey unto their teeth.

6. Our soul is escaped even as a bird out of the snare of the fowler : the snare is broken, and we are delivered.

7. Our help standeth in the Name of the Lord : who hath made heaven and earth.

Meditation

The hills stand about Jerusalem : even so standeth the Lord round about his people, from this time forth for evermore. Psalm 125. 2

MORNING PRAYER (2)

Rend your heart, and not your garments, and turn unto the Lord your God: for he is gracious and merciful, slow to anger, and of great kindness, and repenteth him of the evil. Joel 2. 13

Benedictus. St. Luke 1. 68
From 'Morning Prayer'

BLESSED be the Lord God of Israel: for he hath visited and redeemed his people;

And hath raised up a mighty salvation for us: in the house of his servant David;

As he spake by the mouth of his holy Prophets: which have been since the world began;

That we should be saved from our enemies: and from the hands of all that hate us;

To perform the mercy promised to our forefathers: and to remember his holy Covenant.

To perform the oath which he sware to our forefather Abraham: that he would give us;

That we being delivered out of the hands of our enemies: might serve him without fear;

In holiness and righteousness before him: all the days of our life.

TWO OR THREE GATHERED TOGETHER

Lead me, O Lord, in thy righteousness, because of mine enemies : make thy way plain before my face. Psalm 5. 8

Psalm 5. *Verba mea auribus*

PONDER my words, O Lord : consider my meditation.

2. O hearken thou unto the voice of my calling, my King, and my God : for unto thee will I make my prayer.

3. My voice shalt thou hear betimes, O Lord : early in the morning will I direct my prayer unto thee, and will look up.

4. For thou art the God that hast no pleasure in wickedness : neither shall any evil dwell with thee.

5. Such as be foolish shall not stand in thy sight : for thou hatest all them that work vanity.

6. Thou shalt destroy them that speak leasing : the Lord will abhor both the blood-thirsty and deceitful man.

7. But as for me, I will come into thine house, even upon the multitude of thy mercy : and in thy fear will I worship toward thy holy temple.

8. Lead me, O Lord, in thy righteousness, because of mine enemies : make thy way plain before my face.

9. For there is no faithfulness in his mouth : their inward parts are very wickedness.

10. Their throat is an open sepulchre : they flatter with their tongue.

TRUSTING GOD IN DANGER

My time is in thy hand; deliver me from the hand of mine enemies : and from them that persecute me. Psalm 31. 17

The Gospel. St. Matthew 8. 23
From 'The Fourth Sunday After the Epiphany'

AND when he was entered into a ship, his disciples followed him. And behold, there arose a great tempest in the sea, insomuch that the ship was covered with the waves: but he was asleep. And his disciples came to him, and awoke him, saying, Lord, save us, we perish. And he saith unto them, Why are ye fearful, O ye of little faith? Then he arose, and rebuked the winds and the sea, and there was a great calm. But the men marvelled, saying, What manner of man is this, that even the winds and the sea obey him! And when he was come to the other side into the country of the Gergesenes, there met him two possessed with devils, coming out of the tombs, exceeding fierce, so that no man might pass by that way. And behold, they cried out, saying, What have we to do with thee, Jesus, thou Son of God? art thou come hither to torment us before the time? And there was a good way off from them an herd of many swine, feeding. So the devils besought him, saying, If thou cast us out, suffer us to go away into the herd of swine. And he said unto them, Go. And when they were come out, they went into the herd of swine: and behold, the whole herd of swine ran violently down a steep place into the sea, and perished in the waters.

SAFE IN THE MIDST OF DANGER

For there is no power but of God: the powers that be are ordained of God.
Romans 13. 1

The Collect
From 'The Fourth Sunday After the Epiphany'

O GOD, who knowest us to be set in the midst of so many and great dangers, that by reason of the frailty of our nature we cannot always stand upright; Grant to us such strength and protection, as may support us in all dangers, and carry us through all temptations; through Jesus Christ our Lord. Amen.

The Epistle. Romans 13. 1
From 'The Fourth Sunday After the Epiphany'

L ET every soul be subject unto the higher powers; for there is no power but of God: the powers that be are ordained of God. Whosoever therefore resisteth the power resisteth the ordinance of God: and they that resist shall receive to themselves damnation. For rulers are not a terror to good works, but to the evil. Wilt thou then not be afraid of the power? do that which is good, and thou shalt have praise of the same: for he is the minister of God to thee for good. But if thou do that which is evil, be afraid; for he beareth not the sword in vain: for he is the minister of God, a revenger to execute wrath upon him that doeth evil. Wherefore ye must needs be subject, not only for wrath, but also for conscience sake.

~

THANKING GOD FOR HIS
SPIRITUAL PROVISION

O give thanks unto the Lord, for he is gracious : because his mercy endureth for ever. Psalm 118. 1

Psalm 34. *Benedicam Domino*

I WILL alway give thanks unto the Lord : his praise shall ever be in my mouth.

2. My soul shall make her boast in the Lord : the humble shall hear thereof, and be glad.

3. O praise the Lord with me : and let us magnify his Name together.

4. I sought the Lord, and he heard me : yea, he delivered me out of all my fear.

5. They had an eye unto him, and were lightened : and their faces were not ashamed.

6. Lo, the poor crieth, and the Lord heareth him : yea, and saveth him out of all his troubles.

7. The angel of the Lord tarrieth round about them that fear him : and delivereth them.

8. O taste, and see, how gracious the Lord is : blessed is the man that trusteth in him.

Meditation

I will offer to thee the sacrifice of thanksgiving : and will call upon the Name of the Lord. Psalm 116. 15

JESUS' FIRST VISIT TO
THE TEMPLE (1)

The Lord, whom ye seek, shall suddenly come to his temple. Malachi 3. 1

The Collect
From 'The Presentation of Christ in the Temple, commonly called,
the Purification of Saint Mary the Virgin'

A LMIGHTY and everliving God, we humbly beseech thy Majesty, that, as thy only-begotten Son was this day presented in the temple in substance of our flesh, so we may be presented unto thee with pure and clean hearts, by the same thy Son Jesus Christ our Lord. Amen.

For The Epistle. Malachi 3. 1
From 'The Presentation of Christ in the Temple'

B EHOLD, I will send my messenger, and he shall prepare the way before me: and the Lord, whom ye seek, shall suddenly come to his temple; even the messenger of the covenant, whom ye delight in; behold, he shall come, saith the Lord of hosts. But who may abide the day of his coming? and who shall stand when he appeareth? for he is like a refiner's fire, and like fullers' soap. And he shall sit as a refiner and purifier of silver; and he shall purify the sons of Levi, and purge them as gold and silver, that they may offer unto the Lord an offering in righteousness. Then shall the offerings of Judah and Jerusalem be pleasant unto the Lord, as in the days of old, and as in former years.

JESUS' FIRST VISIT TO
THE TEMPLE (2)

They brought him to Jerusalem, to present him to the Lord. St. Luke 2. 22

The Gospel. St. Luke 2. 22
From 'The Presentation of Christ in the Temple'

AND when the days of her purification, according to the law of Moses, were accomplished, they brought him to Jerusalem, to present him to the Lord ... and to offer a sacrifice, according to that which is said in the Law of the Lord, A pair of turtle-doves, or two young pigeons. And behold, there was a man in Jerusalem, whose name was Simeon; and the same man was just and devout, waiting for the consolation of Israel: and the Holy Ghost was upon him. And it was revealed unto him by the Holy Ghost, that he should not see death, before he had seen the Lord's Christ. And he came by the Spirit into the temple; and when the parents brought in the child Jesus, to do for him after the custom of the Law, then took he him up in his arms, and blessed God, and said, Lord, now lettest thou thy servant depart in peace, according to thy word: for mine eyes have seen thy salvation, which thou hast prepared before the face of all people; a light to lighten the Gentiles, and the glory of thy people Israel. And Joseph and his mother marvelled at those things which were spoken of him. And Simeon blessed them, and said unto Mary his mother, Behold, this child is set for the fall and rising again of many in Israel; and for a sign which shall be spoken against; (yea, a sword shall pierce through thy own soul also;) that the thoughts of many hearts may be revealed.

GOD'S LOVING-KINDNESS

Like as we have heard, so have we seen in the city of the Lord of hosts, in the city of our God : God upholdeth the same for ever. Psalm 48. 7

Psalm 48. *Magnus Dominus*

GREAT is the Lord, and highly to be praised : in the city of our God, even upon his holy hill.

2. The hill of Sion is a fair place, and the joy of the whole earth : upon the north-side lieth the city of the great King; God is well known in her palaces as a sure refuge.

3. For lo, the kings of the earth : are gathered, and gone by together.

4. They marvelled to see such things : they were astonished, and suddenly cast down.

5. Fear came there upon them, and sorrow : as upon a woman in her travail.

6. Thou shalt break the ships of the sea : through the east-wind.

7. Like as we have heard, so have we seen in the city of the Lord of hosts, in the city of our God : God upholdeth the same for ever.

8. We wait for thy loving-kindness, O God : in the midst of thy temple.

9. O God, according to thy Name, so is thy praise unto the world's end : thy right hand is full of righteousness.

10. Let the mount Sion rejoice, and the daughter of Judah be glad : because of thy judgements.

'BEHOLD THE FOWLS OF THE AIR'

Is not the life more than meat, and the body than raiment? St. Matthew 6. 25

The Gospel. *St. Matthew 6. 24–34*
From 'The Fifteenth Sunday after Trinity'

NO man can serve two masters: for either he will hate the one, and love the other; or else he will hold to the one, and despise the other. Ye cannot serve God and mammon. Therefore I say unto you, Take no thought for your life, what ye shall eat, or what ye shall drink; nor yet for your body, what ye shall put on. Is not the life more than meat, and the body than raiment? Behold the fowls of the air: for they sow not, neither do they reap, nor gather into barns; yet your heavenly Father feedeth them. Are ye not much better than they? Which of you by taking thought can add one cubit unto his stature? And why take ye thought for raiment? Consider the lilies of the field, how they grow; they toil not, neither do they spin. And yet I say unto you, That even Solomon in all his glory was not arrayed like one of these. Wherefore, if God so clothe the grass of the field, which to day is, and to morrow is cast into the oven, shall he not much more clothe you, O ye of little faith? Therefore take no thought, saying, What shall we eat? or, What shall we drink? or, Wherewithal shall we be clothed? (For after all these things do the Gentiles seek:) for your heavenly Father knoweth that ye have need of all these things. But seek ye first the kingdom of God, and his righteousness; and all these things shall be added unto you.

THE HEALTH OF GOD'S CHURCH

Forbearing one another, and forgiving one another. Colossians 3. 13

The Collect
From 'The Fifth Sunday After the Epiphany'

O LORD, we bessech thee to keep thy Church and houshold continually in thy true religion; that they who do lean only upon the hope
of thy heavenly grace may evermore be defended by thy mighty power;
through Jesus Christ our Lord. Amen.

The Epistle. *Colossians 3. 12*
From 'The Fifth Sunday After the Epiphany'

P UT on therefore, as the elect of God, holy and beloved, bowels of
mercies, kindness, humbleness of mind, meekness, long-suffering; forbearing one another, and forgiving one another, if any man have a quarrel
against any; even as Christ forgave you, so also do ye. And above all these
things put on charity, which is the bond of perfectness. And let the peace
of God rule in your hearts, to the which also ye are called in one body; and
be ye thankful. Let the word of Christ dwell in you richly in all wisdom,
teaching and admonishing one another in psalms, and hymns, and spiritual
songs, singing with grace in your hearts to the Lord. And whatsoever ye
do, in word or deed, do all in the Name of the Lord Jesus, giving thanks to
God and the Father by him.

GOD'S LIGHT

O send out thy light and thy truth, that they may lead me : and bring me unto thy holy hill, and to thy dwelling. Psalm 43. 3

Psalm 43. *Judica me, Deus*

GIVE sentence with me, O God, and defend my cause against the un-godly people : O deliver me from the deceitful and wicked man.
2. For thou art the God of my strength, why hast thou put me from thee : and why go I so heavily, while the enemy oppresseth me?
3. O send out thy light and thy truth, that they may lead me : and bring me unto thy holy hill, and to thy dwelling.
4. And that I may go unto the altar of God, even unto the God of my joy and gladness : and upon the harp will I give thanks unto thee, O God, my God.
5. Why art thou so heavy, O my soul : and why art thou so disquieted within me?
6. O put thy trust in God : for I will yet give him thanks, which is the help of my countenance, and my God.

The Third Collect, For Aid Against All Perils
From 'Evening Prayer'

LIGHTEN our darkness, we beseech thee, O Lord; and by thy great mercy defend us from all perils and dangers of this night; for the love of thy only Son, our Saviour, Jesus Christ. Amen. Psalm 18. 28

FORGIVENESS OF SINS

Depart from me; for I am a sinful man, O Lord. St. Luke 5. 8

From 'A Commination'

O MOST mighty God, and merciful Father, who hast compassion upon all men, and hatest nothing that thou hast made; who wouldest not the death of a sinner, but that he should rather turn from his sin, and be saved; Mercifully forgive us our trespasses; receive and comfort us, who are grieved and wearied with the burden of our sins. Thy property is always to have mercy; to thee only it appertaineth to forgive sins. Spare us therefore, good Lord, spare thy people, whom thou hast redeemed; enter not into judgement with thy servants, who are vile earth, and miserable sinners; but so turn thine anger from us, who meekly acknowledge our vileness, and truly repent us of our faults, and so make haste to help us in this world, that we may ever live with thee in the world to come; through Jesus Christ our Lord. Amen.

From 'A Commination'

T URN thou us, O good Lord, and so shall we be turned. Be favourable, O Lord, Be favourable to thy people, Who turn to thee in weeping, fasting, and praying. For thou art a merciful God, Full of compassion, Long-suffering, and of great pity. Thou sparest when we deserve punishment, And in thy wrath thinkest upon mercy. Spare thy people good Lord, spare them, And let not thine heritage be brought to confusion.

GOD'S COMFORT FOR THE DYING

Lord, let me know mine end, and the number of my days : that I may be certified how long I have to live. Psalm 39. 5

Psalm 39. *Dixi, custodiam*

I SAID, I will take heed to my ways : that I offend not in my tongue.
2. I will keep my mouth as it were with a bridle : while the ungodly is in my sight.
3. I held my tongue, and spake nothing : I kept silence, yea, even from good words; but it was pain and grief to me.
4. My heart was hot within me, and while I was thus musing the fire kindled : and at the last I spake with my tongue ...
6. Behold, thou hast made my days as it were a span long : and mine age is even as nothing in respect of thee; and verily every man living is altogether vanity.
7. For man walketh in a vain shadow, and disquieteth himself in vain : he heapeth up riches, and cannot tell who shall gather them.
8. And now, Lord, what is my hope : truly my hope is even in thee.

Meditation
Hear my prayer; O Lord, and with thine ears consider my calling : hold not thy peace at my tears. Psalm 39.13

MORNING PRAYER (3)

To the Lord our God belong mercies and forgivenesses, though we have rebelled against him; Neither have we obeyed the voice of the Lord our God, to walk in his laws, which he set before us. Daniel 9. 9–10

The Second Collect, for Peace
From 'Morning Prayer'

O GOD, who art the author of peace and lover of concord, in knowledge of whom standeth our eternal life, whose service is perfect freedom; Defend us thy humble servants in all assaults of our enemies; that we, surely trusting in thy defence, may not fear the power of any adversaries, through the might of Jesus Christ our Lord. Amen.

The Third Collect, for Grace
From 'Morning Prayer'

O LORD, our heavenly Father, Almighty and everlasting God, who hast safely brought us to the beginning of this day; Defend us in the same with thy mighty power; and grant that this day we fall into no sin, neither run into any kind of danger; but that all our doings may be ordered by thy governance, to do always that is righteous in thy sight; through Jesus Christ our Lord. Amen.

Meditation
Repent ye: for the kingdom of heaven is at hand. St. Matthew 3. 2

IN TIMES OF ADVERSITY

One deep calleth another, because of the noise of the water-pipes : all thy waves and storms are gone over me. Psalm 42. 9

Psalm 42. *Quemadmodum*

LIKE as the hart desireth the water-brooks : so longeth my soul after thee, O God.

2. My soul is athirst for God, yea, even for the living God : when shall I come to appear before the presence of God?

3. My tears have been my meat day and night : while they daily say unto me, Where is now thy God?

4. Now when I think thereupon, I pour out my heart by myself : for I went with the multitude, and brought them forth into the house of God;

5. In the voice of praise and thanksgiving : among such as keep holy-day.

6. Why art thou so full of heaviness, O my soul : and why art thou so disquieted within me?

7. O put thy trust in God : for I will yet give him thanks for the help of his countenance.

Meditation

Hear what comfortable words our Saviour Christ saith unto all that truly turn to him: 'Come unto me all that travail and are heavy laden, and I will refresh you' (St. Matthew 11. 28). From 'Holy Communion'

GOD AND HIS WORLD

His dominion shall be also from the one sea to the other : and from the flood unto the world's end. Psalm 72. 8

Psalm 72. *Deus, judicium*

GIVE the King thy judgements, O God : and thy righteousness unto the King's son.

2. Then shall he judge thy people according unto right : and defend the poor.

3. The mountains also shall bring peace : and the little hills righteousness unto the people.

4. He shall keep the simple folk by their right : defend the children of the poor, and punish the wrong doer.

5. They shall fear thee, as long as the sun and moon endureth : from one generation to another.

6. He shall come down like the rain into a fleece of wool : even as the drops that water the earth.

7. In his time shall the righteous flourish : yea, and abundance of peace, so long as the moon endureth.

Meditation

He shall come down like the rain into a fleece of wool : even as the drops that water the earth. Psalm 72. 6

PREPARING FOR CHRIST'S SECOND COMING

Beloved, now are we the sons of God, and it doth not yet appear what we shall be: but we know that, when he shall appear, we shall be like him; for we shall see him as he is. 1 St. John 3. 2

The Gospel. *St. Matthew 24. 23*
From 'The Sixth Sunday After the Epiphany'

THEN if any man shall say unto you, Lo, here is Christ, or there; believe it not. For there shall arise false Christs, and false prophets, and shall shew great signs and wonders; insomuch that (if it were possible) they shall deceive the very elect. Behold, I have told you before. Wherefore if they shall say unto you, Behold, he is in the desert; go not forth: behold, he is in the secret chambers; believe it not. For as the lightning cometh out of the east, and shineth even unto the west; so shall also the coming of the Son of Man be. For wheresoever the carcase is, there will the eagles be gathered together. Immediately after the tribulation of those days shall the sun be darkened, and the moon shall not give her light, and the stars shall fall from heaven, and the powers of the heavens shall be shaken. And then shall appear the sign of the Son of Man in heaven: and then shall all the tribes of the earth mourn, and they shall see the Son of Man coming in the clouds of heaven, with power and great glory. And he shall send his angels with a great sound of a trumpet, and they shall gather together his elect from the four winds, from one end of heaven to the other.

INSTRUCTION FROM GOD'S WORD

Blessed are they that keep his testimonies : and seek him with their whole heart.
Psalm 119. 2

The Collect
From 'The Second Sunday in Advent'

BLESSED Lord, who hast caused all holy Scriptures to be written for our learning; Grant that we may in such wise hear them, read, mark, learn, and inwardly digest them, that by patience, and comfort of thy holy Word, we may embrace, and ever hold fast the blessed hope of everlasting life, which thou hast given us in our Saviour Jesus Christ. Amen.

Psalm 119. *Beati immaculati*

BLESSED are those that are undefiled in the way : and walk in the law of the Lord ...

3. For they who do no wickedness : walk in his ways.

4. Thou hast charged : that we shall diligently keep thy commandments.

5. O that my ways were made so direct : that I might keep thy statutes!

6. So shall I not be confounded : while I have respect unto all thy commandments.

7. I will thank thee with an unfeigned heart : when I shall have learned the judgements of thy righteousness.

8. I will keep thy ceremonies : O forsake me not utterly.

CONTRITION (1)

And I said, It is mine own infirmity : but I will remember the years of the right hand of the most Highest.
Psalm 77. 10

Psalm 77. *Voce mea ad Dominum*

I WILL cry unto God with my voice : even unto God will I cry with my voice, and he shall hearken unto me.

2. In the time of my trouble I sought the Lord : my sore ran, and ceased not in the night-season; my soul refused comfort.

3. When I am in heaviness, I will think upon God : when my heart is vexed, I will complain.

4. Thou holdest mine eyes waking : I am so feeble, that I cannot speak.

5. I have considered the days of old : and the years that are past.

6. I call to remembrance my song : and in the night I commune with mine own heart, and search out my spirits.

7. Will the Lord absent himself for ever : and will he be no more intreated?

8. Is his mercy clean gone for ever : and is his promise come utterly to an end for evermore?

9. Hath God forgotten to be gracious : and will he shut up his loving-kindness in displeasure?

10. And I said, It is mine own infirmity : but I will remember the years of the right hand of the most Highest.

A PRAYER OF THANKS

O praise our God, ye people : and make the voice of his praise to be heard.
Psalm 66. 7

Psalm 66. *Jubilate Deo*

O BE joyful in God, all ye lands : sing praises unto the honour of his Name, make his praise to be glorious.

2. Say unto God, O how wonderful art thou in thy works : through the greatness of thy power shall thine enemies be found liars unto thee.

3. For all the world shall worship thee : sing of thee, and praise thy Name.

4. O come hither, and behold the works of God : how wonderful he is in his doing toward the children of men.

5. He turned the sea into dry land : so that they went through the water on foot; there did we rejoice thereof.

6. He ruleth with his power for ever; his eyes behold the people : and such as will not believe shall not be able to exalt themselves …

8. Who holdeth our soul in life : and suffereth not our feet to slip.

9. For thou, O God, hast proved us : thou also hast tried us, like as silver is tried.

10. Thou broughtest us into the snare : and laidest trouble upon our loins.

11. Thou sufferedst men to ride over our heads : we went through fire and water, and thou broughtest us out into a wealthy place.

STRENGTH FOR THE
INNER LIFE

Defend, O Lord, this thy Child [or this thy Servant] with thy heavenly grace, that he may continue thine for ever; and daily increase in thy holy Spirit more and more, until he come unto thy everlasting kingdom. Amen.
From 'The Order of Confirmation'

Collect
From 'The Order of Confirmation'

ALMIGHTY and everliving God, who makest us both to will and to do those things that be good and acceptable unto thy divine Majesty; We make our humble supplications unto thee for these thy servants, upon whom (after the example of thy holy Apostles) we have now laid our hands, to certify them (by this sign) of thy favour and gracious goodness towards them. Let thy fatherly hand, we beseech thee, ever be over them; let thy Holy Spirit ever be with them; and so lead them in the knowledge and obedience of thy Word, that in the end they may obtain everlasting life; through our Lord Jesus Christ, who with thee and the Holy Ghost liveth and reigneth, ever one God, world without end. Amen.

Meditation
Be still then, and know that I am God : I will be exalted among the heathen, and I will be exalted in the earth. Psalm 46. 10

'BLESS YE THE LORD'

God is very greatly to be feared in the council of the saints : and to be had in reverence of all them that are round about him. Psalm 89. 8

Benedicite, Omnia Opera
From 'Morning Prayer'

O ALL ye Works of the Lord, bless ye the Lord : praise him, and magnify him for ever.

O ye Angels of the Lord, bless ye the Lord : praise him, and magnify him for ever.

O ye Heavens, bless ye the Lord : praise him, and magnify him for ever.

O ye Waters that be above the Firmament, bless ye the Lord : praise him, and magnify him for ever.

O all ye Powers of the Lord, bless ye the Lord : praise him, and magnify him for ever.

O ye Sun, and Moon, bless ye the Lord : praise him, and magnify him for ever.

O ye Stars of Heaven, bless ye the Lord : praise him, and magnify him for ever.

O ye Showers, and Dew, bless ye the Lord : praise him, and magnify him for ever.

O ye Winds of God, bless ye the Lord : praise him, and magnify him for ever.

CREATION PRAISES THE CREATOR

Let every thing that hath breath : praise the Lord. Psalm 150. 6

Benedicite, Omnia Opera
From 'Morning Prayer'

O YE Nights and Days, bless ye the Lord : praise him, and magnify him for ever.

O ye Light and Darkness, bless ye the Lord : praise him, and magnify him for ever.

O ye Lightnings and Clouds, bless ye the Lord : praise him, and magnify him for ever.

O let the Earth bless the Lord : yea, let it praise him, and magnify him for ever.

O ye Mountains and Hills, bless ye the Lord : praise him, and magnify him for ever.

O all ye Green Things upon the Earth, bless ye the Lord : praise him, and magnify him for ever.

O ye Wells, bless ye the Lord : praise him, and magnify him for ever.

O ye Seas and Floods, bless ye the Lord : praise him, and magnify him for ever.

O ye Whales, and all that move in the Waters, bless ye the Lord : praise him, and magnify him for ever.

O all ye Fowls of the Air, bless ye the Lord : praise him, and magnify him for ever.

THE KINGDOM OF HEAVEN

So the last shall be first, and the first last. St. Matthew 20. 16

The Gospel. *St. Matthew 20. 1*
From 'The Sunday Called Septuagesima'

THE kingdom of heaven is like unto a man that is an householder, which went out early in the morning to hire labourers into his vineyard. And when he had agreed with the labourers for a penny a day, he sent them into his vineyard … And about the eleventh hour he went out, and found others standing idle … He saith unto them, Go ye also into the vineyard, and whatsoever is right, that shall ye receive. So when even was come, the lord of the vineyard saith unto his steward, Call the labourers, and give them their hire, beginning from the last unto the first. And when they came that were hired about the eleventh hour, they received every man a penny. But when the first came, they supposed that they should have received more; and they likewise received every man a penny. And when they had received it, they murmured against the good-man of the house, saying, These last have wrought but one hour, and thou hast made them equal unto us, which have borne the burden and heat of the day. But he answered one of them, and said, Friend, I do thee no wrong; didst not thou agree with me for a penny? Take that thine is, and go thy way; I will give unto this last, even as unto thee. Is it not lawful for me to do what I will with mine own? Is thine eye evil, because I am good?

EVENING PRAYER (1)

If we say that we have no sin, we deceive ourselves, and the truth is not in us; but if we confess our sins, God is faithful and just to forgive us our sins, and to cleanse us from all unrighteousness. 1 St. John 1. 8–9

The Lord's Prayer
From 'Evening Prayer'

OUR Father, which art in heaven, Hallowed be thy Name. Thy kingdom come. Thy will be done, in earth as it is in heaven. Give us this day our daily bread. And forgive us our trespasses, As we forgive them that trespass against us. And lead us not into temptation; But deliver us from evil: For thine is the kingdom, The power, and the glory, For ever and ever. Amen.

> *Priest.* O Lord, open thou our lips.
> *Answer.* And our mouth shall shew forth thy praise.
> *Priest.* O God, make speed to save us.
> *Answer.* O Lord, make haste to help us.
> *Priest.* Glory be to the Father, and to the Son: and to the Holy Ghost;
> *Answer.* As it was in the beginning, is now, and ever shall be: world without end. Amen.
> *Priest.* Praise ye the Lord.
> *Answer.* The Lord's Name be praised.

IN DEEP TROUBLE (1)

My heart is disquieted within me : and the fear of death is fallen upon me.
Psalm 55. 4

Psalm 55. *Exaudi, Deus*

HEAR my prayer, O God : and hide not thyself from my petition.
2. Take heed unto me, and hear me : how I mourn in my prayer, and am vexed.

3. The enemy crieth so, and the ungodly cometh on so fast : for they are minded to do me some mischief; so maliciously are they set against me.

4. My heart is disquieted within me : and the fear of death is fallen upon me.

5. Fearfulness and trembling are come upon me : and an horrible dread hath overwhelmed me.

6. And I said, O that I had wings like a dove : for then would I flee away, and be at rest.

7. Lo, then would I get me away far off : and remain in the wilderness.

8. I would make haste to escape : because of the stormy wind and tempest.

9. Destroy their tongues, O Lord, and divide them : for I have spied unrighteousness and strife in the city.

10. Day and night they go about within the walls thereof : mischief also and sorrow are in the midst of it.

THE MESSIAH IN THE PSALMS (1)

God will declare the Messiah to be his Son

I will rehearse the decree : the Lord hath said unto me, Thou art my Son, this day have I begotten thee. Psalm 2. 7

Psalm 2. *Quare fremuerunt gentes?*

WHY do the heathen so furiously rage together : and why do the people imagine a vain thing?

2. The kings of the earth stand up, and the rulers take counsel together : against the Lord, and against his Anointed.

3. Let us break their bonds asunder : and cast away their cords from us.

4. He that dwelleth in heaven shall laugh them to scorn : the Lord shall have them in derision.

5. Then shall he speak unto them in his wrath : and vex them in his sore displeasure.

6. Yet have I set my King : upon my holy hill of Sion.

7. I will preach the law, whereof the Lord hath said unto me : Thou art my Son, this day have I begotten thee.

8. Desire of me, and I shall give thee the heathen for thine inheritance : and the utmost parts of the earth for thy possession.

9. Thou shalt bruise them with a rod of iron : and break them in pieces like a potter's vessel.

10. Be wise now therefore, O ye kings : be learned, ye that are judges of the earth.

11. Serve the Lord in fear : and rejoice unto him with reverence.

SAINT MATTHIAS'S DAY (1)

And they gave forth their lots; and the lot fell upon Matthias. Acts 1. 26

For the Epistle. *Acts 1. 15*
From 'Saint Matthias's Day'

IN those days Peter stood up in the midst of the disciples, and said, (the number of the names together were about an hundred and twenty,) Men and brethren, this scripture must needs have been fulfilled, which the Holy Ghost by the mouth of David spake before concerning Judas, which was guide to them that took Jesus: for he was numbered with us, and had obtained part of this ministry. Now this man purchased a field with the reward of iniquity; and falling headlong, he burst asunder in the midst, and all his bowels gushed out ... Wherefore, of these men which have companied with us all the time that the Lord Jesus went in and out among us, beginning from the baptism of John, unto that same day that he was taken up from us, must one be ordained to be a witness with us of his resurrection. And they appointed two, Joseph called Barsabas, who was surnamed Justus, and Matthias. And they prayed, and said, Thou, Lord, which knowest the hearts of all men, shew whether of these two thou hast chosen; that he may take part of this ministry and apostleship, from which Judas by transgression fell, that he might go to his own place. And they gave forth their lots; and the lot fell upon Matthias, and he was numbered with the eleven Apostles.

SAINT MATTHIAS'S DAY (2)

I am a stranger upon earth : O hide not thy commandments from me.
Psalm 119. 19

The Collect
From 'Saint Matthias's Day'

OALMIGHTY God, who into the place of the traitor Judas didst choose thy faithful servant Matthias to be of the number of the twelve Apostles; Grant that thy Church, being alway preserved from false Apostles, may be ordered and guided by faithful and true pastors; through Jesus Christ our Lord. Amen.

The Gospel. *St. Matthew 11. 25*
From 'Saint Matthias's Day'

AT that time Jesus answered and said, I thank thee, O Father, Lord of heaven and earth, because thou hast hid these things from the wise and prudent, and hast revealed them unto babes. Even so, Father, for so it seemed good in thy sight. All things are delivered unto me of my Father: and no man knoweth the Son, but the Father; neither knoweth any man the Father, save the Son, and he to whomsoever the Son will reveal him. Come unto me, all ye that labour and are heavy laden, and I will give you rest. Take my yoke upon you, and learn of me; for I am meek and lowly in heart: and ye shall find rest unto your souls. For my yoke is easy, and my burden is light.

THE WAY OF PEACE

Peace be to this house, and to all that dwell in it.
From 'The Visitation of the Sick'

Benedictus. *St. Luke 1. 68*
From 'Morning Prayer'

Blessed be the Lord God of Israel : for he hath visited and redeemed his people;

And hath raised up a mighty salvation for us : in the house of his servant David;

As he spake by the mouth of his holy Prophets : which have been since the world began;

That we should be saved from our enemies : and from the hand of all that hate us;

To perform the mercy promised to our forefathers : and to remember his holy Covenant;

To perform the oath which he sware to our forefather Abraham : that he would give us;

That we being delivered out of the hand of our enemies : might serve him without fear;

In holiness and righteousness before him : all the days of our life.

Meditation
To guide our feet into the way of peace. St. Luke 1. 79

THE ORIGIN OF DIVINE POWER

I am wiser than the aged : because I keep thy commandments. Psalm 119. 100

The Gospel. *St. Luke 8. 4*
From 'The Sunday Called Sexagesima'

WHEN much people were gathered together, and were come to him out of every city, he spake by a parable: A sower went out to sow his seed; and as he sowed, some fell by the way-side; and it was trodden down, and the fowls of the air devoured it. And some fell upon a rock, and as soon as it was sprung up, it withered away, because it lacked moisture. And some fell among thorns, and the thorns sprang up with it, and choked it. And other fell on good ground, and sprang up, and bare fruit an hundredfold. And when he had said these things, he cried, He that hath ears to hear, let him hear ... Now the parable is this: The seed is the Word of God. Those by the way-side are they that hear; then cometh the devil, and taketh away the word out of their hearts, lest they should believe and be saved. They on the rock are they, which, when they hear, receive the word with joy; and these have no root, which for a while believe, and in time of temptation fall away. And that which fell among thorns are they, which, when they have heard, go forth, and are choked with cares, and riches, and pleasures of this life, and bring no fruit to perfection. But that on the good ground, are they, which in an honest and good heart, having heard the word, keep it, and bring forth fruit with patience.

BOASTING IN THE LORD

My soul shall make her boast in the Lord : the humble shall hear thereof, and be glad. Psalm 34. 2

The Epistle. *2 Corinthians 11. 19–31*
From 'The Sunday called Sexagesima'

YE suffer fools gladly, seeing ye yourselves are wise. For ye suffer, if a man bring you into bondage, if a man devour you, if a man take of you, if a man exalt himself, if a man smite you on the face. I speak as concerning reproach, as though we had been weak. Howbeit whereinsoever any is bold, (I speak foolishly,) I am bold also. Are they Hebrews? so am I. Are they Israelites? so am I. Are they the seed of Abraham? so am I. Are they ministers of Christ? (I speak as a fool) I am more; in labours more abundant, in stripes above measure, in prisons more frequent, in deaths oft. Of the Jews five times received I forty stripes save one. Thrice was I beaten with rods, once was I stoned, thrice I suffered shipwreck, a night and a day I have been in the deep; In journeyings often, in perils of waters, in perils of robbers, in perils by mine own countrymen, in perils by the heathen, in perils in the city, in perils in the wilderness, in perils in the sea, in perils among false brethren; In weariness and painfulness, in watchings often, in hunger and thirst, in fastings often, in cold and nakedness. Beside those things that are without, that which cometh upon me daily, the care of all the churches. Who is weak, and I am not weak? who is offended, and I burn not?

FATHER OF MERCIES

O praise the Lord, all ye nations : praise him, all ye peoples. Psalm 117. 1

A Prayer for a Sick Person, when there appeareth small hope of recovery
From 'The Visitation of the Sick'

O FATHER of mercies, and God of all comfort, our only help in time of need; We fly unto thee for succour in behalf of this thy servant, here lying under thy hand in great weakness of body. Look graciously upon him, O Lord; and the more the outward man decayeth, strengthen him, we beseech thee, so much the more continually with thy grace and Holy Spirit in the inner man. Give him unfeigned repentance for all the errors of his life past, and stedfast faith in thy Son Jesus; that his sins may be done away by thy mercy, and his pardon sealed in heaven, before he go hence, and be no more seen. We know, O Lord, that there is no word impossible with thee; and that, if thou wilt, thou canst even yet raise him up, and grant him a longer continuance amongst us: Yet, forasmuch as in all appearance the time of his dissolution draweth near, so fit and prepare him, we beseech thee, against the hour of death, that after his departure hence in peace, and in thy favour, his soul may be received into thine everlasting kingdom, through the merits and mediation of Jesus Christ, thine only Son, our Lord and Saviour. Amen.

REVERENCE BEFORE GOD

The Lord is nigh unto them that are of a contrite heart : and will save such as be of an humble spirit. Psalm 34. 18

Psalm 147. *Laudate Dominum*

O PRAISE the Lord, for it is a good thing to sing praises unto our God : yea, a joyful and pleasant thing it is to be thankful.

2. The Lord doth build up Jerusalem : and gather together the outcasts of Israel.

3. He healeth those that are broken in heart : and giveth medicine to heal their sickness.

4. He telleth the number of the stars : and calleth them all by their names.

5. Great is our Lord, and great is his power : yea, and his wisdom is infinite.

6. The Lord setteth up the meek : and bringeth the ungodly down to the ground.

7. O sing unto the Lord with thanksgiving : sing praises upon the harp unto our God;

8. Who covereth the heaven with clouds, and prepareth rain for the earth : and maketh the grass to grow upon the mountains, and herb for the use of men.

HUMILITY BEFORE GOD

Lo, the poor crieth, and the Lord heareth him : yea, and saveth him out of all his troubles. Psalm 34. 6

From 'The Visitation of the Sick'

O SAVIOUR of the world, who by thy Cross and precious Blood hast redeemed us, Save us, and help us, we humbly beseech thee, O Lord.

THE Almighty Lord, who is a most strong tower to all them that put their trust in him, to whom all things in heaven, in earth, and under the earth, do bow and obey, be now and evermore thy defence; and make thee know and feel, that there is none other Name under heaven given to man, in whom, and through whom, thou mayest receive health and salvation, but only the Name of our Lord Jesus Christ. Amen.

Psalm 16. *Conserva me, Domine*

PRESERVE me, O God : for in thee have I put my trust.
2. O my soul, thou hast said unto the Lord : Thou art my God; I have no good like unto thee.
3. All my delight is upon the saints that are in the earth : and upon such as excel in virtue.
4. But they that run after another god : shall have great trouble.

CONSOLATION IN GOD

But as for me, I shall behold thy presence in righteousness : and when I awake up after thy likeness, I shall be satisfied. Psalm 17. 16

Psalm 73. *Quam bonus Israel!*

ALL the day long have I been punished : and chastened every morning.
14. Yea, and I had almost said even as they : but lo, then I should have condemned the generation of thy children.

15. Then thought I to understand this : but it was too hard for me,

16. Until I went into the sanctuary of God : then understood I the end of these men;

17. Namely, how thou dost set them in slippery places : and castest them down, and destroyest them.

18. Oh, how suddenly do they consume : perish, and come to a fearful end!

19. Yea, even like as a dream when one awaketh : so shalt thou make their image to vanish out of the city.

20. Thus my heart was grieved : and it went even through my reins.

21. So foolish was I, and ignorant : even as it were a beast before thee.

22. Nevertheless, I am alway by thee : for thou hast holden me by my right hand.

23. Thou shalt guide me with thy counsel : and after that receive me with glory.

EVENING PRAYER (2)

When the wicked man turneth away from his wickedness that he hath committed, and doeth that which is lawful and right, he shall save his soul alive.

Ezekiel 18. 27

Cantate Domino. *Psalm 98*
From 'Evening Prayer'

O SING unto the Lord a new song : for he hath done marvellous things.

With his own right hand, and with his holy arm : hath he gotten himself the victory.

The Lord declared his salvation : his righteousness hath he openly showed in the sight of the heathen.

He hath remembered his mercy and truth toward the house of Israel : and all the ends of the world have seen the salvation of our God.

Show yourselves joyful unto the Lord, all ye lands : sing, rejoice, and give thanks.

Praise the Lord upon the harp : sing to the harp with a psalm of thanksgiving.

With trumpets also and shawms : O shew yourselves joyful before the Lord the King.

Let the sea make a noise, and all that therein is : the round world, and they that dwell therein.

LOVE

Though I speak with the tongues of men and of angels, and have not charity, I am become as sounding brass, or a tinkling cymbal. 1 Corinthians 13. 1

The Epistle. *1 Corinthians 13. 1*
From 'The Sunday Called Quinquagesima'

THOUGH I speak with the tongues of men and of angels, and have not charity, I am become as sounding brass, or a tinkling cymbal. And though I have the gift of prophecy, and understand all mysteries, and all knowledge; and though I have all faith, so that I could remove mountains, and have not charity, I am nothing. And though I bestow all my goods to feed the poor, and though I give my body to be burned, and have not charity, it profiteth me nothing. Charity suffereth long, and is kind; charity envieth not; charity vaunteth not itself, is not puffed up, doth not behave itself unseemly, seeketh not her own, is not easily provoked, thinketh no evil; rejoiceth not in iniquity, but rejoiceth in the truth; beareth all things, believeth all things, hopeth all things, endureth all things. Charity never faileth: but whether there be prophecies, they shall fail; whether there be tongues, they shall cease; whether there be knowledge, it shall vanish away. For we know in part, and we prophesy in part. But when that which is perfect is come, then that which is in part shall be done away ... For now we see through a glass, darkly; but then face to face: now I know in part; but then shall I know even as also I am known. And now abideth faith, hope, charity, these three; but the greatest of these is charity.

INSTRUCTION FROM GOD'S WORD (2)

Open thou mine eyes : that I may see the wondrous things of thy law.

Psalm 119. 18

The Collect
From 'The Second Sunday in Advent'

BLESSED Lord, who hast caused all holy Scriptures to be written for our learning: Grant that we may in such wise hear them, read, mark, learn, and inwardly digest them, that by patience and comfort of thy holy Word, we may embrace and ever hold fast the blessed hope of everlasting life, which thou hast given us in our Saviour Jesus Christ. Amen.

Psalm 119. *Adhaesit pavimento*

MY soul cleaveth to the dust : O quicken thou me, according to thy word.

26. I have acknowledged my ways, and thou heardest me : O teach me thy statutes.

27. Make me to understand the way of thy commandments : and so shall I talk of thy wondrous works.

28. My soul melteth away for very heaviness : comfort thou me according unto thy word.

29. Take from me the way of lying : and cause thou me to make much of thy law.

THE MESSIAH IN THE PSALMS (2)

All things will be put under his feet

Thou makest him to have dominion of the works of thy hands : and thou hast put all things in subjection under his feet. Psalm 8. 6

Psalm 8. *Domine, Dominus noster*

O LORD our Governor, how excellent is thy Name in all the world : thou that hast set thy glory above the heavens!

2. Out of the mouth of very babes and sucklings hast thou ordained strength, because of thine enemies : that thou mightest still the enemy and the avenger.

3. For I will consider thy heavens, even the works of thy fingers : the moon and the stars, which thou hast ordained.

4. What is man, that thou art mindful of him : and the son of man, that thou visitest him?

5. Thou madest him lower than the angels : to crown him with glory and worship.

6. Thou makest him to have dominion of the works of thy hands : and thou hast put all things in subjection under his feet;

7. All sheep and oxen : yea, and the beasts of the field;

8. The fowls of the air, and the fishes of the sea : and whatsoever walketh through the paths of the seas.

9. O Lord our Governor : how excellent is thy Name in all the world!

ASH-WEDNESDAY

Turn ye even to me with all your heart, and with fasting, and with weeping, and with mourning. Joel 2. 12

The Collect
From 'Ash-Wednesday'

A LMIGHTY and everlasting God, who hatest nothing that thou hast made and dost forgive the sins of all them that are penitent : Create and make in us new and contrite hearts, that we, worthily lamenting our sins, and acknowledging our wretchedness, may obtain of thee, the God of all mercy, perfect remission and forgiveness; through Jesus Christ our Lord. Amen.

The Gospel. *St. Matthew 6. 16*
From 'Ash-Wednesday'

W HEN ye fast, be not, as the hypocrites, of a sad countenance : for they disfigure their faces, that they may appear unto men to fast. Verily I say unto you, They have their reward. But thou, when thou fastest, anoint thine head, and wash thy face; That thou appear not unto men to fast, but unto thy Father which is in secret : and thy Father, which seeth in secret, shall reward thee openly. Lay not up for yourselves treasures upon earth, where moth and rust doth corrupt, and where thieves break through and steal : But lay up for yourselves treasures in heaven, where neither moth nor rust doth corrupt ...

FORGIVEN SIN

Blessed is he whose unrighteousness is forgiven : and whose sin is covered.

Psalm 32. 1

The Collect
From 'Ash-Wednesday'

ALMIGHTY and everlasting God, who hatest nothing that thou hast made and dost forgive the sins of all them that are penitent: Create and make in us new and contrite hearts, that we, worthily lamenting our sins, and acknowledging our wretchedness, may obtain of thee, the God of all mercy, perfect remission and forgiveness; through Jesus Christ our Lord. Amen.

Psalm 6. *Domine, ne in furore*

O LORD, rebuke me not in thine indignation : neither chasten me in thy displeasure.

2. Have mercy upon me, O Lord, for I am weak : O Lord, heal me, for my bones are vexed.

3. My soul also is sore troubled : but, Lord, how long wilt thou punish me?

4. Turn thee, O Lord, and deliver my soul : O save me, for thy mercy's sake.

5. For in death no man remembereth thee : and who will give thee thanks in the pit?

MOURNING OVER SIN

I am brought into so great trouble and misery : that I go mourning all the day long.

Psalm 38. 6

Psalm 38. *Domine, ne in furore*

PUT me not to rebuke, O Lord, in thine anger : neither chasten me in thy heavy displeasure.

2. For thine arrows stick fast in me : and thy hand presseth me sore.

3. There is no health in my flesh, because of thy displeasure : neither is there any rest in my bones, by reason of my sin.

4. For my wickednesses are gone over my head : and are like a sore burden, too heavy for me to bear.

5. My wounds stink, and are corrupt : through my foolishness.

6. I am brought into so great trouble and misery : that I go mourning all the day long ...

9. Lord, thou knowest all my desire : and my groaning is not hid from thee.

10. My heart panteth, my strength hath failed me : and the light of mine eyes is gone from me.

11. My lovers and my neighbours did stand looking upon my trouble : and my kinsmen stood afar off.

12. They also that sought after my life laid snares for me : and they that went about to do me evil talked of wickedness, and imagined deceit all the day long.

REVERENCE FOR GOD

Hide not thy face from me in the time of my trouble : incline thine ear unto me when I call; O hear me, and that right soon. Psalm 102. 8

Psalm 102. *Domine, exaudi*

WHEN he turneth him unto the prayer of the poor destitute : and despiseth not their desire.

18. This shall be written for those that come after : and the people which shall be born shall praise the Lord.

19. For he hath looked down from his sanctuary : out of the heaven did the Lord behold the earth;

20. That he might hear the mournings of such as are in captivity : and deliver them that are appointed unto death;

21. That they may declare the Name of the Lord in Sion : and his worship at Jerusalem;

22. When the peoples are gathered together : and the kingdoms also, to serve the Lord.

23. He brought down my strength in my journey : and shortened my days.

24. But I said, O my God, take me not away in the midst of mine age : as for thy years, they endure throughout all generations.

25. Thou, Lord, in the beginning hast laid the foundation of the earth : and the heavens are the work of thy hands.

FASTING AND TEMPTATION

Then was Jesus led up of the Spirit into the wilderness to be tempted of the devil.

St. Matthew 4. 1

The Gospel. *St. Matthew 4. 1*
From 'The First Sunday in Lent'

THEN was Jesus led up of the Spirit into the wilderness to be tempted of the devil. And when he had fasted forty days and forty nights, he was afterward anhungred. And when the tempter came to him, he said, If thou be the Son of God, command that these stones be made bread. But he answered and said, It is written, Man shall not live by bread alone, but by every word that proceedeth out of the mouth of God. Then the devil taketh him up into the holy city, and setteth him on a pinnacle of the temple, And saith unto him, If thou be the Son of God, cast thyself down: for it is written, He shall give his angels charge concerning thee: and in their hands they shall bear thee up, lest at any time thou dash thy foot against a stone. Jesus said unto him, It is written again, Thou shalt not tempt the Lord thy God. Again, the devil taketh him up into an exceeding high mountain, and sheweth him all the kingdoms of the world, and the glory of them; And saith unto him, All these things will I give thee, if thou wilt fall down and worship me. Then saith Jesus unto him, Get thee hence, Satan: for it is written, Thou shalt worship the Lord thy God, and him only shalt thou serve. Then the devil leaveth him, and behold, angels came and ministered unto him.

FASTING AND PRAYER

In watchings, in fastings… 2 Corinthians 6. 5

The Collect
From 'Ash-Wednesday'

ALMIGHTY and everlasting God, who hatest nothing that thou hast made and dost forgive the sins of all them that are penitent: Create and make in us new and contrite hearts, that we, worthily lamenting our sins, and acknowledging our wretchedness, may obtain of thee, the God of all mercy, perfect remission and forgiveness; through Jesus Christ our Lord. Amen.

The Epistle. *2 Corinthians 6. 1*
From 'The First Sunday in Lent'

WE then, as workers together with him, beseech you also that ye receive not the grace of God in vain … Giving no offence in any thing, that the ministry be not blamed: But in all things approving ourselves as the ministers of God, in much patience, in afflictions, in necessities, in distresses, in stripes, in imprisonments, in tumults, in labours, in watchings, in fastings; by pureness, by knowledge, by long-suffering, by kindness, by the Holy Ghost, by love unfeigned, by the word of truth, by the power of God, by the armour of righteousness on the right hand and on the left, by honour and dishonour, by evil report and good report: as deceivers, and yet true; as unknown, and yet well known; as dying, and behold, we live.

OUR TROUBLES AND ADVERSITIES

Graciously look upon our afflictions. From 'The Ordering of Deacons'

From 'The Ordering of Deacons'

O GOD, merciful Father, that despisest not the sighing of a contrite heart, nor the desire of such as are sorrowful; Mercifully assist our prayers which we make before thee in all our troubles and adversities, whensoever they oppress us; and graciously hear us, that those evils which the craft and subtilty of the devil or man worketh be brought to nought; and by the providence of thy goodness they may be dispersed; that we thy servants, being hurt by no persecutions, may evermore give thanks unto thee in thy holy Church; through Jesus Christ our Lord.

O Lord, arise, help us, and deliver us for thy Name's sake.

WE humbly beseech thee, O Father, mercifully to look upon our in-firmities; and, for the glory of thy Name, turn from us all those evils that we most justly have deserved; and grant, that in all our troubles we may put our whole trust and confidence in thy mercy, and evermore serve thee in holiness and pureness of living, to thy honour and glory; through our only Mediator and Advocate, Jesus Christ our Lord. Amen.

KEEP ALL THY PEOPLE

That it may please thee to bless and keep all thy people; We beseech thee to hear us, good Lord. From 'The Ordering of Deacons'

From 'The Ordering of Deacons'
That it may please thee to give to all nations unity, peace, and concord;
    We beseech thee to hear us, good Lord.
    That it may please thee to give us an heart to love and dread thee, and diligently to live after thy commandments;
    We beseech thee to hear us, good Lord.
    That it may please thee to give to all thy people increase of grace to hear meekly thy Word, and to receive it with pure affection, and to bring forth the fruits of the Spirit;
    We beseech thee to hear us, good Lord.
    That it may please thee to bring into the way of truth all such as have erred, and are deceived;
    We beseech thee to hear us, good Lord.

EVENING PRAYER (3)

Enter not into judgment with thy servant, O Lord; for in thy sight shall no man living be justified. Psalm 143. 2

Deus Misereatur. *Psalm 67*
From 'Evening Prayer'

GOD be merciful unto us, and bless us : and shew us the light of his countenance, and be merciful unto us;

That thy way may be known upon earth : thy saving health among all nations.

Let the peoples praise thee, O God : yea, let all the peoples praise thee.

O let the nations rejoice and be glad : for thou shalt judge the folk righteously, and govern the nations upon earth.

Let the people praise thee, O God : yea, let all the people praise thee.

Then shall the earth bring forth her increase : and God, even our own God, shall give us his blessing.

God shall bless us : and all the ends of the world shall fear him.

Glory be to the Father, and to the Son : and to the Holy Ghost;

As it was in the beginning, is now, and ever shall be : world without end. Amen.

Meditation
God be merciful unto us, and bless us : and shew us the light of his countenance, and be merciful unto us. Psalm 67. 1

EVENING PRAYER (4)

I will arise and go to my father, and will say unto him, Father, I have sinned against heaven, and before thee, and am no more worthy to be called thy son.

St. Luke 15. 18–19

The Second Collect
From 'Evening Prayer'

O GOD, from whom all holy desires, all good counsels, and all just works do proceed; Give unto thy servants that peace which the world cannot give; that both our hearts may be set to obey thy commandments, and also that by thee we being defended from the fear of our enemies may pass our time in rest and quietness; through the merits of Jesus Christ our Saviour. Amen.

The Third Collect, For Aid Against All Perils
From 'Evening Prayer'

L IGHTEN our darkness, we beseech thee, O Lord; and by thy great mercy defend us from all perils and dangers of this night; for the love of thy only Son, our Saviour, Jesus Christ. Amen.

Meditation
Take not thy Holy Spirit from us. From 'Evening Prayer'

THE MESSIAH IN THE PSALMS (3)

He will be raised from the dead

Wherefore my heart is glad, and my glory rejoiceth : my flesh also shall rest in hope.
Psalm 16. 10

Psalm 16. *Conserva me, Domine*

PRESERVE me, O God : for in thee have I put my trust.
2. O my soul, thou hast said unto the Lord : Thou are my God, my goods are nothing unto thee.

3. All my delight is upon the saints, that are in the earth : and upon such as excel in virtue.

4. But they that run after another god : shall have great trouble.

5. Their drink–offerings of blood will I not offer : neither make mention of their names within my lips.

6. The Lord himself is the portion of mine inheritance, and of my cup : thou shalt maintain my lot.

7. The lot is fallen unto me in a fair ground : yea, I have a goodly heritage.

8. I will thank the Lord for giving me warning : my reins also chasten me in the night-season.

9. I have set God always before me : for he is on my right hand, therefore I shall not fall.

10. Wherefore my heart is glad, and my glory rejoiceth : my flesh also shall rest in hope.

WALKING IN GOD'S WAYS

For this is the will of God, even your sanctification. 1 Thessalonians 4. 3

The Collect
From 'The Second Sunday in Lent'

ALMIGHTY God, who seest that we have no power of ourselves to help ourselves; Keep us both outwardly in our bodies and inwardly in our souls; that we may be defended from all adversities which may happen to the body and from all evil thoughts which may assault and hurt the soul; through Jesus Christ our Lord. Amen.

The Epistle. *1 Thessalonians 4. 1*
From 'The Second Sunday in Lent'

WE beseech you, brethren, and exhort you by the Lord Jesus, that as ye have received of us how ye ought to walk and to please God, so ye would abound more and more. For ye know what commandments we gave you by the Lord Jesus. For this is the will of God, even your sanctification, that ye should abstain from fornication; that every one of you should know how to possess his vessel in sanctification and honour; not in the lust of concupiscence, even as the Gentiles which know not God: that no man go beyond and defraud his brother in any matter; because that the Lord is the avenger of all such, as we also have forewarned you, and testified. For God hath not called us unto uncleanness, but unto holiness.

INSTRUCTION FROM GOD'S WORD (3)

Give me understanding, and I shall keep thy law : yea, I shall keep it with my whole heart. Psalm 119. 34

The Collect
From 'The Second Sunday in Advent'

BLESSED Lord, who hast caused all holy Scriptures to be written for our learning; Grant that we may in such wise hear them, read, mark, learn, and inwardly digest them, that by patience and comfort of thy holy Word, we may embrace, and ever hold fast the blessed hope of everlasting life, which thou hast given us in our Saviour Jesus Christ. Amen.

Psalm 119. *Legem pone*

TEACH me, O Lord, the way of thy statutes : and I shall keep it unto the end.

34. Give me understanding, and I shall keep thy law : yea, I shall keep it with my whole heart.

35. Make me to go in the path of thy commandments : for therein is my desire.

36. Incline my heart unto thy testimonies : and not to covetousness.

37. O turn away mine eyes, lest they behold vanity : and quicken thou me in thy way.

38. O stablish thy word in thy servant : that I may fear thee.

'REMEMBER NOT, LORD,
OUR OFFENCES'

O God the Son, Redeemer of the world : have mercy upon us miserable sinners.
From 'The Litany'

From 'The Litany'

O GOD the Father of heaven: have mercy upon us miserable sinners.
O God the Father of heaven: have mercy upon us miserable sinners.

O God the Son, Redeemer of the world: have mercy upon us miserable sinners.

O God the Son, Redeemer of the world: have mercy upon us miserable sinners.

O God the Holy Ghost, proceeding from the Father and the Son: have mercy upon us miserable sinners.

O God the Holy Ghost, proceeding from the Father and the Son: have mercy upon us miserable sinners.

O holy, blessed, and glorious Trinity, three Persons and one God: have mercy upon us miserable sinners.

O holy, blessed, and glorious Trinity, three Persons and one God: have mercy upon us miserable sinners.

Remember not, Lord, our offences, nor the offences of our forefathers; neither take thou vengeance of our sins: spare us, good Lord, spare thy people, whom thou hast redeemed with thy most precious blood, and be not angry with us for ever.

Spare us, good Lord...

PSALMS OF PRAISE AND THANKSGIVING (1)

What is man?

What is man, that thou art mindful of him : and the son of man, that thou visitest him? Psalm 8. 4

Psalm 8. *Domine, Dominus noster*

O LORD our Governor, how excellent is thy Name in all the world : thou that hast set thy glory above the heavens!

2. Out of the mouth of very babes and sucklings hast thou ordained strength, because of thine enemies : that thou mightest still the enemy, and the avenger.

3. When I consider thy heavens, even the work of thy fingers : the moon and the stars, which thou hast ordained;

4. What is man, that thou art mindful of him : and the son of man, that thou visitest him?

5. Thou madest him lower than the angels : to crown him with glory and worship.

6. Thou makest him to have dominion of the works of thy hands : and thou hast put all things in subjection under his feet;

7. All sheep and oxen : yea, and the beasts of the field;

8. The fowls of the air, and the fishes of the sea : and whatsoever walketh through the paths of the seas.

9. O Lord our Governor : how excellent is thy Name in all the world!

PSALMS OF PRAISE AND THANKSGIVING (2)

The King of Glory

Who is the King of glory : it is the Lord strong and mighty, even the Lord mighty in battle. Psalm 24. 8

Psalm 24. *Domini est terra*

THE earth is the Lord's, and all that therein is : the compass of the world, and they that dwell therein.

2. For he hath founded it upon the seas : and prepared it upon the floods.

3. Who shall ascend into the hill of the Lord : or who shall rise up in his holy place?

4. Even he that hath clean hands, and a pure heart : and that hath not lift up his mind unto vanity, nor sworn to deceive his neighbour.

5. He shall receive the blessing from the Lord : and righteousness from the God of his salvation.

6. This is the generation of them that seek him : even of them that seek thy face, O Jacob.

7. Lift up your heads, O ye gates; and be ye lift up, ye everlasting doors : and the King of glory shall come in.

8. Who is the King of glory : it is the Lord strong and mighty, even the Lord mighty in battle.

9. Lift up your heads, O ye gates; and be ye lift up, ye everlasting doors : and the King of glory shall come in.

10. Who is the King of glory : even the Lord of hosts, he is the King of glory.

A VIRGIN SHALL CONCEIVE

Behold, a virgin shall be with child, and shall bring forth a son, and they shall call his name Emmanuel, which being interpreted is, God with us.

St. Matthew 1. 23

The Collect
From 'The Annunciation of the Blessed Virgin Mary'

WE beseech thee, O Lord, pour thy grace into our hearts; that, as we have known the incarnation of thy Son Jesus Christ by the message of an angel, so by his cross and passion we may be brought unto the glory of his resurrection; through the same Jesus Christ our Lord. Amen.

For the Epistle. *Isaiah 7. 10*
From 'The Annunciation of the Blessed Virgin Mary'

MOREOVER, the Lord spake again unto Ahaz, saying, Ask thee a sign of the Lord thy God; ask it either in the depth, or in the height above. But Ahaz said, I will not ask, neither will I tempt the Lord. And he said, Hear ye now, O house of David; Is it a small thing for you to weary men, but will ye weary my God also? Therefore the Lord himself shall give you a sign; Behold, a virgin shall conceive, and bear a son, and shall call his name Immanuel. Butter and honey shall he eat, that he may know to refuse the evil, and choose the good.

GABRIEL'S MESSAGE

Fear not, Mary : for thou hast found favour with God. St. Luke 1. 30

The Gospel. *St. Luke 1. 26*
From 'The Annunciation of the Blessed Virgin Mary'

AND in the sixth month the angel Gabriel was sent from God unto a city of Galilee, named Nazareth, to a Virgin espoused to a man whose name was Joseph, of the house of David; and the Virgin's name was Mary. And the angel came in unto her, and said, Hail, thou that art highly favoured, the Lord is with thee: blessed art thou among women. And when she saw him, she was troubled at his saying, and cast in her mind what manner of salutation this should be. And the angel said unto her, Fear not, Mary; for thou hast found favour with God. And, behold, thou shalt conceive in thy womb, and bring forth a Son, and shalt call his name JESUS. He shall be great, and shall be called the Son of the Highest; and the Lord God shall give unto him the throne of his father David. And he shall reign over the house of Jacob for ever; and of his kingdom there shall be no end. Then said Mary unto the angel, How shall this be, seeing I know not a man? And the angel answered and said unto her, The Holy Ghost shall come upon thee, and the power of the Highest shall overshadow thee: therefore also that holy thing which shall be born of thee shall be called the Son of God. And behold, thy cousin Elisabeth, she hath also conceived a son in her old age; and this is the sixth month with her who was called barren: for with God nothing shall be impossible.

GOODNESS AND RIGHTEOUSNESS

For the fruit of the Spirit is in all goodness and righteousness and truth.

Ephesians 5. 9

The Epistle. *Ephesians 5. 1*
From 'The Third Sunday in Lent'

BE ye therefore followers of God, as dear children; and walk in love, as Christ also hath loved us, and hath given himself for us, an offering and a sacrifice to God for a sweet-smelling savour. But fornication, and all un-cleanness, or covetousness, let it not be once named amongst you, as be-cometh saints; neither filthiness, nor foolish-talking, nor jesting, which are not convenient; but rather giving of thanks: for this ye know, that no whoremonger, nor unclean person, nor covetous man, who is an idolater, hath any inheritance in the kingdom of Christ, and of God. Let no man deceive you with vain words : for because of these things cometh the wrath of God upon the children of disobedience. Be not ye therefore partakers with them: for ye were sometimes darkness, but now are ye light in the Lord : walk as children of light; (for the fruit of the Spirit is in all goodness, and righteousness, and truth;) proving what is acceptable unto the Lord. And have no fellowship with the unfruitful works of darkness, but rather reprove them : for it is a shame even to speak of those things which are done of them in secret … Wherefore he saith, Awake, thou that sleepest, and arise from the dead, and Christ shall give thee light.

DIVINE POWER

But if I with the finger of God cast out devils, no doubt the kingdom of God is come upon you. St. Luke 11. 20

The Gospel. *St. Luke 11. 14*
From 'The Third Sunday in Lent'

JESUS was casting out a devil, and it was dumb. And it came to pass, when the devil was gone out, the dumb spake; and the people wondered. But some of them said, He casteth out devils through Beelzebub, the chief of the devils. And others, tempting him, sought of him a sign from heaven. But he, knowing their thoughts, said unto them, Every kingdom divided against itself is brought to desolation; and a house divided against a house falleth. If Satan also be divided against himself, how shall his kingdom stand? because ye say, that I cast out devils through Beelzebub. And if I by Beelzebub cast out devils, by whom do your sons cast them out? therefore shall they be your judges. But if I with the finger of God cast out devils, no doubt the kingdom of God is come upon you. When a strong man armed keepeth his palace, his goods are in peace; but when a stronger than he shall come upon him, and overcome him, he taketh from him all his armour wherein he trusted, and divideth his spoils. He that is not with me is against me: and he that gathereth not with me scattereth.

PSALMS OF PRAISE AND THANKSGIVING (3)
Honour God

Give the Lord the honour due unto his Name : worship the Lord with holy worship. Psalm 29. 2

Psalm 29. *Afferte Domino*

BRING unto the Lord, O ye mighty, bring young rams unto the Lord : ascribe unto the Lord worship and strength.

2. Give the Lord the honour due unto his Name : worship the Lord with holy worship.

3. It is the Lord, that commandeth the waters : it is the glorious God, that maketh the thunder.

4. It is the Lord, that ruleth the sea; the voice of the Lord is mighty in operation : the voice of the Lord is a glorious voice.

5. The voice of the Lord breaketh the cedar-trees : yea, the Lord breaketh the cedars of Libanus.

6. He maketh them also to skip like a calf : Libanus also, and Sirion, like a young unicorn.

7. The voice of the Lord divideth the flames of fire; the voice of the Lord shaketh the wilderness : yea, the Lord shaketh the wilderness of Cades.

8. The voice of the Lord maketh the hinds to bring forth young, and discovereth the thick bushes : in his temple doth every man speak of his honour.

9. The Lord sitteth above the water-flood : and the Lord remaineth a King for ever.

THE MESSIAH IN THE PSALMS (4)

God will forsake him in his hour of need

My God, my God, look upon me; why hast thou forsaken me : and art so far from my health, and from the words of my complaint? O my God, I cry in the day-time, but thou hearest not : and in the night-season also I take no rest. Psalm 22. 1

The Gospel. *St. Matthew 27. 45–54*
From 'The Sunday before Easter'

NOW from the sixth hour there was darkness over all the land unto the ninth hour. And about the ninth hour Jesus cried with a loud voice, saying, Eli, Eli, lama sabachthani? that is to say, My God, my God, why hast thou forsaken me? Some of them that stood there, when they heard that, said, This man calleth for Elias. And straightway one of them ran, and took a spunge, and filled it with vinegar, and put it on a reed, and gave him to drink. The rest said, Let be, let us see whether Elias will come to save him. Jesus, when he had cried again with a loud voice, yielded up the ghost. And, behold, the veil of the temple was rent in twain from the top to the bottom; and the earth did quake, and the rocks rent; And the graves were opened; and many bodies of the saints which slept arose, And came out of the graves after his resurrection, and went into the holy city, and appeared unto many. Now when the centurion, and they that were with him, watching Jesus, saw the earthquake, and those things that were done, they feared greatly, saying, Truly this was the Son of God.

IN DEEP TROUBLE (2)

Thou art my helper, and my redeemer : O Lord, make no long tarrying.

Psalm 70. 6

Psalm 141. *Domine, clamavi*

LORD, I call upon thee, haste thee unto me : and consider my voice when I cry unto thee.

2. Let my prayer be set forth in thy sight as the incense : and let the lifting up of my hands be an evening sacrifice.

3. Set a watch, O Lord, before my mouth : and keep the door of my lips.

4. O let not mine heart be inclined to any evil thing : let me not be occupied in ungodly works with the men that work wickedness, lest I eat of such things as please them.

5. Let the righteous rather smite me friendly : and reprove me.

6. But let not their precious balms break my head : yea, I will pray yet against their wickedness.

7. Let their judges be overthrown in stony places : that they may hear my words, for they are sweet.

8. Our bones lie scattered before the pit : like as when one breaketh and heweth wood upon the earth.

9. But mine eyes look unto thee, O Lord God : in thee is my trust, O cast not out my soul.

10. Keep me from the snare that they have laid for me : and from the traps of the wicked doers.

PSALMS OF PRAISE AND
THANKSGIVING (4)

God is over all

Let all the earth fear the Lord : stand in awe of him, all ye that dwell in the world.
Psalm 33. 8

Psalm 33. *Exultate, justi*

REJOICE in the Lord, O ye righteous : for it becometh well the just to be thankful.

2. Praise the Lord with harp : sing praises unto him with the lute, and instrument of ten strings.

3. Sing unto the Lord a new song : sing praises lustily unto him with a good courage.

4. For the word of the Lord is true : and all his works are faithful.

5. He loveth righteousness and judgement : the earth is full of the goodness of the Lord.

6. By the word of the Lord were the heavens made : and all the host of them by the breath of his mouth.

7. He gathereth the waters of the sea together, as it were upon an heap : and layeth up the deep, as in a treasure-house.

8. Let all the earth fear the Lord : stand in awe of him, all ye that dwell in the world.

9. For he spake, and it was done : he commanded, and it stood fast.

10. The Lord bringeth the counsel of the heathen to nought: and maketh the devices of the people to be of none effect, and casteth out the counsels of princes.

PSALMS OF PRAISE AND THANKSGIVING (5)

Our refuge and strength

God is our hope and strength : a very present help in trouble. Psalm 46. 1

Psalm 46. *Deus noster refugium*

GOD is our hope and strength : a very present help in trouble.

2. Therefore will we not fear, though the earth be moved : and though the hills be carried into the midst of the sea.

3. Though the waters thereof rage and swell : and though the mountains shake at the tempest of the same.

4. The rivers of the flood thereof shall make glad the city of God : the holy place of the tabernacle of the most Highest.

5. God is in the midst of her, therefore shall she not be removed : God shall help her, and that right early.

6. The heathen make much ado, and the kingdoms are moved : but God hath shewed his voice, and the earth shall melt away.

7. The Lord of hosts is with us : the God of Jacob is our refuge.

8. O come hither, and behold the works of the Lord : what destruction he hath brought upon the earth.

9. He maketh wars to cease in all the world : he breaketh the bow, and knappeth the spear in sunder, and burneth the chariots in the fire.

10. Be still then, and know that I am God : I will be exalted among the heathen, and I will be exalted in the earth.

11. The Lord of hosts is with us : the God of Jacob is our refuge.

TWO COVENANTS

Now we, brethren, as Isaac was, are the children of promise. Galatians 4. 28

The Epistle. *Galatians 4. 21*
From 'The Fourth Sunday in Lent'

TELL me, ye that desire to be under the law, do ye not hear the law? For it is written, that Abraham had two sons, the one by a bond-maid, the other by a free-woman. But he who was of the bond-woman was born after the flesh; but he of the free-woman was by promise. Which things are an allegory: for these are the two covenants; the one from the mount Sinai, which gendereth to bondage, which is Agar. For this Agar is mount Sinai in Arabia, and answereth to Jerusalem which now is, and is in bondage with her children. But Jerusalem which is above is free; which is the mother of us all. For it is written, Rejoice, thou barren that bearest not; break forth and cry, thou that travailest not: for the desolate hath many more children than she which hath an husband. Now we, brethren, as Isaac was, are the children of promise. But as then he that was born after the flesh persecuted him that was born after the Spirit; even so it is now. Nevertheless, what saith the Scripture? Cast out the bond-woman and her son; for the son of the bond-woman shall not be heir with the son of the free-woman. So then, brethren, we are not children of the bond-woman, but of the free.

'FIVE BARLEY LOAVES, AND TWO SMALL FISHES'

There is a lad here, which hath five barley loaves, and two small fishes: but what are they among so many? St. John 6. 9

The Gospel. *St. John 6. 1*
From 'The Fourth Sunday in Lent'

JESUS went over the sea of Galilee, which is the sea of Tiberias. And a great multitude followed him, because they saw his miracles which he did on them that were diseased. And Jesus went up into a mountain, and there he sat with his disciples. And the Passover, a feast of the Jews, was nigh. When Jesus then lifted up his eyes, and saw a great company come unto him, he saith unto Philip, Whence shall we buy bread, that these may eat? (And this he said to prove him; for he himself knew what he would do.) Philip answered him, Two hundred pennyworth of bread is not sufficient for them, that every one of them may take a little. One of his disciples, Andrew, Simon Peter's brother, saith unto him, There is a lad here, which hath five barley loaves, and two small fishes: but what are they among so many? And Jesus said, Make the men sit down. Now there was much grass in the place. So the men sat down, in number about five thousand. And Jesus took the loaves, and when he had given thanks he distributed to the disciples, and the disciples to them that were set down; and likewise of the fishes as much as they would. When they were filled, he said unto his disciples, Gather up the fragments that remain, that nothing be lost.

A HYMN OF PRAISE AND THANKSGIVING

The Lord is gracious and full of compassion : slow to anger, and of great mercy.

Psalm 103.8

From 'Forms of Prayer to be Used at Sea'

O COME, let us give thanks unto the Lord, for he is gracious : and his mercy endureth for ever.

Great is the Lord, and greatly to be praised; let the redeemed of the Lord say so : whom he hath delivered from the merciless rage of the sea.

The Lord is gracious and full of compassion : slow to anger, and of great mercy.

He hath not dealt with us according to our sins : neither rewarded us according to our iniquities.

But as the heaven is high above the earth : so great hath been his mercy towards us.

We found trouble and heaviness : we were even at death's door.

The waters of the sea had well-nigh covered us : the proud waters had well-nigh gone over our soul.

The sea roared : and the stormy wind lifted up the waves thereof.

We were carried up as it were to heaven, and then down again into the deep : our soul melted within us, because of trouble;

Then cried we unto thee, O Lord : and thou didst deliver us out of our distress.

INSTRUCTION FROM GOD'S WORD (4)

I have thought upon thy Name, O Lord, in the night-season : and have kept thy law. Psalm 119. 55

The Collect
From 'The Second Sunday in Advent'

BLESSED Lord, who hast caused all holy Scriptures to be written for our learning: Grant that we may in such wise hear them, read, mark, learn, and inwardly digest them, that by patience and comfort of thy holy Word, we may embrace, and ever hold fast the blessed hope of everlasting life, which thou hast given us in our Saviour Jesus Christ. Amen.

Psalm 119. *Memor esto servi tui*

O THINK upon thy servant, as concerning thy word : wherein thou hast caused me to put my trust.

50. The same is my comfort in my trouble : for thy word hath quickened me.

51. The proud have had me exceedingly in derision : yet have I not shrinked from thy law.

52. For I remembered thine everlasting judgements, O Lord : and received comfort.

53. I am horribly afraid : for the ungodly that forsake thy law.

54. Thy statutes have been my songs : in the house of my pilgrimage.

PSALMS OF PRAISE AND
THANKSGIVING (6)

Sing praise to our God

O sing praises, sing praises unto our God : O sing praises, sing praises unto our King. Psalm 47. 6

Psalm 47. *Omnes gentes, plaudite*

O CLAP your hands together, all ye people : O sing unto God with the voice of melody.

2. For the Lord is high, and to be feared : he is the great King upon all the earth.

3. He shall subdue the people under us : and the nations under our feet.

4. He shall choose out an heritage for us : even the excellency of Jacob, whom he loved.

5. God is gone up with a merry noise : and the Lord with the sound of the trump.

6. O sing praises, sing praises unto our God : O sing praises, sing praises unto our King.

7. For God is the King of all the earth : sing ye praises with understanding.

8. God reigneth over the heathen : God sitteth upon his holy seat.

9. The princes of the peoples are joined unto the people of the God of Abraham : for God, which is very high exalted, doth defend the earth, as it were with a shield.

PSALMS OF PRAISE AND THANKSGIVING (7)
God and his city

The hill of Sion is a fair place, and the joy of the whole earth : upon the north-side lieth the city of the great King; God is well known in her palaces as a sure refuge.

Psalm 48. 2

Psalm 48. *Magnus Dominus*

GREAT is the Lord, and highly to be praised : in the city of our God, even upon his holy hill ...

3. For lo, the kings of the earth : were gathered, and gone by together.

4. They marvelled to see such things : they were astonished, and suddenly cast down.

5. Fear came there upon them, and sorrow : as upon a woman in her travail.

6. Thou dost break the ships of the sea : through the east-wind.

7. Like as we have heard, so have we seen in the city of the Lord of hosts, in the city of our God : God upholdeth the same for ever.

8. We wait for thy loving-kindness, O God : in the midst of thy temple.

9. O God, according to thy Name, so is thy praise unto the world's end : thy right hand is full of righteousness.

Meditation
For this God is our God for ever and ever : he shall be our guide unto death.

Psalm 48. 13

PSALMS OF PRAISE AND THANKSGIVING (8)

Harvest Thanksgiving

The river of God is full of water : thou preparest their corn, for so thou providest for the earth. Psalm 65. 10

Psalm 65. *Te decet hymnus*

THOU, O God, art praised in Sion : and unto thee shall the vow be performed in Jerusalem.

2. Thou that hearest the prayer : unto thee shall all flesh come.

3. My misdeeds prevail against me : O be thou merciful unto our sins.

4. Blessed is the man whom thou choosest, and receivest unto thee : he shall dwell in thy court, and shall be satisfied with the pleasures of thy house, even of thy holy temple.

5. Thou shalt shew us wonderful things in thy righteousness, O God of our salvation : thou that art the hope of all the ends of the earth, and of them that remain in the broad sea.

6. Who in his strength setteth fast the mountains : and is girded about with power.

7. Who stilleth the raging of the sea : and the noise of his waves, and the madness of the people.

8. They also that dwell in the uttermost parts of the earth shall be afraid at thy tokens : thou that makest the outgoings of the morning and evening to praise thee.

9. Thou visitest the earth, and blessest it : thou makest it very plenteous.

ETERNAL REDEMPTION

By his own blood he entered in once into the holy place, having obtained eternal redemption for us. Hebrews 9. 12

The Collect
From 'The Fifth Sunday in Lent'

WE beseech thee, Almighty God, mercifully to look upon thy people; that by thy great goodness they may be governed and preserved evermore, both in body and soul; through Jesus Christ our Lord. Amen.

The Epistle. *Hebrews 9. 11*
From 'The Fifth Sunday in Lent'

CHRIST being come an High Priest of good things to come, by a greater and more perfect tabernacle, not made with hands; that is to say, not of this building; neither by the blood of goats and calves; but by his own blood he entered in once into the holy place, having obtained eternal redemption for us. For if the blood of bulls and of goats, and the ashes of an heifer sprinkling the unclean, sanctifieth to the purifying of the flesh; how much more shall the blood of Christ, who, through the eternal Spirit, offered himself without spot to God, purge your conscience from dead works to serve the living God? And for this cause he is the mediator of the new testament, that by means of death, for the redemption of the transgressions that were under the first testament, they which are called might receive the promise of eternal inheritance.

CHRIST AND ABRAHAM

If a man keep my saying, he shall never taste of death. John 8. 51

The Gospel. *St. John 8. 46*
From 'The Fifth Sunday in Lent'

JESUS said, Which of you convinceth me of sin? and if I say the truth, why do ye not believe me? He that is of God heareth God's words; ye therefore hear them not, because ye are not of God. Then answered the Jews, and said unto him, Say we not well, that thou art a Samaritan, and hast a devil? Jesus answered, I have not a devil; but I honour my Father, and ye do dishonour me. And I seek not mine own glory; there is one that seeketh and judgeth. Verily, verily, I say unto you, If a man keep my saying, he shall never see death. Then said the Jews unto him, Now we know that thou hast a devil. Abraham is dead, and the prophets; and thou sayest, If a man keep my saying, he shall never taste of death. Art thou greater than our father Abraham, which is dead? and the prophets are dead: whom makest thou thyself? Jesus answered, If I honour myself, my honour is nothing; it is my Father that honoureth me, of whom ye say, that he is your God: yet ye have not known him; but I know him: and if I should say, I know him not, I shall be a liar like unto you; but I know him, and keep his saying. Your father Abraham rejoiced to see my day, and he saw it, and was glad. Then said the Jews unto him, Thou art not yet fifty years old, and hast thou seen Abraham? Jesus said unto them, Verily, verily, I say unto you, before Abraham was, I am.

THE MESSIAH IN THE PSALMS (5)

He will be scorned and mocked

All they that see me laugh me to scorn : they shoot out their lips, and shake their heads, saying, He trusted in God, that he would deliver him : let him deliver him, if he will have him. Psalm 22. 7–8

Psalm 22. *Deus, Deus meus*

MY God, my God, look upon me; why has thou forsaken me : and art so far from my health, and from the words of my complaint?

2. O my God, I cry in the day-time, but thou hearest not : and in the night-season also I take no rest.

3. And thou continuest holy : O thou worship of Israel.

4. Our fathers hoped in thee : they trusted in thee, and thou didst deliver them.

5. They called upon thee, and were holpen : they put their trust in thee, and were not confounded.

6. But as for me, I am a worm, and no man : a very scorn of men, and the out-cast of the people.

Meditation

And the people stood beholding. And the rulers also with them derided him, saying, He saved others; let him save himself, if he be Christ, the chosen of God. And the soldiers also mocked him. St. Luke 23. 35–36

'THEY GAPE UPON ME'

All they that see me laugh me to scorn. Psalm 22. 7

Psalm 22. *Deus, Deus meus*

But thou art he that took me out of my mother's womb : thou wast my hope, when I hanged yet upon my mother's breasts.

10. I have been left unto thee ever since I was born : thou art my God even from my mother's womb.

11. O go not from me, for trouble is hard at hand : and there is none to help me.

12. Many oxen are come about me : fat bulls of Basan close me in on every side.

13. They gape upon me with their mouths : as it were a ramping and a roaring lion.

14. I am poured out like water, and all my bones are out of joint : my heart also in the midst of my body is even like melting wax.

15. My strength is dried up like a potsherd, and my tongue cleaveth to my gums : and thou bringest me into the dust of death.

16. For many dogs are come about me : and the council of the wicked layeth siege against me.

Meditation
They shoot out their lips, and shake their heads. Psalm 22. 7

'THEY PIERCED MY HANDS'

They pierced my hands and my feet; I may tell all my bones : they stand staring and looking upon me. Psalm 22. 17

Psalm 22. *Deus, Deus meus*

THEY pierced my hands and my feet; I may tell all my bones : they stand staring and looking upon me.

18. They part my garments among them : and cast lots upon my vesture.

19. But be not thou far from me, O Lord : thou art my succour, haste thee to help me.

20. Deliver my soul from the sword : my darling from the power of the dog.

21. Save me from the lion's mouth : thou hast heard me also from among the horns of the unicorns.

22. I will declare thy Name unto my brethren : in the midst of the congregation will I praise thee.

23. O praise the Lord, ye that fear him : magnify him, all ye of the seed of Jacob, and fear him, all ye seed of Israel.

24. For he hath not despised, nor abhorred, the low estate of the poor : he hath not hid his face from him, but when he called unto him he heard him.

25. My praise is of thee in the great congregation : my vows will I perform in the sight of them that fear him.

26. The poor shall eat, and be satisfied : they that seek after the Lord shall praise him; your heart shall live for ever.

'I WAITED PATIENTLY
FOR THE LORD'

And he hath put a new song in my mouth : even a thanksgiving unto our God.

Psalm 40. 3

Psalm 40. *Expectans expectavi*

I WAITED patiently for the Lord : and he inclined unto me, and heard my calling.

2. He brought me also out of the horrible pit, out of the mire and clay : and set my feet upon the rock, and ordered my goings.

3. And he hath put a new song in my mouth : even a thanksgiving unto our God.

4. Many shall see it, and fear : and shall put their trust in the Lord.

5. Blessed is the man that hath set his hope in the Lord : and turned not unto the proud, and to such as go about with lies.

6. O Lord my God, great are the wondrous works which thou hast done, like as be also thy thoughts which are to us-ward : and yet there is no man that ordereth them unto thee.

7. If I should declare them, and speak of them : they should be more than I am able to express.

8. Sacrifice, and meat-offering, thou wouldest not : but mine ears hast thou opened.

THE HUMILITY OF JESUS

Who ... took upon him the form of a servant, and was made in the likeness of men.
Philippians 2. 6–7

The Collect
From 'The Sunday Next Before Easter'

ALMIGHTY and everlasting God, who, of thy tender love towards mankind, hast sent thy Son, our Saviour Jesus Christ, to take upon him our flesh, and to suffer death upon the cross, that all mankind should follow the example of his great humility; Mercifully grant, that we may both follow the example of his patience, and also be made partakers of his resurrection; through the same Jesus Christ our Lord. Amen.

The Epistle. *Philippians 2. 5*
From 'The Sunday Next Before Easter'

LET this mind be in you, which was also in Christ Jesus : who, being in the form of God, thought it not robbery to be equal with God; but made himself of no reputation, and took upon him the form of a servant, and was made in the likeness of men : and being found in fashion as a man, he humbled himself, and became obedient unto death, even the death of the cross. Wherefore God also hath highly exalted him, and given him a Name which is above every name; that at the Name of Jesus every knee should bow, of things in heaven, and things in earth, and things under the earth; and that every tongue should confess that Jesus Christ is Lord ...

JUDAS THE BETRAYER

[Judas] then, having received the sop, went immediately out; and it was night.

John 13. 30

The Gospel. *St. Matthew 27. 3*
From 'The Sunday Next Before Easter'

Then Judas who had betrayed him, when he saw that he was condemned, repented himself, and brought again the thirty pieces of silver to the chief priests and elders, saying, I have sinned, in that I have betrayed the innocent blood. And they said, What is that to us? see thou to that. And he cast down the pieces of silver in the temple, and departed, and went and hanged himself. And the chief priests took the silver pieces, and said, It is not lawful for to put them into the treasury, because it is the price of blood. And they took counsel, and bought with them the potter's field, to bury strangers in. Wherefore that field was called, The field of blood, unto this day ... And Jesus stood before the governor; and the governor asked him, saying, Art thou the King of the Jews? And Jesus said unto him, Thou sayest. And when he was accused of the chief priests and elders, he answered nothing. Then said Pilate unto him, Hearest thou not how many things they witness against thee? And he answered him to never a word, insomuch that the governor marvelled greatly.

'WHEREFORE ART THOU
RED IN THINE APPAREL?'

Who is this that cometh from Edom, with dyed garments from Bozrah? this that is glorious in his apparel, travelling in the greatness of his strength? I that speak in righteousness, mighty to save. Isaiah 63. 1

For the Epistle. *Isaiah 63. 7*
From 'Monday Before Easter'

I WILL mention the loving-kindnesses of the Lord, and the praises of the Lord, according to all that the Lord hath bestowed on us, and the great goodness towards the house of Israel, which he hath bestowed on them according to his mercies, and according to the multitude of his loving-kindnesses. For he said, Surely they are my people, children that will not lie: so he was their Saviour. In all their affliction he was afflicted, and the angel of his presence saved them: in his love, and in his pity, he redeemed them, and he bare them, and carried them all the days of old. But they rebelled, and vexed his Holy Spirit; therefore he was turned to be their enemy, and he fought against them. Then he remembered the days of old, Moses and his people, saying, Where is he that brought them up out of the sea with the shepherd of his flock? where is he that put his Holy Spirit within him? that led them by the right hand of Moses, with his glorious arm, dividing the water before them, to make himself an everlasting Name? that led them through the deep as an horse in the wilderness, that they should not stumble?

'I GAVE MY BACK
TO THE SMITERS'

I gave my back to the smiters, and my cheeks to them that plucked off the hair: I hid not my face from shame and spitting. Isaiah 50. 6

For the Epistle. *Isaiah 50. 5*
From 'Tuesday Before Easter'

THE Lord God hath opened mine ear, and I was not rebellious, neither turned away back. I gave my back to the smiters, and my cheeks to them that plucked off the hair: I hid not my face from shame and spitting. For the Lord God will help me, therefore shall I not be confounded: therefore have I set my face like a flint, and I know that I shall not be ashamed. He is near that justifieth me; who will contend with me? Let us stand together; who is mine adversary? let him come near to me. Behold, the Lord God will help me; who is he that shall condemn me? Lo, they all shall wax old as a garment: the moth shall eat them up. Who is among you that feareth the Lord, that obeyeth the voice of his servant, that walketh in darkness, and hath no light? let him trust in the Name of the Lord, and stay upon his God. Behold, all ye that kindle a fire, that compass yourselves about with sparks; walk in the light of your fire, and in the sparks that ye have kindled. This shall ye have of mine hand, ye shall lie down in sorrow.

Meditation
For the Lord God will help me; therefore shall I not be confounded: therefore have I set my face like a flint, and I know that I shall not be ashamed. Isaiah 50. 7

THE SHEDDING OF BLOOD

Without shedding of blood is no remission. Hebrews 9. 22

The Epistle. *Hebrews 9. 16*
From 'Wednesday Before Easter'

WHERE a testament is, there must also of necessity be the death of the testator. For a testament is of force after men are dead: otherwise it is of no strength at all while the testator liveth. Whereupon neither the first testament was dedicated without blood. For when Moses had spoken every precept to all the people according to the law, he took the blood of calves and of goats, with water, and scarlet wool, and hyssop, and sprinkled both the book, and all the people, saying, This is the blood of the testament which God hath enjoined unto you. Moreover, he sprinkled with blood both the tabernacle, and all the vessels of the ministry. And almost all things are by the law purged with blood; and without shedding of blood is no remission. It was therefore necessary that the patterns of things in the heavens should be purified with these; but the heavenly things themselves with better sacrifices than these. For Christ is not entered into the holy places made with hands, which are the figures of the true, but into heaven itself, now to appear in the presence of God for us; nor yet that he should offer himself often, as the high priest entereth into the holy place every year with blood of others: for then must he often have suffered since the foundation of the world; but now once in the end of the world hath he appeared to put away sin by the sacrifice of himself.

MAUNDY THURSDAY

Christ our passover is sacrificed for us: Therefore let us keep the feast.
1 Corinthians 5. 7

The Epistle. *1 Corinthians 11. 17*
From 'Thursday Before Easter'

IN this that I declare unto you, I praise you not; that ye come together not for the better, but for the worse. For first of all, when ye come together in the church, I hear that there be divisions among you, and I partly believe it. For there must be also heresies among you, that they who are approved may be made manifest among you. When ye come together therefore into one place, this is not to eat the Lord's supper: for in eating every one taketh before other his own supper; and one is hungry, and another is drunken. What, have ye not houses to eat and to drink in? or despise ye the church of God, and shame them that have not? What shall I say to you? shall I praise you in this? I praise you not. For I have received of the Lord that which also I delivered unto you, That the Lord Jesus, the same night in which he was betrayed, took bread; and when he had given thanks, he brake it, and said, Take, eat; this is my body, which is broken for you: this do in remembrance of me. After the same manner also he took the cup, when he had supped, saying, This cup is the new testament in my blood: this do ye, as oft as ye drink it, in remembrance of me. For as often as ye eat this bread, and drink this cup, ye do shew the Lord's death till he come.

GOOD FRIDAY

By the which will we are sanctified through the offering of the body of Jesus Christ once for all. Hebrews 10. 10

The Epistle. *Hebrews 10. 1*
From 'Good Friday'

THE law having a shadow of good things to come, and not the very image of the things, can never with those sacrifices which they offered year by year continually make the comers thereunto perfect: for then would they not have ceased to be offered? because that the worshippers once purged should have had no more conscience of sins. But in those sacrifices there is a remembrance again made of sins every year. For it is not possible that the blood of bulls and of goats should take away sins. Wherefore, when he cometh into the world, he saith, Sacrifice and offering thou wouldest not, but a body hast thou prepared me: In burnt-offerings and sacrifices for sin thou hast had no pleasure: Then said I, Lo, I come (in the volume of the book it is written of me) to do thy will, O God. Above, when he said, Sacrifice and offering, and burnt-offerings, and offering for sin thou wouldest not, neither hadst pleasure therein, which are offered by the Law: then said he, Lo, I come to do thy will, O God. He taketh away the first, that he may establish the second. By the which will we are sanctified through the offering of the body of Jesus Christ once for all. And every priest standeth daily ministering and offering oftentimes the same sacrifices, which can never take away sins.

CHRIST WHO DIED FOR US

For Christ also hath once suffered for sins, the just for the unjust, that he might bring us to God. 1 St. Peter 3. 18

The Collect
From 'Easter Even'

GRANT, O Lord, that as we are baptized into the death of thy blessed Son our Saviour Jesus Christ, so by continual mortifying our corrupt affections we may be buried with him: and that through the grave, and gate of death, we may pass to our joyful resurrection; for his merits, who died, and was buried, and rose again for us, thy Son Jesus Christ our Lord. Amen.

The Epistle. *1 St. Peter 3. 17*
From 'Easter Even'

IT is better, if the will of God be so, that ye suffer for well-doing, than for evil-doing. For Christ also hath once suffered for sins, the just for the unjust, that he might bring us to God, being put to death in the flesh, but quickened by the Spirit. By which also he went and preached unto the spirits in prison; which sometime were disobedient, when once the long-suffering of God waited in the days of Noah, while the ark was a preparing; wherein few, that is, eight souls, were saved by water.

EASTER-DAY

Christ is risen from the dead: and become the first-fruits of them that sleep.
1 Corinthians 15. 20

The Gospel. *St. John 20. 1*
From 'Easter-Day'

THE first day of the week cometh Mary Magdalen early, when it was yet dark, unto the sepulchre, and seeth the stone taken away from the sepulchre. Then she runneth and cometh to Simon Peter, and to the other disciple whom Jesus loved, and saith unto them, They have taken away the Lord out of the sepulchre, and we know not where they have laid him. Peter therefore went forth, and that other disciple, and came to the sepulchre. So they ran both together; and the other disciple did outrun Peter, and came first to the sepulchre; and he, stooping down and looking in, saw the linen clothes lying; yet went he not in. Then cometh Simon Peter following him, and went into the sepulchre, and seeth the linen clothes lie; and the napkin that was about his head, not lying with the linen clothes, but wrapped together in a place by itself. Then went in also that other disciple which came first to the sepulchre, and he saw, and believed. For as yet they knew not the Scripture, that he must rise again from the dead. Then the disciples went away again unto their own home.

Meditation
Christ being raised from the dead dieth no more. Romans 6. 9

THE OPEN GATE

Art thou only a stranger in Jerusalem, and hast not known the things which are come to pass there in these days? St. Luke 24. 18

The Gospel. *St. Luke 24. 13*
From 'Monday in Easter-Week'

BEHOLD, two of them went that same day to a village called Emmaus, which was from Jerusalem about three-score furlongs. And they talked together of all these things which had happened. And it came to pass, that, while they communed together and reasoned, Jesus himself drew near, and went with them. But their eyes were holden that they should not know him. And he said unto them, What manner of communications are these that ye have one to another, as ye walk, and are sad? And the one of them, whose name was Cleopas, answering, said unto him, Art thou only a stranger in Jerusalem, and hast not known the things which are come to pass there in these days? And he said unto them, What things? And they said unto him, Concerning Jesus of Nazareth, which was a prophet mighty in deed and word, before God and all the people: and how the chief priests and our rulers delivered him to be condemned to death, and have crucified him. But we trusted that it had been he which should have redeemed Israel: and besides all this, to-day is the third day since these things were done...

THE MISSING BODY

They found not his body. St. Luke 24. 23

The Gospel. *St. Luke 24. 22*
From 'Monday in Easter-Week'

Yea, and certain women also of our company made us astonished, which were early at the sepulchre; and when they found not his body, they came, saying, that they had also seen a vision of angels, which said that he was alive. And certain of them which were with us went to the sepulchre, and found it even so as the women had said; but him they saw not. Then he said unto them, O fools, and slow of heart to believe all that the prophets have spoken: ought not Christ to have suffered these things, and to enter into his glory? And beginning at Moses, and all the prophets, he expounded unto them in all the Scriptures the things concerning himself. And they drew nigh unto the village whither they went; and he made as though he would have gone further: but they constrained him, saying, Abide with us, for it is towards evening, and the day is far spent. And he went in to tarry with them. And it came to pass, as he sat at meat with them, he took bread, and blessed it, and brake, and gave to them. And their eyes were opened, and they knew him, and he vanished out of their sight. And they said one to another, Did not our heart burn within us, while he talked with us by the way, and while he opened to us the Scriptures?

PREACHING WITH RESURRECTION POWER

And he commanded us to preach unto the people, and to testify that it is he which was ordained of God to be the Judge of quick and dead. Acts 10. 42

Proper Preface Upon Easter-Day
From 'Holy Communion'

IT is very meet, right, and our bounden duty, that we should at all times, and in all places, give thanks unto thee, O Lord, Holy Father, Almighty, Everlasting God.

But chiefly are we bound to praise thee for the glorious Resurrection of thy Son Jesus Christ our Lord: for he is the very Paschal Lamb, which was offered for us, and hath taken away the sin of the world; who by his death hath destroyed death, and by his rising to life again hath restored to us everlasting life.

Therefore with Angels and Archangels, and with all the company of heaven, we laud and magnify thy glorious Name; evermore praising thee, and saying, Holy, holy, holy, Lord God of hosts, heaven and earth are full of thy glory: Glory be to thee, O Lord most High. Amen.

Meditation
Him God raised up the third day, and shewed him openly. Acts 10. 40

'IF YE THEN BE RISEN
WITH CHRIST'

For as in Adam all die; even so in Christ shall all be made alive.

1 Corinthians 15. 20

The Collect
From 'Easter-Day'

ALMIGHTY God, who through thine only-begotten Son Jesus Christ overcame death and opened unto us the gate of everlasting life; We humbly beseech thee, that as by thy special grace preventing us thou dost put into our minds good desires, so by thy continual help we may bring the same to good effect; through Jesus Christ our Lord, who liveth and reigneth with thee and the Holy Ghost, ever one God, world without end. Amen.

The Epistle. *Colossians 3. 1–6*
From 'Easter-Day'

IF ye then be risen with Christ, seek those things which are above, where Christ sitteth on the right hand of God. Set your affection on things above, not on things on the earth: For ye are dead, and your life is hid with Christ in God. When Christ, who is our life, shall appear, then shall ye also appear with him in glory. Mortify therefore your members which are upon the earth; fornication, uncleanness, inordinate affection, evil concupiscence, and covetousness, which is idolatry: For which things' sake the wrath of God cometh on the children of disobedience.

'BUT GOD RAISED HIM FROM THE DEAD'

He was seen many days of them which came up with him from Galilee to Jerusalem, who are his witnesses unto the people. Acts 13. 31

For the Epistle. *Acts 13. 26–35*
From 'Tuesday in Easter-Week'

MEN and brethren, children of the stock of Abraham, and whosoever among you feareth God, to you is the word of this salvation sent. For they that dwell at Jerusalem, and their rulers, because they knew him not, nor yet the voices of the prophets which are read every sabbath-day, they have fulfilled them in condemning him. And though they found no cause of death in him, yet desired they Pilate that he should be slain. And when they had fulfilled all that was written of him, they took him down from the tree, and laid him in a sepulchre. But God raised him from the dead: And he was seen many days of them which came up with him from Galilee to Jerusalem, who are his witnesses unto the people. And we declare unto you glad tidings, how that the promise which was made unto the fathers, God hath fulfilled the same unto us their children, in that he hath raised up Jesus again; as it is also written in the second Psalm, Thou art my Son, this day have I begotten thee. And as concerning that he raised him up from the dead, now no more to return to corruption, he said on this wise, I will give you the sure mercies of David. Wherefore he saith also in another Psalm, Thou shalt not suffer thine Holy One to see corruption.

'JESUS STOOD IN THEIR MIDST'

Then said Jesus to them again, Peace be unto you. St. John 20. 19

The Gospel. *St. John 20. 19*
From 'The First Sunday After Easter'

THE same day at evening, being the first day of the week, when the doors were shut, where the disciples were assembled for fear of the Jews, came Jesus and stood in the midst, and saith unto them, Peace be unto you. And when he had so said, he shewed unto them his hands and his side. Then were the disciples glad when they saw the Lord. Then said Jesus to them again, Peace be unto you: As my Father hath sent me, even so send I you. And when he had said this, he breathed on them, and saith unto them, Receive ye the Holy Ghost. Whosesoever sins ye remit, they are remitted unto them; and whosesoever sins ye retain, they are retained.

Psalm 145. *Exaltabo te, Deus*

I WILL magnify thee, O God, my King : and I will praise thy Name for ever and ever.

2. Every day will I give thanks unto thee : and praise thy Name for ever and ever.

3. Great is the Lord, and marvellous worthy to be praised : there is no end of his greatness.

4. One generation shall praise thy works unto another : and declare thy power.

PURENESS OF LIVING

Whatsoever is born of God overcometh the world : and this is the victory that overcometh the world, even our faith. 1 St. John 5. 4

The Epistle. *1 St. John 5. 4*
From 'The First Sunday After Easter'

WHATSOEVER is born of God overcometh the world: and this is the victory that overcometh the world, even our faith. Who is he that overcometh the world, but he that believeth that Jesus is the Son of God? This is he that came by water and blood, even Jesus Christ; not by water only, but by water and blood. And it is the Spirit that beareth witness, because the Spirit is truth. For there are three that bear record in heaven, the Father, the Word, and the Holy Ghost: and these three are one. And there are three that bear witness in earth, the spirit, and the water, and the blood: and these three agree in one. If we receive the witness of men, the witness of God is greater: for this is the witness of God, which he hath testified of his Son. He that believeth on the Son of God hath the witness in himself: he that believeth not God hath made him a liar, because he believeth not the record that God gave of his Son. And this is the record, that God hath given to us eternal life; and this life is in his Son. He that hath the Son hath life; and he that hath not the Son hath not life.

JAMES, A SERVANT OF GOD

If any of you lack wisdom, let him ask of God, that giveth to all men liberally.

St. James 1. 5

The Epistle. *St. James 1. 1*
From 'Saint Philip and Saint James's Day'

JAMES, a servant of God and of the Lord Jesus Christ, to the twelve tribes which are scattered abroad, greeting. My brethren, count it all joy when ye fall into divers temptations; knowing this, that the trying of your faith worketh patience. But let patience have her perfect work, that ye may be perfect and entire, wanting nothing. If any of you lack wisdom, let him ask of God, that giveth to all men liberally, and upbraideth not; and it shall be given him. But let him ask in faith, nothing wavering: for he that wavereth is like a wave of the sea, driven with the wind, and tossed. For let not that man think that he shall receive any thing of the Lord. A double-minded man is unstable in all his ways. Let the brother of low degree rejoice in that he is exalted; but the rich, in that he is made low; because as the flower of the grass he shall pass away. For the sun is no sooner risen with a burning heat, but it withereth the grass, and the flower thereof falleth, and the grace of the fashion of it perisheth: so also shall the rich man fade away in his ways. Blessed is the man that endureth temptation; for when he is tried, he shall receive the crown of life, which the Lord hath promised to them that love him.

PHILIP'S REQUEST

Philip saith unto him, Lord, shew us the Father, and it sufficeth us.

St. John 14. 8

The Gospel. *St. John 14. 1*
From 'Saint Philip and Saint James's Day'

AND Jesus said unto his disciples, Let not your heart be troubled; ye believe in God, believe also in me. In my Father's house are many mansions; if it were not so, I would have told you. I go to prepare a place for you: and if I go and prepare a place for you I will come again, and receive you unto myself, that where I am, there ye may be also. And whither I go ye know, and the way ye know. Thomas saith unto him, Lord, we know not whither thou goest, and how can we know the way? Jesus saith unto him, I am the way, the truth, and the life: no man cometh unto the Father but by me. If ye had known me, ye should have known my Father also: and from henceforth ye know him, and have seen him. Philip saith unto him, Lord, shew us the Father, and it sufficeth us. Jesus saith unto him, Have I been so long time with you, and yet hast thou not known me, Philip? He that hath seen me hath seen the Father; and how sayest thou then, Shew us the Father? Believest thou not that I am in the Father, and the Father in me? The words that I speak unto you I speak not of myself; but the Father that dwelleth in me, he doeth the works. Believe me, that I am in the Father, and the Father in me; or else believe me for the very works' sake.

I BELIEVE

Lord, I believe; help thou mine unbelief. St. Mark 9. 24

From 'A Catechism'

WHAT did your Godfathers and Godmothers then for you?

Answer. They did promise and vow three things in my name. First, that I should renounce the devil and all his works, the pomps and vanity of this wicked world, and all the sinful lusts of the flesh. Secondly, that I should believe all the articles of the Christian faith. And thirdly, that I should keep God's holy will and commandments, and walk in the same all the days of my life.

Question. Dost thou not think that thou art bound to believe, and to do, as they have promised for thee?

Answer. Yes verily: and by God's help so I will. And I heartily thank our heavenly Father, that he hath called me to this state of salvation, through Jesus Christ our Saviour. And I pray unto God to give me his grace, that I may continue in the same unto my life's end.

Catechist. Rehearse the Articles of thy Belief.

Answer. I believe in God the Father Almighty, Maker of heaven and earth …

I believe in the Holy Ghost; The holy Catholick Church; The Communion of Saints; The Forgiveness of sins; The Resurrection of the body; And the life everlasting. Amen.

'PEACE BE UNTO YOU'

Then opened he their understanding, that they might understand the scriptures.

St. Luke 24. 45

The Gospel. *St. Luke 24. 36–48*
From 'Tuesday in Easter Week'

JESUS himself stood in the midst of them, and saith unto them, Peace be unto you. But they were terrified and affrighted, and supposed that they had seen a spirit. And he said unto them, Why are ye troubled, and why do thoughts arise in your hearts? Behold my hands and my feet, that it is I myself: handle me, and see; for a spirit hath not flesh and bones, as ye see me have. And when he had thus spoken, he shewed them his hands and his feet. And while they yet believed not for joy, and wondered, he said unto them, Have ye here any meat? And they gave him a piece of a broiled fish, and of an honey-comb. And he took it, and did eat before them. And he said unto them, These are the words which I spake unto you, while I was yet with you, that all things must be fulfilled, which were written in the law of Moses, and in the prophets, and in the psalms concerning me. Then opened he their understanding, that they might understand the Scriptures, and said unto them, Thus it is written, and thus it behoved Christ to suffer, and to rise from the dead the third day; and that repentance and remission of sins should be preached in his name among all nations, beginning at Jerusalem. And ye are witnesses of these things.

'ESTABLISHED IN
THY HOLY GOSPEL'

Grow up into him in all things, which is the head, even Christ. Ephesians 4. 15

The Collect

The Epistle. *Ephesians 4. 7*
From 'Saint Mark's Day'

UNTO every one of us is given grace, according to the measure of the gift of Christ. Wherefore he saith, When he ascended up on high, he led captivity captive, and gave gifts unto men ... And he gave some Apostles, and some Prophets, and some Evangelists, and some Pastors and Teachers; for the perfecting of the saints for the work of the ministry, for the edifying of the body of Christ; till we all come, in the unity of the faith and of the knowledge of the Son of God, unto a perfect man, unto the measure of the stature of the fulness of Christ: that we henceforth be no more children, tossed to and fro, and carried about with every wind of doctrine, by the sleight of men, and cunning craftiness, whereby they lie in wait to deceive; but speaking the truth in love, may grow up into him in all things, which is the head, even Christ: from whom the whole body fitly joined together and compacted by that which every joint supplieth, according to the effectual working in the measure of every part, maketh increase of the body, unto the edifying of itself in love.

THE TRUE VINE

I am the vine, ye are the branches. He that abideth in me, and I in him, the same bringeth forth much fruit. St. John 15. 5

The Gospel. *St. John 15. 1*
From 'Saint Mark's Day'

I AM the true vine, and my Father is the husbandman. Every branch in me that beareth not fruit he taketh away; and every branch that beareth fruit, he purgeth it, that it may bring forth more fruit. Now ye are clean through the word which I have spoken unto you. Abide in me, and I in you. As the branch cannot bear fruit of itself, except it abide in the vine; no more can ye, except ye abide in me. I am the vine, ye are the branches. He that abideth in me, and I in him, the same bringeth forth much fruit; for without me ye can do nothing. If a man abide not in me, he is cast forth as a branch, and is withered; and men gather them, and cast them into the fire, and they are burned. If ye abide in me, and my words abide in you, ye shall ask what ye will, and it shall be done unto you. Herein is my Father glorified, that ye bear much fruit; so shall ye be my disciples. As the Father hath loved me, so have I loved you: continue ye in my love. If ye keep my commandments, ye shall abide in my love; even as I have kept my Father's commandments, and abide in his love. These things have I spoken unto you, that my joy might remain in you, and that your joy might be full.

HIS MOST HOLY LIFE

Who did no sin, neither was guile found in his mouth. 1 St. Peter 2. 22

The Collect
From 'The Second Sunday After Easter'

ALMIGHTY God, who hast given thine only Son to be unto us both a sacrifice for sin, and also an ensample of godly life: Give us grace that we may always most thankfully receive that his inestimable benefit, and also daily endeavour ourselves to follow the blessed steps of his most holy life; through the same Jesus Christ our Lord. Amen.

The Epistle. *1 St. Peter 2. 19*
From 'The Second Sunday After Easter'

THIS is thank-worthy, if a man for conscience toward God endure grief, suffering wrongfully. For what glory is it, if, when ye be buffeted for your faults, ye shall take it patiently? but if, when ye do well, and suffer for it, ye take it patiently, this is acceptable with God. For even hereunto were ye called: because Christ also suffered for us, leaving us an example, that ye should follow his steps: who did no sin, neither was guile found in his mouth: who, when he was reviled, reviled not again; when he suffered, he threatened not; but committed himself to him that judgeth righteously: who his own self bare our sins in his own body on the tree, that we, being dead to sins, should live unto righteousness: by whose stripes ye were healed.

THE RESURRECTION OF CHRIST

The same stone which the builders refused : is become the head-stone in the corner.

Psalm 118. 22

Psalm 118. *Confitemini Domino*

O GIVE thanks unto the Lord, for he is gracious : because his mercy endureth for ever.

2. Let Israel now confess that he is gracious : and that his mercy endureth for ever.

3. Let the house of Aaron now confess : that his mercy endureth for ever.

4. Yea, let them now that fear the Lord confess : that his mercy endureth for ever.

5. I called upon the Lord in trouble : and the Lord heard me at large.

6. The Lord is on my side : I will not fear what man doeth unto me.

7. The Lord taketh my part with them that help me : therefore shall I see my desire upon mine enemies.

8. It is better to trust in the Lord : than to put any confidence in man.

9. It is better to trust in the Lord : than to put any confidence in princes.

10. All nations compassed me round about : but in the Name of the Lord will I destroy them.

11. They kept me in on every side, they kept me in, I say, on every side : but in the Name of the Lord will I destroy them.

12. They came about me like bees, and are extinct even as the fire among the thorns : for in the Name of the Lord I will destroy them.

INSTRUCTION FROM GOD'S WORD (5)

Before I was troubled, I went wrong : but now have I kept thy word.

Psalm 119. 67

Psalm 119. *Manus tuae fecerunt me*

THY hands have made me and fashioned me : O give me understanding, that I may learn thy commandments.

74. They that fear thee will be glad when they see me : because I have put my trust in thy word.

75. I know, O Lord, that thy judgements are right : and that thou of very faithfulness hast caused me to be troubled.

76. O let thy merciful kindness be my comfort : according to thy word unto thy servant.

77. O let thy loving mercies come unto me, that I may live : for thy law is my delight.

78. Let the proud be confounded, for they go wickedly about to destroy me : but I will be occupied in thy commandments.

79. Let such as fear thee, and have known thy testimonies : be turned unto me.

80. O let my heart be sound in thy statutes : that I be not ashamed.

Meditation

O let thy merciful kindness be my comfort : according to thy word unto thy servant.

Psalm 119. 76

IN DEEP TROUBLE (3)

My strength will I ascribe unto thee : for thou art the God of my refuge.

Psalm 59. 9

Psalm 59. *Eripe me de inimicis*

DELIVER me from mine enemies, O God : defend me from them that rise up against me.

2. O deliver me from the wicked doers : and save me from the blood-thirsty men.

3. For lo, they lie waiting for my soul : the mighty men are gathered against me, without any offence or fault of me, O Lord.

4. They run and prepare themselves without my fault : arise thou therefore to help me, and behold.

5. Stand up, O Lord God of hosts, thou God of Israel, to visit all the heathen : and be not merciful unto them that offend of malicious wickedness.

6. They go to and fro in the evening : they grin like a dog, and run about through the city.

7. Behold, they speak with their mouth, and swords are in their lips : for who doth hear?

8. But thou, O Lord, shalt have them in derision : and thou shalt laugh all the heathen to scorn.

9. My strength will I ascribe unto thee : for thou art the God of my refuge.

'A CERTAIN BLIND MAN'

Jesus of Nazareth passeth by. St. Luke 18. 37

The Gospel. *St. Luke 18. 31*
From 'Quinquagesima'

THEN Jesus took unto him the twelve, and said unto them, Behold, we go up to Jerusalem, and all things that are written by the prophets concerning the Son of Man shall be accomplished. For he shall be delivered unto the Gentiles, and shall be mocked, and spitefully entreated, and spitted on: and they shall scourge him, and put him to death: and the third day he shall rise again. And they understood none of these things: and this saying was hid from them, neither knew they the things which were spoken. And it came to pass, that as he was come nigh unto Jericho, a certain blind man sat by the way-side begging: and hearing the multitude pass by, he asked what it meant. And they told him, that Jesus of Nazareth passeth by. And he cried, saying, Jesus, thou Son of David, have mercy on me. And they which went before rebuked him, that he should hold his peace: but he cried so much the more, Thou Son of David, have mercy on me. And Jesus stood, and commanded him to be brought unto him: and when he was come near, he asked him, saying, What wilt thou that I shall do unto thee? And he said, Lord, that I may receive my sight. And Jesus said unto him, Receive thy sight; thy faith hath saved thee. And immediately he received his sight, and followed him, glorifying God: and all the people, when they saw it, gave praise unto God.

THE MESSIAH IN THE PSALMS (6)
His hands and feet will be pierced

They pierced my hands and my feet; I may tell all my bones : they stand staring and looking upon me. Psalm 22. 17

The Gospel. *St. John 20. 24*
From 'Saint Thomas the Apostle'

THOMAS, one of the twelve, called Didymus, was not with them when Jesus came. The other disciples therefore said unto him, We have seen the Lord. But he said unto them, Except I shall see in his hands the print of the nails, and put my finger into the print of the nails, and thrust my hand into his side, I will not believe. And after eight days again his disciples were within, and Thomas with them: then came Jesus, the doors being shut, and stood in the midst, and said, Peace be unto you. Then saith he to Thomas, Reach hither thy finger, and behold my hands; and reach hither thy hand, and thrust it into my side: and be not faithless, but believing. And Thomas answered and said unto him, My Lord, and my God. Jesus saith unto him, Thomas, because thou hast seen me, thou hast believed: blessed are they that have not seen, and yet have believed. And many other signs truly did Jesus in the presence of his disciples, which are not written in this book: But these are written, that ye might believe that Jesus is the Christ, the Son of God; and that believing ye might have life through his name.

PSALMS OF PRAISE AND THANKSGIVING (9)
God's mercy

He is a father of the fatherless, and defendeth the cause of the widows : even God in his holy habitation. Psalm 68. 5

Psalm 68. *Exurgat Deus*

LET God arise, and let his enemies be scattered : let them also that hate him flee before him.

2. Like as the smoke vanisheth, so shalt thou drive them away : and like as wax melteth at the fire, so let the ungodly perish at the presence of God.

3. But let the righteous be glad, and rejoice before God : let them also be merry and joyful.

4. O sing unto God, and sing praises unto his Name : magnify him that rideth upon the heavens, as it were upon a horse; praise him in his Name JAH, and rejoice before him.

5. He is a father of the fatherless, and defendeth the cause of the widows : even God in his holy habitation.

6. He is the God that maketh men to be of one mind in an house, and bringeth the prisoners out of captivity : but letteth the runagates continue in scarceness.

7. O God, when thou wentest forth before the people : when thou wentest through the wilderness;

8. The earth shook, and the heavens dropped at the presence of God : even as Sinai also was moved at the presence of God, who is the God of Israel.

ESCHEWING AND FOLLOWING

… abstain from fleshly lusts, which war against the soul. 1 St. Peter 2. 11

The Collect
From 'The Third Sunday After Easter'

ALMIGHTY God, who shewest to them that be in error the light of thy truth, to the intent that they may return into the way of righteousness: Grant unto all them that are admitted into the fellowship of Christ's religion, that they may eschew those things that are contrary to their profession, and follow all such things as are agreeable to the same; through our Lord Jesus Christ. Amen.

Psalm 16. *Conserva me, Domine*

PRESERVE me, O God : for in thee have I put my trust.

2. O my soul, thou hast said unto the Lord : Thou art my God; my goods are nothing unto thee.

3. All my delight is upon the saints, that are in the earth : and upon such as excel in virtue.

4. But they that run after another god : shall have great trouble.

5. Their drink-offerings of blood will I not offer : neither make mention of their names within my lips.

6. The Lord himself is the portion of mine inheritance, and of my cup : thou shalt maintain my lot.

'A LITTLE WHILE'

Your joy no man taketh from you. St. John 16. 22

The Gospel. *St. John 16. 16*
From 'The Third Sunday After Easter'

JESUS said to his disciples, A little while and ye shall not see me; and again a little while and ye shall see me; because I go to the Father. Then said some of his disciples among themselves, What is this that he saith unto us, A little while and ye shall not see me; and again a little while and ye shall see me; and, Because I go to the Father? They said therefore, What is this that he saith, A little while? we cannot tell what he saith. Now Jesus knew that they were desirous to ask him, and said unto them, Do ye inquire among yourselves of that I said, A little while and ye shall not see me; and again a little while and ye shall see me? Verily, verily I say unto you, that ye shall weep and lament, but the world shall rejoice: and ye shall be sorrowful, but your sorrow shall be turned into joy. A woman, when she is in travail, hath sorrow, because her hour is come: but as soon as she is delivered of the child, she remembereth no more the anguish, for joy that a man is born into the world. And ye now therefore have sorrow: but I will see you again, and your heart shall rejoice, and your joy no man taketh from you.

PSALMS OF PRAISE AND THANKSGIVING (10)
God's majesty

It is well seen, O God, how thou goest : how thou, my God and King, goest in the sanctuary. Psalm 68. 24

Psalm 68. *Exurgat Deus*

THE chariots of God are twenty thousand, even thousands of angels : and the Lord is among them, as in the holy place of Sinai.

18. Thou art gone up on high, thou hast led captivity captive, and received gifts for men : yea, even for thine enemies, that the Lord God might dwell among them.

19. Praised be the Lord daily : even the God who helpeth us, and poureth his benefits upon us.

20. He is our God, even the God of whom cometh salvation : God is the Lord, by whom we escape death...

26. Give thanks, O Israel, unto God the Lord in the congregations from the ground of the heart.

27. There is little Benjamin their ruler, and the princes of Judah their counsel : the princes of Zabulon, and the princes of Nephthali.

28. Thy God hath sent forth strength for thee : stablish the thing, O God, that thou hast wrought in us,

29. For thy temple's sake at Jerusalem : so shall kings bring presents unto thee.

IN GOD'S SERVICE

My help cometh even from the Lord : who hath made heaven and earth.

Psalm 121. 2

Psalm 121. *Levavi oculos*

I WILL lift up mine eyes unto the hills : from whence cometh my help.
2. My help cometh even from the Lord : who hath made heaven and earth.
3. He will not suffer thy foot to be moved : and he that keepeth thee will not sleep.
4. Behold, he that keepeth Israel : shall neither slumber nor sleep.
5. The Lord himself is thy keeper : the Lord is thy defence upon thy right hand;
6. So that the sun shall not burn thee by day : neither the moon by night.
7. The Lord shall preserve thee from all evil : yea, it is even he that shall keep thy soul.
8. The Lord shall preserve thy going out, and thy coming in : from this time forth for evermore.

Meditation
O Holy Ghost, into our minds send down thy heav'nly light;
Kindle our hearts with fervent zeal to serve God day and night.

From 'The Ordering of Priests'

THE GIFT OF CHRIST

Unto every one of us is given grace, according to the measure of the gift of Christ.
Ephesians 4. 7

From 'The Ordering of Priests'

OUR weakness strengthen and confirm, (for, Lord, thou know'st us
frail;)
That neither devil, world, nor flesh, against us may prevail.
Put back our enemy far from us, and help us to obtain
Peace in our hearts with God and man, (the best, the truest gain;)
And grant that thou being, O Lord, our leader and our guide,
We may escape the snares of sin, and never from thee slide.
Such measures of thy powerful grace grant, Lord, to us, we pray;
That thou may'st be our Comforter at the last dreadful day.
Of strife and of dissension dissolve, O Lord, the bands,
And knit the knots of peace and love throughout all Christian lands.
Grant us the grace that we may know the Father of all might,
That we of his beloved Son may gain the blissful sight;
And that we may with perfect faith ever acknowledge thee,
The Spirit of Father, and of Son, One God in Persons Three.
To God the Father laud and praise, and to his blessed Son,
And to the Holy Spirit of grace, co-equal Three in One.
And pray we, that our only Lord would please his Spirit to send
On all that shall profess his Name, from hence to the world's end. Amen.

THE MESSIAH IN THE PSALMS (7)

Others will gamble for his clothes

They part my garments among them : and cast lots upon my vesture.

Psalm 22. 18

Psalm 22. *Deus, Deus meus*

THEY part my garments among them : and cast lots upon my vesture. 19. But be not thou far from me, O Lord : thou art my succour, haste thee to help me.

20. Deliver my soul from the sword : my darling from the power of the dog.

21. Save me from the lion's mouth : thou hast heard me also from among the horns of the unicorns.

22. I will declare thy Name unto my brethren : in the midst of the congregation will I praise thee.

23. O praise the Lord, ye that fear him, magnify him, all ye of the seed of Jacob ; and fear him, all ye seed of Israel.

24. For he hath not despised nor abhorred, the low estate of the poor : he hath not hid his face from him, but when he called unto him he heard him.

25. My praise is of thee in the great congregation : my vows will I perform in the sight of them that fear him.

26. The poor shall eat and be satisfied : they that seek after the Lord shall praise him; your heart shall live for ever.

THE TEN COMMANDMENTS

I learn two things: my duty towards God, and my duty towards my Neighbour.

From 'A Catechism'

From 'A Catechism'

WHAT dost thou chiefly learn by these Commandments?

Answer. I learn two things: my duty towards God, and my duty towards my Neighbour.

Question. What is thy duty towards God?

Answer. My duty towards God is to believe in him, to fear him, and to love him, with all my heart, with all my mind, with all my soul, and with all my strength; to worship him, to give him thanks, to put my whole trust in him, to call upon him, to honour his holy Name and his Word, and to serve him truly all the days of my life.

Question. What is thy duty towards thy Neighbour?

Answer. My duty towards my Neighbour is to love him as myself, and to do to all men as I would they should do unto me: To love, honour, and succour my father and mother: To honour and obey the Queen, and all that are put in authority under her: To submit myself to all my governors, teachers, spiritual pastors and masters: To order myself lowly and reverently to all my betters: To hurt no body by word nor deed: To be true and just in all my dealing: To bear no malice nor hatred in my heart: To keep my hands from picking and stealing, and my tongue from evil-speaking, lying, and slandering.

GIFTS FROM ABOVE

Do well, O Lord : unto those that are good and true of heart. Psalm 125. 4

The Collect
From 'The Fourth Sunday After Easter'

O ALMIGHTY God, who alone canst order the unruly wills and affections of sinful men: Grant unto thy people, that they may love the
thing which thou commandest, and desire that which thou dost promise;
that so, among the sundry and manifold changes of the world, our hearts
may surely there be fixed, where true joys are to be found; through Jesus
Christ our Lord. Amen.

The Epistle. *St. James 1. 17*
From 'The Fourth Sunday After Easter'

EVERY good gift and every perfect gift is from above, and cometh
down from the Father of lights, with whom is no variableness, neither
shadow of turning. Of his own will begat he us with the word of truth,
that we should be a kind of first-fruits of his creatures. Wherefore, my
beloved brethren, let every man be swift to hear, slow to speak, slow
to wrath; for the wrath of man worketh not the righteousness of God.
Wherefore lay apart all filthiness and superfluity of naughtiness, and receive
with meekness the engrafted word, which is able to save your souls.

THE COMFORTER

It is expedient for you that I go away. St. John 16. 7

The Gospel. *St. John 16. 5*
From 'The Fourth Sunday After Easter'
JESUS said unto his disciples, Now I go my way to him that sent me, and none of you asketh me, Whither goest thou? But, because I have said these things unto you, sorrow hath filled your heart. Nevertheless, I tell you the truth; it is expedient for you that I go away: for if I go not away, the Comforter will not come unto you; but if I depart, I will send him unto you. And when he is come, he will reprove the world of sin, and of righteousness, and of judgement: of sin, because they believe not on me; of righteousness, because I go to my Father, and ye see me no more; of judgement, because the prince of this world is judged. I have yet many things to say unto you, but ye cannot bear them now. Howbeit, when he, the Spirit of truth, is come, he will guide you into all truth: for he shall not speak of himself; but whatsoever he shall hear, that shall he speak: and he will shew you things to come. He shall glorify me: for he shall receive of mine, and shall shew it unto you.

Meditation
But when the Comforter is come ... he shall testify of me. St. John 15. 26

PSALMS OF PRAISE AND THANKSGIVING (11)
God is in control

And why? God is the Judge : he putteth down one, and setteth up another.
Psalm 75. 8

Psalm 75. *Confitebimur tibi*

UNTO thee, O God, do we give thanks : yea, unto thee do we give thanks.

2. Thy Name also is so nigh : and that do thy wondrous works declare.

3. When I receive the congregation : I shall judge according unto right.

4. The earth is weak, and all the inhabiters thereof : I bear up the pillars of it.

5. I said unto the fools, Deal not so madly : and to the ungodly, Set not up your horn.

6. Set not up your horn on high : and speak not with a stiff neck.

7. For promotion cometh neither from the east, nor from the west : nor yet from the south ...

9. For in the hand of the Lord there is a cup, and the wine is red : it is full mixed, and he poureth out of the same.

10. As for the dregs thereof : all the ungodly of the earth shall drink them, and suck them out.

11. But I will talk of the God of Jacob : and praise him for ever.

12. All the horns of the ungodly also will I break : and the horns of the righteous shall be exalted.

PSALMS OF PRAISE AND THANKSGIVING (12)

Reverence is due to God

Thou, even thou art to be feared : and who may stand in thy sight when thou art angry? Psalm 76. 7

Psalm 76. *Notus in Judaea*

IN Jewry is God known : his Name is great in Israel.
2. At Salem is his tabernacle : and his dwelling in Sion.
3. There brake he the arrows of the bow : the shield, the sword, and the battle.
4. Thou art of more honour and might : than the hills of the robbers.
5. The proud are robbed, they have slept their sleep : and all the men whose hands were mighty have found nothing.
6. At thy rebuke, O God of Jacob : both the chariot and horse are fallen.
7. Thou, even thou art to be feared : and who may stand in thy sight when thou art angry?
8. Thou didst cause thy judgement to be heard from heaven : the earth trembled, and was still;
9. When God arose to judgement : and to help all the meek upon earth.
10. The fierceness of man shall turn to thy praise : and the fierceness of them shalt thou refrain.
11. Promise unto the Lord your God, and keep it, all ye that are round about him : bring presents unto him that ought to be feared.

THE MESSIAH IN THE PSALMS (8)

Not one of his bones will be broken

He keepeth all his bones : so that not one of them is broken. Psalm 34. 20

Psalm 34. *Benedicam Domino*

THE angel of the Lord tarrieth round about them that fear him : and delivereth them.

8. O taste, and see, how gracious the Lord is : blessed is the man that trusteth in him.

9. O fear the Lord, ye that are his saints : for they that fear him lack nothing ...

11. Come, ye children, and hearken unto me : I will teach you the fear of the Lord...

15. The eyes of the Lord are over the righteous : and his ears are open unto their prayers.

16. The countenance of the Lord is against them that do evil : to root out the remembrance of them from the earth.

17. The righteous cry, and the Lord heareth them : and delivereth them out of all their troubles.

18. The Lord is nigh unto them that are of a contrite heart : and will save such as be of an humble spirit.

19. Great are the troubles of the righteous : but the Lord delivereth him out of all.

20. He keepeth all his bones : so that not one of them is broken.

INSTRUCTION FROM GOD'S WORD (6)

All thy commandments are true : they persecute me falsely; O be thou my help.

Psalm 119. 86

The Collect
From 'The Second Sunday in Advent'

BLESSED Lord, who hast caused all holy Scriptures to be written for our learning: Grant that we may in such wise hear them, read, mark, learn, and inwardly digest them, that by patience and comfort of thy holy Word, we may embrace and ever hold fast the blessed hope of everlasting life, which thou hast given us in our Saviour Jesus Christ. Amen.

Psalm 119. *Defecit anima mea*

MY soul hath longed for thy salvation : and I have a good hope because of thy word.

82. Mine eyes long sore for thy word : saying, O when wilt thou comfort me?

83. For I am become like a bottle in the smoke : yet do I not forget thy statutes.

84. How many are the days of thy servant : when wilt thou be avenged of them that persecute me?

85. The proud have digged pits for me : which are not after thy law...

88. O quicken me after thy loving-kindness : and so shall I keep the testimonies of thy mouth.

THANKSGIVING

With his own right hand, and with his holy arm : hath he gotten himself the victory. Psalm 98. 2

Psalm 8. *Domine, Dominus noster*

O LORD our Governor, how excellent is thy Name in all the world : thou that hast set thy glory above the heavens!

2. Out of the mouth of very babes and sucklings hast thou ordained strength, because of thine enemies : that thou mightest still the enemy and the avenger.

3. For I will consider thy heavens, even the works of thy fingers : the moon and the stars, which thou hast ordained.

4. What is man, that thou art mindful of him : and the son of man, that thou visitest him?

5. Thou madest him lower than the angels : to crown him with glory and worship.

6. Thou madest him to have dominion of the works of thy hands : and thou hast put all things in subjection under his feet;

7. All sheep and oxen : yea, and the beasts of the field;

8. The fowls of the air, and the fishes of the sea : and whatsoever walketh through the paths of the seas.

9. O Lord our Governor : how excellent is thy Name in all the world!

PURE RELIGION

Pure religion and undefiled before God and the Father is this, To visit the fatherless and widows in their affliction, and to keep himself unspotted from the world.

St. James 1. 27

The Collect
From 'The Fifth Sunday After Easter'

O LORD, from whom all good things do come; Grant to us thy humble servants, that by thy holy inspiration we may think those things that be good, and by thy merciful guiding may perform the same; through our Lord Jesus Christ. Amen.

The Epistle. *St. James 1. 22*
From 'The Fifth Sunday After Easter'

B E ye doers of the word, and not hearers only, deceiving your own selves. For if any be a hearer of the word, and not a doer, he is like unto a man beholding his natural face in a glass. For he beholdeth himself, and goeth his way, and straightway forgetteth what manner of man he was. But whoso looketh into the perfect law of liberty, and continueth therein, he being not a forgetful hearer, but a doer of the work, this man shall be blessed in his deed. If any man among you seem to be religious, and bridleth not his tongue, but deceiveth his own heart, this man's religion is vain.

PEACE

These things I have spoken unto you, that in me ye might have peace. In the world ye shall have tribulation; but be of good cheer, I have overcome the world.

St. John 16. 33

The Gospel. *St. John 16. 23*
From 'The Fifth Sunday After Easter'

VERILY, verily I say unto you, Whatsoever ye shall ask the Father in my name, he will give it you. Hitherto have ye asked nothing in my name: ask, and ye shall receive, that your joy may be full. These things have I spoken unto you in proverbs: the time cometh when I shall no more speak unto you in proverbs, but I shall shew you plainly of the Father. At that day ye shall ask in my name: and I say not unto you, that I will pray the Father for you: for the Father himself loveth you, because ye have loved me, and have believed that I came out from God. I came forth from the Father, and am come into the world: again, I leave the world, and go to the Father. His disciples said unto him, Lo, now speakest thou plainly, and speakest no proverb. Now are we sure that thou knowest all things, and needest not that any man should ask thee: by this we believe that thou camest forth from God. Jesus answered them, Do ye now believe? Behold, the hour cometh, yea, is now come, that ye shall be scattered, every man to his own, and shall leave me alone: and yet I am not alone, because the Father is with me.

THE BIBLE

Holy Scripture containeth all things necessary to salvation.
From the 'Articles of Religion'

From the 'Articles of Religion'
VI. Of the Sufficiency of the holy Scriptures for salvation

HOLY Scripture containeth all things necessary to salvation: so that whatsoever is not read therein, nor may be proved thereby, is not to be required of any man, that it should be believed as an article of the Faith, or be thought requisite or necessary to salvation. In the name of the holy Scripture we do understand those Canonical Books of the Old and New Testament, of whose authority was never any doubt in the Church.

Psalm 119. *Lucerna pedibus meis*

THY word is a lantern unto my feet : and a light unto my paths.
106. I have sworn, and am stedfastly purposed : to keep thy righteous judgements.
107. I am troubled above measure : quicken me, O Lord, according to thy word.
108. Let the free-will offerings of my mouth please thee, O Lord : and teach me thy judgements.
109. My soul is alway in my hand : yet do I not forget thy law.

LIVING WITH THE END IN VIEW

The end of all things is at hand : be ye therefore sober, and watch unto prayer.
                                                                1 St. Peter 4. 7

The Proper Preface Upon Ascension Day
From 'Holy Communion'

IT is very meet, right, and our bounden duty, that we should at all times, and in all places, give thanks unto thee, O Lord, Holy Father, Almighty, Everlasting God.

Through thy most dearly beloved Son Jesus Christ our Lord; who after his most glorious Resurrection manifestly appeared to all his Apostles, and in their sight ascended up into heaven to prepare a place for us; that where he is, thither we might also ascend, and reign with him in glory.

Therefore with Angels and Archangels and with all the company of heaven, we laud and magnify thy glorious Name; evermore praising thee, and saying: Holy, holy, holy, Lord God of hosts, heaven and earth are full of thy glory: Glory be to thee, O Lord most High. Amen.

Meditation
And that, knowing the time, that now it is high time to awake out of sleep : for now is our salvation nearer than when we believed. Romans 13. 11

CHRIST'S ASCENSION

And when he had spoken these things, while they beheld, he was taken up, and a cloud received him out of their sight. Acts 1. 9

For the Epistle. *Acts 1. 1*
From 'Ascension Day'

THE former treatise have I made, O Theophilus, of all that Jesus began both to do and teach, until the day in which he was taken up, after that he through the Holy Ghost had given commandments unto the Apostles whom he had chosen: to whom also he shewed himself alive after his passion, by many infallible proofs; being seen of them forty days, and speaking of the things pertaining to the kingdom of God: and, being assembled together with them, commanded them that they should not depart from Jerusalem, but wait for the promise of the Father, which, saith he, ye have heard of me. For John truly baptized with water, but ye shall be baptized with the Holy Ghost not many days hence. When they therefore were come together, they asked of him, saying, Lord, wilt thou at this time restore again the kingdom to Israel? And he said unto them, It is not for you to know the times or the seasons, which the Father hath put in his own power. But ye shall receive power after that the Holy Ghost is come upon you; and ye shall be witnesses unto me, both in Jerusalem, and in all Judaea, and in Samaria, and unto the uttermost part of the earth. And when he had spoken these things, while they beheld, he was taken up, and a cloud received him out of their sight.

POWER FROM ON HIGH

...he was received up into heaven, and sat on the right hand of God.

St. Mark 16. 19

The Gospel. *St. Mark 16. 14*
From 'Ascension Day'

JESUS appeared unto the eleven as they sat at meat, and upbraided them with their unbelief and hardness of heart, because they believed not them which had seen him after he was risen. And he said unto them, Go ye into all the world, and preach the Gospel to every creature. He that believeth and is baptized shall be saved; but he that believeth not shall be damned. And these signs shall follow them that believe: In my name shall they cast out devils; they shall speak with new tongues; they shall take up serpents; and if they drink any deadly thing, it shall not hurt them; they shall lay hands on the sick, and they shall recover. So then after the Lord had spoken unto them, he was received up into heaven, and sat on the right hand of God. And they went forth and preached every where, the Lord working with them, and confirming the word with signs following.

Meditation
Go ye into all the world, and preach the Gospel to every creature.

St. Mark 16. 15

'ASCENDED ... TO PREPARE A PLACE FOR US'

Thou art gone up on high, thou hast led captivity captive, and received gifts for men : yea, even for thine enemies, that the Lord God might dwell among them.

Psalm 68. 18

Psalm 8. *Domine, Dominus noster*

O LORD our Governor, how excellent is thy Name in all the world : thou that hast set thy glory above the heavens!

2. Out of the mouth of very babes and sucklings hast thou ordained strength, because of thine enemies : that thou mightest still the enemy and the avenger.

3. For I will consider thy heavens, even the works of thy fingers : the moon and the stars, which thou hast ordained.

4. What is man, that thou art mindful of him : and the son of man, that thou visitest him?

5. Thou madest him lower than the angels : to crown him with glory and worship.

6. Thou makest him to have dominion of the works of thy hands : and thou hast put all things in subjection under his feet;

7. All sheep and oxen : yea, and the beasts of the field;

8. The fowls of the air, and the fishes of the sea : and whatsoever walketh through the paths of the seas.

9. O Lord our Governor : how excellent is thy Name in all the world!

THE COMFORTER

Who shall ascend into the hill of the Lord : or who shall rise up in his holy place?
Psalm 24. 3

The Collect
From 'The Sunday After Ascension Day'

O GOD the King of glory, who hast exalted thine only Son Jesus Christ
with great triumph unto thy kingdom in heaven : We beseech thee,
leave us not comfortless; but send to us thine Holy Ghost to comfort us,
and exalt us unto the same place whither our Saviour Christ is gone before,
who liveth and reigneth with thee and the Holy Ghost, one God, world
without end. Amen.

The Gospel. *St. John 15. 26*
From 'The Sunday After Ascension Day'

WHEN the Comforter is come, whom I will send unto you from the
Father, even the Spirit of truth, which proceedeth from the Father,
he shall testify of me; and ye also shall bear witness, because ye have been
with me from the beginning. These things have I spoken unto you, that ye
should not be offended. They shall put you out of the synagogues: yea, the
time cometh, that whosoever killeth you will think that he doeth God
service. And these things will they do unto you, because they have not
known the Father, nor me. But these things have I told you, that, when
the time shall come, ye may remember that I told you of them.

BUILDING UP CHRIST'S BODY

Unto every one of us is given grace, according to the measure of the gift of Christ.
Ephesians 4. 7

The Epistle. *Ephesians 4. 1*
From 'The Seventeenth Sunday after Trinity' and 'Saint Mark's Day'

I THEREFORE the prisoner of the Lord beseech you, that ye walk worthy of the vocation wherewith ye are called, with all lowliness and meekness, with long-suffering, forbearing one another in love; endeavouring to keep the unity of the Spirit in the bond of peace. There is one body, and one Spirit, even as ye are called in one hope of your calling; one Lord, one faith, one baptism, one God and Father of all, who is above all, and through all, and in you all. Unto every one of us is given grace, according to the measure of the gift of Christ. Wherefore he saith, When he ascended up on high, he led captivity captive, and gave gifts unto men. And he gave some Apostles, and some Prophets, and some Evangelists, and some Pastors and Teachers; for the perfecting of the saints for the work of the ministry, for the edifying of the body of Christ; till we all come, in the unity of the faith and of the knowledge of the Son of God, unto a perfect man, unto the measure of the stature of the fulness of Christ: that we henceforth be no more children, tossed to and fro, and carried about with every wind of doctrine, by the sleight of men, and cunning craftiness, whereby they lie in wait to deceive; but speaking the truth in love, may grow up into him in all things, which is the head, even Christ.

ASCENDED IN HEART AND MIND

Set up thyself, O God, above the heavens : and thy glory above all the earth.

Psalm 108. 5

The Collect
From 'Ascension Day'

GRANT, we beseech thee, Almighty God, that like as we do believe thy only-begotten Son our Lord Jesus Christ to have ascended into the heavens; so we may also in heart and mind thither ascend, and with him continually dwell, who liveth and reigneth with thee and the Holy Ghost, one God, world without end. Amen.

Psalm 108. *Paratum cor meum*

O GOD, my heart is ready, my heart is ready : I will sing and give praise with the best member that I have.

2. Awake, thou lute and harp : I myself will awake right early.

3. I will give thanks unto thee, O Lord, among the people : I will sing praises unto thee among the nations.

4. For thy mercy is greater than the heavens : and thy truth reacheth unto the clouds ...

7. God hath spoken in his holiness : I will rejoice therefore, and divide Sichem, and mete out the valley of Succoth.

8. Gilead is mine, and Manasses is mine : Ephraim also is the strength of my head ...

TAKEN UP INTO HEAVEN

While he blessed them, he was parted from them, and carried up into heaven.
St. Luke 24. 51

Psalm 21. *Domine, in virtute tua*

THE King shall rejoice in thy strength, O Lord : exceeding glad shall he be of thy salvation.

2. Thou hast given him his heart's desire : and hast not denied him the request of his lips.

3. For thou shalt prevent him with the blessings of goodness : and shalt set a crown of pure gold upon his head.

4. He asked life of thee, and thou gavest him a long life : even for ever and ever.

5. His honour is great in thy salvation : glory and great worship shalt thou lay upon him.

6. For thou shalt give him everlasting felicity : and make him glad with the joy of thy countenance.

7. And why? because the King putteth his trust in the Lord : and in the mercy of the most Highest he shall not miscarry.

8. All thine enemies shall feel thine hand : thy right hand shall find out them that hate thee...

13. Be thou exalted, Lord, in thine own strength : so will we sing, and praise thy power.

COME, HOLY SPIRIT

Thou art the very Comforter in grief and all distress.

From 'The Ordering of Priests'

From 'The Ordering of Priests'
COME, Holy Ghost, our souls inspire,
And lighten with celestial fire.
Thou the anointing Spirit art,
Who dost thy seven-fold gifts impart.
Thy blessed Unction from above
Is comfort, life, and fire of love.
Enable with perpetual light
The dulness of our blinded sight.
Anoint and cheer our soiled face
With the abundance of thy grace.
Keep far our foes, give peace at home :
Where thou art guide, no ill can come.
Teach us to know the Father, Son,
And thee, of both, to be but One.
That, through the ages all along,
This may be our endless song:
Praise to thy eternal merit,
Father, Son, and Holy Spirit.

BARNABAS' CARE FOR PAUL

Then departed Barnabas to Tarsus, for to seek Saul. Acts 11. 25

For the Epistle. *Acts 11. 22*
From 'Saint Barnabas the Apostle'

TIDINGS of these things came unto the ears of the Church which was in Jerusalem; and they sent forth Barnabas, that he should go as far as Antioch. Who, when he came, and had seen the grace of God, was glad and exhorted them all, that with purpose of heart they would cleave unto the Lord. For he was a good man, and full of the Holy Ghost and of faith: and much people was added unto the Lord. Then departed Barnabas to Tarsus, for to seek Saul. And when he had found him, he brought him unto Antioch. And it came to pass, that a whole year they assembled themselves with the Church, and taught much people: and the disciples were called Christians first in Antioch. And in these days came prophets from Jerusalem unto Antioch. And there stood up one of them named Agabus, and signified by the Spirit that there should be great dearth throughout all the world : which came to pass in the days of Claudius Caesar. Then the disciples, every man according to his ability, determined to send relief unto the brethren which dwelt in Judaea: which also they did, and sent it to the elders by the hands of Barnabas and Saul.

TRUE FRIENDSHIP

Henceforth I call you not servants: for the servant knoweth not what his lord doeth: but I have called you friends. St. John 15. 15

Psalm 112. *Beatus vir*

BLESSED is the man that feareth the Lord : he hath great delight in his commandments.

2. His seed shall be mighty upon earth : the generation of the faithful shall be blessed.

3. Riches and plenteousness shall be in his house : and his righteousness endureth for ever.

4. Unto the godly there ariseth up light in the darkness : he is merciful, loving, and righteous …

7. He will not be afraid of any evil tidings : for his heart standeth fast, and believeth in the Lord …

9. He hath dispersed abroad, and given to the poor : and his righteousness remaineth for ever; his horn shall be exalted with honour.

10. The ungodly shall see it, and it shall grieve him : he shall gnash with his teeth, and consume away; the desire of the ungodly shall perish.

Meditation
A good man is merciful, and lendeth : and will guide his words with discretion. For he shall never be moved : and the righteous shall be had in everlasting remembrance.

Psalm 112. 5–6

THE HOLY SPIRIT

And they were all filled with the Holy Ghost, and began to speak with other tongues, as the Spirit gave them utterance. Acts 2. 4

For the Epistle. *Acts 2. 1*
From 'Whitsunday'

WHEN the day of Pentecost was fully come, they were all with one accord in one place. And suddenly there came a sound from heaven, as of a rushing mighty wind, and it filled all the house where they were sitting. And there appeared unto them cloven tongues, like as of fire, and it sat upon each of them: and they were all filled with the Holy Ghost, and began to speak with other tongues, as the Spirit gave them utterance. And there were dwelling at Jerusalem Jews, devout men, out of every nation under heaven. Now when this was noised abroad, the multitude came together, and were confounded, because that every man heard them speak in his own language. And they were all amazed, and marvelled, saying one to another, Behold, are not all these which speak Galilaeans? And how hear we every man in our own tongue wherein we were born? Parthians, and Medes, and Elamites, and the dwellers in Mesopotamia, and in Judaea, and Cappadocia, in Pontus, and Asia, Phrygia, and Pamphylia, in Egypt, and in the parts of Libya about Cyrene, and strangers of Rome, Jews and proselytes, Cretes and Arabians, we do hear them speak in our tongues the wonderful works of God.

THE COMFORTER

But the Comforter, which is the Holy Ghost, whom the Father will send in my name, he shall teach you all things, and bring all things to your remembrance, whatsoever I have said unto you. St. John 14. 26

The Gospel. *St. John 14. 15*
From 'Whitsunday'

JESUS said unto his disciples, If ye love me, keep my commandments. And I will pray the Father, and he shall give you another Comforter, that he may abide with you for ever; even the Spirit of truth, whom the world cannot receive, because it seeth him not, neither knoweth him: but ye know him; for he dwelleth with you, and shall be in you. I will not leave you comfortless: I will come to you. Yet a little while, and the world seeth me no more; but ye see me: because I live, ye shall live also. At that day ye shall know that I am in my Father, and ye in me, and I in you. He that hath my commandments, and keepeth them, he it is that loveth me; and he that loveth me shall be loved of my Father, and I will love him, and will manifest myself to him. Judas saith unto him, (not Iscariot,) Lord, how is it that thou wilt manifest thyself unto us, and not unto the world? Jesus answered and said unto him, If a man love me, he will keep my words, and my Father will love him, and we will come unto him, and make our abode with him. He that loveth me not keepeth not my sayings: and the word which ye hear is not mine, but the Father's which sent me.

ANOINTED

How God anointed Jesus of Nazareth with the Holy Ghost and with power.

Acts 10. 38

For the Epistle. *Acts 10. 34*
From 'Monday in Whitsun Week'

THEN Peter opened his mouth, and said, Of a truth I perceive that God is no respecter of persons; but in every nation he that feareth him, and worketh righteousness, is accepted with him. The word which God sent unto the children of Israel, preaching peace by Jesus Christ ... that word, I say, ye know, which was published throughout all Judaea, and began from Galilee, after the baptism which John preached: how God anointed Jesus of Nazareth with the Holy Ghost, and with power; who went about doing good, and healing all that were oppressed of the devil: for God was with him. And we are witnesses of all things which he did, both in the land of the Jews, and in Jerusalem; whom they slew, and hanged on a tree: him God raised up the third day, and shewed him openly: not to all the people, but unto witnesses chosen before God, even to us, who did eat and drink with him after he rose from the dead ... To him give all the prophets witness, that through his name whosoever believeth in him shall receive remission of sins. While Peter yet spake these words, the Holy Ghost fell on all them which heard the word. And they of the circumcision which believed were astonished, as many as came with Peter, because that on the Gentiles also was poured out the gift of the Holy Ghost.

'I KNOW MY SHEEP'

I am the door of the sheep. St. John 10. 7

The Gospel. *St. John 10. 1*
From 'Tuesday in Whitsun Week'

VERILY, verily I say unto you, He that entereth not by the door into the sheepfold, but climbeth up some other way, the same is a thief and a robber. But he that entereth in by the door is the shepherd of the sheep: to him the porter openeth; and the sheep hear his voice, and he calleth his own sheep by name, and leadeth them out. And, when he putteth forth his own sheep, he goeth before them, and the sheep follow him; for they know his voice. And a stranger will they not follow but will flee from him; for they know not the voice of strangers. This parable spake Jesus unto them: but they understood not what things they were which he spake unto them. Then said Jesus unto them again; Verily, verily I say unto you, I am the door of the sheep. All that ever came before me are thieves and robbers; but the sheep did not hear them. I am the door; by me if any man enter in, he shall be saved, and shall go in and out, and find pasture. The thief cometh not but for to steal, and to kill, and to destroy: I am come that they might have life, and that they might have it more abundantly.

Meditation
He ... shall go in and out, and find pasture. St. John 10. 9

TAUGHT BY THE SPIRIT

Then laid they their hands on them, and they received the Holy Ghost.

Acts 8. 17

The Collect
From 'Tuesday in Whitsun Week'

O GOD, who as at this time didst teach the hearts of thy faithful people, by the sending to them the light of thy Holy Spirit: Grant us by the same Spirit to have a right judgement in all things, and evermore to rejoice in his holy comfort; through the merits of Christ Jesus our Saviour, who liveth and reigneth with thee, in the unity of the same Spirit, one God, world without end. Amen.

For the Epistle. *Acts 8. 14*
From 'Tuesday in Whitsun Week'

WHEN the Apostles, which were at Jerusalem, heard that Samaria had received the word of God, they sent unto them Peter and John; who, when they were come down, prayed for them, that they might receive the Holy Ghost: (for as yet he was fallen upon none of them; only they were baptized in the name of the Lord Jesus.) Then laid they their hands on them, and they received the Holy Ghost.

Meditation
But ye shall receive power, after that the Holy Ghost is come upon you. Acts 1. 8

'TO LEAD THEM TO ALL TRUTH'

Great is the Lord, and marvellous worthy to be praised : there is no end of his greatness. Psalm 145. 3

The Proper Preface Upon Whitsunday
From 'Holy Communion'

IT is very meet, right, and our bounden duty, that we should at all times, and in all places, give thanks unto thee, O Lord, Holy Father, Almighty, Everlasting God.

Through Jesus Christ our Lord; according to whose most true promise, the Holy Ghost came down as at this time from heaven with a sudden great sound, as it had been a mighty wind, in the likeness of fiery tongues, lighting upon the Apostles, to teach them, and to lead them to all truth; giving them both the gift of divers languages, and also boldness with fervent zeal constantly to preach the Gospel unto all nations; whereby we have been brought out of darkness and error into the clear light and true knowledge of thee, and of thy Son Jesus Christ.

Therefore with Angels and Archangels, and with all the company of heaven, we laud and magnify thy glorious Name; evermore praising thee, and saying: Holy, holy, holy, Lord God of hosts, heaven and earth are full of thy glory: Glory be to thee, O Lord most High. Amen.

THE TRINITY

Holy, holy, holy, Lord God Almighty, which was, and is, and is to come.

Revelation 4. 8

For the Epistle. *Revelation 4. 1*
From 'Trinity Sunday'

AFTER this I looked, and behold, a door was opened in heaven: and the first voice which I heard was as it were of a trumpet talking with me; which said, Come up hither, and I will shew thee things which must be hereafter. And immediately I was in the spirit; and behold, a throne was set in heaven, and one sat on the throne: and he that sat was to look upon like a jasper and a sardine stone: and there was a rainbow round about the throne, in sight like unto an emerald. And round about the throne were four and twenty seats; and upon the seats I saw four and twenty elders sitting, clothed in white raiment; and they had on their heads crowns of gold: and out of the throne proceeded lightnings and thunderings and voices. And there were seven lamps of fire burning before the throne, which are the seven Spirits of God. And before the throne there was a sea of glass like unto crystal: and in the midst of the throne, and round about the throne, were four beasts full of eyes before and behind. And the first beast was like a lion, and the second beast like a calf, and the third beast had a face as a man, and the fourth beast was like a flying eagle. And the four beasts had each of them six wings about him; and they were full of eyes within.

SPIRITUAL BIRTH

Except a man be born of water and of the Spirit, he cannot enter into the kingdom of God. St. John 3. 5

The Gospel. *St. John 3. 1*
From 'Trinity Sunday'

THERE was a man of the Pharisees, named Nicodemus, a ruler of the Jews: the same came to Jesus by night, and said unto him, Rabbi, we know that thou art a teacher come from God: for no man can do these miracles that thou doest, except God be with him. Jesus answered and said unto him, Verily, verily I say unto thee, Except a man be born again, he cannot see the kingdom of God. Nicodemus saith unto him, How can a man be born when he is old? can he enter the second time into his mother's womb, and be born? Jesus answered, Verily, verily I say unto thee, Except a man be born of water and of the Spirit, he cannot enter into the kingdom of God. That which is born of the flesh is flesh; and that which is born of the Spirit is spirit. Marvel not that I said unto thee, Ye must be born again. The wind bloweth where it listeth, and thou hearest the sound thereof, but canst not tell whence it cometh, and whither it goeth: so is every one that is born of the Spirit. Nicodemus answered and said unto him, How can these things be? Jesus answered and said unto him, Art thou a master of Israel, and knowest not these things? Verily, verily I say unto thee, We speak that we do know, and testify that we have seen; and ye receive not our witness.

THREE PERSONS,
ONE SUBSTANCE

Holy, Holy, Holy : Lord God of Sabaoth;
Heaven and earth are full of the Majesty : of thy glory.

From 'Te Deum Laudamus'

From the 'Articles of Religion'
I. Of Faith in the Holy Trinity

THERE is but one living and true God, everlasting, without body, parts, or passions; of infinite power, wisdom, and goodness; the Maker, and Preserver of all things both visible and invisible. And in unity of this Godhead there be three Persons, of one substance, power, and eternity; the Father, the Son, and the Holy Ghost.

The Proper Preface Upon the Feast of Trinity
From 'Holy Communion'

IT is very meet, right, and our bounden duty, that we should at all times, and in all places, give thanks unto thee, O Lord, Holy Father, Almighty, Everlasting God.

Who art one God, one Lord; not one only Person, but three Persons in one Substance. For that which we believe of the glory of the Father, the same we believe of the Son, and of the Holy Ghost, without any difference or inequality.

THE TRIUNE GOD

Holy, holy, holy, Lord God of hosts, heaven and earth are full of thy glory : Glory be to thee, O Lord most High. Amen. From 'Holy Communion'

From 'The Litany'

O GOD the Father of heaven : have mercy upon us miserable sinners.

O God the Father of heaven : have mercy upon us miserable sinners.

O God the Son, Redeemer of the world : have mercy upon us miserable sinners.

O God the Son, Redeemer of the world : have mercy upon us miserable sinners.

O God the Holy Ghost, proceeding from the Father and the Son : have mercy upon us miserable sinners.

O God the Holy Ghost, proceeding from the Father and the Son : have mercy upon us miserable sinners.

O holy, blessed, and glorious Trinity, three Persons and one God : have mercy upon us miserable sinners.

Meditation

O holy, blessed, and glorious Trinity, three Persons and one God : have mercy upon us miserable sinners. From 'The Litany'

THE CREED OF ATHANASIUS

But the Godhead of the Father, of the Son, and of the Holy Ghost, is all one.

From 'At Morning Prayer'

Quicunque Vult. *The Creed of Saint Athanasius*
From 'At Morning Prayer'

WHOSOEVER will be saved : before all things it is necessary that he hold the Catholick Faith.

Which Faith except every one do keep whole and undefiled : without doubt he shall perish everlastingly.

And the Catholick Faith is this : That we worship one God in Trinity, and Trinity in Unity;

Neither confounding the Persons : nor dividing the Substance.

For there is one Person of the Father, another of the Son : and another of the Holy Ghost.

But the Godhead of the Father, of the Son, and of the Holy Ghost, is all one : the Glory equal, the Majesty co-eternal.

Such as the Father is, such is the Son : and such is the Holy Ghost.

The Father uncreate, the Son uncreate : and the Holy Ghost uncreate.

The Father incomprehensible, the Son incomprehensible : and the Holy Ghost incomprehensible.

The Father eternal, the Son eternal : and the Holy Ghost eternal.

And yet they are not three eternals : but one eternal.

PREPARE YE THE WAY OF THE LORD

Behold your God! Behold, the Lord God will come with strong hand.

Isaiah 40. 9–10

For the Epistle. *Isaiah 40. 1*
From 'Saint John Baptist's Day'

COMFORT ye, comfort ye my people, saith your God. Speak ye comfortably to Jerusalem, and cry unto her, that her warfare is accomplished, that her iniquity is pardoned: for she hath received of the Lord's hand double for all her sins. The voice of him that crieth in the wilderness, Prepare ye the way of the Lord, make straight in the desert a highway for our God. Every valley shall be exalted, and every mountain and hill shall be made low, and the crooked shall be made straight, and the rough places plain. And the glory of the Lord shall be revealed, and all flesh shall see it together: for the mouth of the Lord hath spoken it. The voice said, Cry. And he said, What shall I cry? All flesh is grass, and all the goodliness thereof is as the flower of the field. The grass withereth, the flower fadeth, because the spirit of the Lord bloweth upon it: surely the people is grass. The grass withereth, the flower fadeth; but the word of our God shall stand for ever. O Zion, that bringest good tidings, get thee up into the high mountain: O Jerusalem, that bringest good tidings, lift up thy voice with strength; lift it up, be not afraid: say unto the cities of Judah, Behold your God. Behold, the Lord God will come with strong hand, and his arm shall rule for him: behold, his reward is with him, and his work before him.

'HE SHALL BE CALLED JOHN'

And the hand of the Lord was with him. St. Luke 1. 66

The Gospel. *St. Luke 1. 57*
From 'Saint John Baptist's Day'

ELISABETH'S full time came that she should be delivered; and she brought forth a son. And her neighbours and her cousins heard how the Lord had shewed great mercy upon her; and they rejoiced with her. And it came to pass, that on the eighth day they came to circumcise the child; and they called him Zacharias, after the name of his father. And his mother answered and said, Not so; but he shall be called John. And they said unto her, There is none of thy kindred that is called by this name. And they made signs to his father, how he would have him called. And he asked for a writing-table, and wrote, saying, His name is John. And they marvelled all. And his mouth was opened immediately, and his tongue loosed, and he spake, and praised God. And fear came on all that dwelt round about them; and all these sayings were noised abroad throughout all the hill-country of Judaea. And all they that heard them laid them up in their hearts, saying, What manner of child shall this be? And the hand of the Lord was with him.

Meditation
Turn us again, O Lord God of hosts : shew the light of thy countenance, and we shall be whole. Psalm 80. 19

ZACHARIAS' PROPHECY

Blessed be the Lord God of Israel; for he hath visited and redeemed his people, And hath raised up an horn of salvation for us in the house of his servant David.

St. Luke 1. 68–69

The Gospel. *St. Luke 1. 67*
From 'Saint John Baptist's Day'

AND his father Zacharias was filled with the Holy Ghost, and prophe-
sied, saying, Blessed be the Lord God of Israel: for he hath visited and
redeemed his people, and hath raised up an horn of salvation for us in the
house of his servant David; as he spake by the mouth of his holy prophets,
which have been since the world began; that we should be saved from
our enemies, and from the hand of all that hate us; to perform the mercy
promised to our fathers, and to remember his holy covenant; the oath
which he sware to our father Abraham, that he would grant unto us, that
we, being delivered out of the hands of our enemies, might serve him
without fear, in holiness and righteousness before him all the days of our
life. And thou, child, shalt be called the Prophet of the Highest: for thou
shalt go before the face of the Lord to prepare his ways; to give knowledge
of salvation unto his people, by the remission of their sins, through the tender mercy of our God, whereby the day-spring from on high hath visited
us; to give light to them that sit in darkness and in the shadow of death
to guide our feet into the way of peace. And the child grew, and waxed
strong in spirit and was in the deserts till the day of his shewing unto Israel.

THE HELP OF GOD'S GRACE

Love is of God. 1 St. John 4. 7

The Epistle. *1 St. John 4. 7*
From 'The First Sunday After Trinity'

BELOVED, let us love one another: for love is of God, and every one that loveth is born of God, and knoweth God. He that loveth not knoweth not God; for God is love. In this was manifested the love of God towards us, because that God sent his only begotten Son into the world, that we might live through him. Herein is love, not that we loved God, but that he loved us, and sent his Son to be the propitiation for our sins. Beloved, if God so loved us, we ought also to love one another. No man hath seen God at any time. If we love one another, God dwelleth in us, and his love is perfected in us. Hereby know we that we dwell in him, and he in us; because he hath given us of his Spirit. And we have seen, and do testify, that the Father sent the Son to be the Saviour of the world. Whosoever shall confess that Jesus is the Son of God, God dwelleth in him, and he in God. And we have known and believed the love that God hath to us. God is love; and he that dwelleth in love dwelleth in God, and God in him. Herein is our love made perfect, that we may have boldness in the day of judgement; because as he is, so are we in this world. There is no fear in love; but perfect love casteth out fear.

KEEPING GOD'S
COMMANDMENTS

Pure religion and undefiled before God and the Father is this, To visit the fatherless and widows in their affliction. St. James 1. 27

The Gospel. *St. Luke 16. 19*
From 'The First Sunday After Trinity'

THERE was a certain rich man, which was clothed in purple and fine linen, and fared sumptuously every day. And there was a certain beggar named Lazarus, which was laid at his gate full of sores, and desiring to be fed with the crumbs which fell from the rich man's table: moreover the dogs came and licked his sores. And it came to pass, that the beggar died, and was carried by the angels into Abraham's bosom. The rich man also died, and was buried: and in hell he lift up his eyes, being in torments, and seeth Abraham afar off, and Lazarus in his bosom. And he cried and said, Father Abraham, have mercy on me, and send Lazarus, that he may dip the tip of his finger in water, and cool my tongue; for I am tormented in this flame. But Abraham said, Son, remember that thou in thy life-time receivedst thy good things, and likewise Lazarus evil things; but now he is comforted, and thou art tormented … Then he said, I pray thee therefore, father, that thou wouldest send him to my father's house: for I have five brethren; that he may testify unto them, lest they also come into this place of torment. Abraham saith unto him, They have Moses and the prophets; let them hear them.

GO BEFORE US, O LORD

The right hand of the Lord hath the pre-eminence : the right hand of the Lord bringeth mighty things to pass. Psalm 118. 16

Psalm 118. *Confitemini Domino*

O GIVE thanks unto the Lord, for he is gracious : because his mercy endureth for ever.

2. Let Israel now confess that he is gracious : and that his mercy endureth for ever.

3. Let the house of Aaron now confess : that his mercy endureth for ever.

4. Yea, let them now that fear the Lord confess : that his mercy endureth for ever.

5. I called upon the Lord in trouble : and the Lord heard me at large.

6. The Lord is on my side : I will not fear what man doeth unto me.

7. The Lord taketh my part with them that help me : therefore shall I see my desire upon mine enemies.

8. It is better to trust in the Lord : than to put any confidence in man.

9. It is better to trust in the Lord : than to put any confidence in princes ...

13. Thou hast thrust sore at me, that I might fall : but the Lord was my help.

14. The Lord is my strength, and my song : and is become my salvation.

15. The voice of joy and health is in the dwellings of the righteous : the right hand of the Lord bringeth mighty things to pass.

PSALMS OF PRAISE AND THANKSGIVING (13)

Learning from what God has done

I eased his shoulder from the burden : and his hands were delivered from making the pots. Psalm 81. 6

Psalm 81. *Exultate Deo*

SING we merrily unto God our strength : make a cheerful noise unto the God of Jacob.

2. Take the psalm, bring hither the tabret : the merry harp with the lute.

3. Blow up the trumpet in the new-moon : even in the time appointed, and upon our solemn feast-day.

4. For this was made a statute for Israel : and a law of the God of Jacob.

5. This he ordained in Joseph for a testimony : when he came out of the land of Egypt, and had heard a strange language.

6. I eased his shoulder from the burden : and his hands were delivered from making the pots.

7. Thou calledst upon me in troubles, and I delivered thee : and heard thee what time as the storm fell upon thee.

8. I proved thee also : at the waters of strife.

9. Hear, O my people, and I will assure thee, O Israel : if thou wilt hearken unto me,

10. There shall no strange god be in thee : neither shalt thou worship any other god.

11. I am the Lord thy God, who brought thee out of the land of Egypt : open thy mouth wide, and I shall fill it.

PETER'S MIRACULOUS
ESCAPE FROM PRISON

And, behold, the angel of the Lord came upon him, and a light shined in the prison : and he smote Peter on the side, and raised him up, saying, Arise up quickly. And his chains fell off from his hands. Acts 12. 7

For the Epistle. *Acts 12. 1*
From 'Saint Peter's Day'

ABOUT that time Herod the king stretched forth his hands to vex certain of the Church. And he killed James the brother of John with the sword. And because he saw it pleased the Jews, he proceeded further to take Peter also. (Then were the days of unleavened bread.) And when he had apprehended him, he put him in prison, and delivered him to four quaternions of soldiers to keep him, intending after Easter to bring him forth to the people. Peter therefore was kept in prison; but prayer was made without ceasing of the Church unto God for him. And when Herod would have brought him forth, the same night Peter was sleeping between two soldiers, bound with two chains; and the keepers before the door kept the prison. And behold, the angel of the Lord came upon him, and a light shined in the prison; and he smote Peter on the side, and raised him up, saying, Arise up quickly. And his chains fell off from his hands. And the angel said unto him, Gird thyself, and bind on thy sandals: and so he did. And he saith unto him, Cast thy garment about thee, and follow me. And he went out and followed him; and wist not that it was true which was done by the angel; but thought he saw a vision.

181

PETER'S DECLARATION

And Simon Peter answered and said, Thou art the Christ, the Son of the living God. St. Matthew 16. 16

The Collect
From 'Saint Peter's Day'

O ALMIGHTY God, who by thy Son Jesus Christ didst give to thy Apostle Saint Peter many excellent gifts, and commandest him earnestly to feed thy flock: Make, we beseech thee, all Bishops and Pastors diligently to preach thy holy Word, and the people obediently to follow the same, that they may receive the crown of everlasting glory; through Jesus Christ our Lord. Amen.

The Gospel. *St. Matthew 16. 13*
From 'Saint Peter's Day'

WHEN Jesus came into the coasts of Caesarea Philippi, he asked his disciples, saying, Whom do men say that I, the Son of man, am? And they said, Some say that thou art John the Baptist, some, Elias, and others Jeremias, or one of the prophets. He saith unto them, But whom say ye that I am? And Simon Peter answered and said, Thou art Christ, the Son of the living God. And Jesus answered and said unto him, Blessed art thou, Simon Bar-jona: for flesh and blood hath not revealed it unto thee, but my Father which is in heaven. And I say also unto thee, that thou art Peter, and upon this rock I will build my Church.

PSALMS OF PRAISE AND THANKSGIVING (14)

Zion, city of our God

Her foundations are upon the holy hills : the Lord loveth the gates of Sion more than all the dwellings of Jacob. Psalm 87. 1

Psalm 87. *Fundamenta ejus*

HER foundations are upon the holy hills : the Lord loveth the gates of Sion more than all the dwellings of Jacob.

2. Very excellent things are spoken of thee : thou city of God.

3. I will make think upon Rahab and Babylon : with them that know me …

5. And of Sion it shall be reported that he was born in her : and the most High shall stablish her.

6. The Lord shall rehearse it, when he writeth up the people : that he was born there.

7. The singers also and trumpeters shall rehearse : All my fresh springs shall be in thee.

A Prayer of Saint Chrysostom
From 'Morning Prayer'

ALMIGHTY God, who hast given us grace at this time with one accord to make our common supplications unto thee; and dost promise that when two or three are gathered together in thy Name thou wilt grant their requests: Fulfil now, O Lord, the desires and petitions of thy servants, as may be most expedient for them; granting us in this world knowledge of thy truth, and in the world to come life everlasting. Amen.

FEAR AND LOVE

We know that we have passed from death unto life, because we love the brethren.

1 St. John 3. 14

The Epistle. *1 St. John 3. 13*
From 'The Second Sunday After Trinity'

MARVEL not, my brethren, if the world hate you. We know that we have passed from death unto life, because we love the brethren. He that loveth not his brother abideth in death. Whosoever hateth his brother is a murderer: and ye know that no murderer hath eternal life abiding in him. Hereby perceive we the love of God, because he laid down his life for us: and we ought to lay down our lives for the brethren. But whoso hath this world's good, and seeth his brother have need, and shutteth up his bowels of compassion from him; how dwelleth the love of God in him? My little children, let us not love in word, neither in tongue; but in deed, and in truth. And hereby we know that we are of the truth, and shall assure our hearts before him. For if our heart condemn us, God is greater than our heart, and knoweth all things. Beloved, if our heart condemn us not, then have we confidence towards God. And whatsoever we ask, we receive of him, because we keep his commandments, and do those things that are pleasing in his sight. And this is his commandment, That we should believe on the name of his Son Jesus Christ, and love one another, as he gave us commandment.

THE HEAVENLY BANQUET

A certain man made a great supper, and bade many. St. Luke 14. 16

The Gospel. *St. Luke 14. 16*
From 'The Second Sunday After Trinity'

A CERTAIN man made a great supper, and bade many; and sent his servant at supper-time to say to them that were bidden, Come, for all things are now ready. And they all with one consent began to make excuse. The first said unto him, I have bought a piece of ground, and I must needs go and see it; I pray thee have me excused. And another said, I have bought five yoke of oxen, and I go to prove them; I pray thee have me excused. And another said, I have married a wife, and therefore I cannot come. So that servant came and shewed his lord these things. Then the master of the house being angry said to his servant, Go out quickly into the streets and lanes of the city, and bring in hither the poor, and the maimed, and the halt, and the blind. And the servant said, Lord, it is done as thou hast commanded, and yet there is room. And the lord said unto the servant, Go out into the high-ways and hedges, and compel them to come in, that my house may be filled. For I say unto you, That none of those men which were bidden shall taste of my supper.

Meditation
Deliver my soul, O Lord, from lying lips : and from a deceitful tongue.

Psalm 120. 2

SPARE US, GOOD LORD

Thou didst turn thy face from me : and I was troubled. Psalm 30. 7

Psalm 30. *Exaltabo te, Domine*

I WILL magnify thee, O Lord, for thou hast set me up : and not made my foes to triumph over me.

2. O Lord my God, I cried unto thee : and thou hast healed me.

3. Thou, Lord, hast brought my soul out of hell : thou hast kept my life from them that go down to the pit.

4. Sing praises unto the Lord, O ye saints of his : and give thanks unto him for a remembrance of his holiness.

5. For his wrath endureth but the twinkling of an eye, and in his pleasure is life : heaviness may endure for a night, but joy cometh in the morning.

6. And in my prosperity I said, I shall never be removed : thou, Lord, of thy goodness hast made my hill so strong.

7. Thou didst turn thy face from me : and I was troubled.

8. Then cried I unto thee, O Lord : and gat me to my Lord right humbly.

9. What profit is there in my blood : when I go down to the pit?

10. Shall the dust give thanks unto thee : or shall it declare thy truth?

11. Hear, O Lord, and have mercy upon me : Lord, be thou my helper.

12. Thou hast turned my heaviness into joy : thou hast put off my sack-cloth, and girded me with gladness.

IN DEEP TROUBLE (4)

When I was in trouble, I called upon the Lord : and he heard me. Psalm 120. 1

Psalm 140. *Eripe me, Domine*

DELIVER me, O Lord, from the evil man : and preserve me from the wicked man.

2. Who imagine mischief in their hearts : and stir up strife all the day long.

3. They have sharpened their tongues like a serpent : adders' poison is under their lips.

4. Keep me, O Lord, from the hands of the ungodly : preserve me from the wicked men, who are purposed to overthrow my goings.

5. The proud have laid a snare for me, and spread a net abroad with cords : yea, and set traps in my way.

6. I said unto the Lord, Thou art my God : hear the voice of my prayers, O Lord.

7. O Lord God, thou strength of my health : thou hast covered my head in the day of battle.

8. Let not the ungodly have his desire, O Lord : let not his mischievous imagination prosper, lest they be too proud …

12. Sure I am that the Lord will avenge the poor : and maintain the cause of the helpless.

13. The righteous also shall give thanks unto thy Name : and the just shall continue in thy sight.

INSTRUCTION FROM
GOD'S WORD (7)

I have refrained my feet from every evil way : that I may keep thy word.

Psalm 119. 101

The Collect
From 'The Second Sunday in Advent'

BLESSED Lord, who hast caused all holy Scriptures to be written for our learning: Grant that we may in such wise hear them, read, mark, learn, and inwardly digest them, that by patience and comfort of thy holy Word, we may embrace and ever hold fast the blessed hope of everlasting life, which thou hast given us in our Saviour Jesus Christ. Amen.

Psalm 119. *Quomodo dilexi!*

LORD, what love have I unto thy law : all the day long is my study in it.

98. Thou through thy commandments hast made me wiser than mine enemies : for they are ever with me.

99. I have more understanding than my teachers : for thy testimonies are my study.

100. I am wiser than the aged : because I keep thy commandments.

101. I have refrained my feet from every evil way : that I may keep thy word.

102. I have not shrunk from thy judgements : for thou teachest me.

HOLY COMMUNION

The Supper of the Lord is ... a Sacrament of our Redemption by Christ's death.
From the 'Articles of Religion'

The Collect
From 'Holy Communion'

ALMIGHTY God, unto whom all hearts be open, all desires known, and from whom no secrets are hid: Cleanse the thoughts of our hearts by the inspiration of thy Holy Spirit, that we may perfectly love thee, and worthily magnify thy holy Name; through Christ our Lord. Amen.

From the 'Articles of Religion'
XXVIII. Of the Lord's Supper

THE Supper of the Lord is not only a sign of the love that Christians ought to have among themselves one to another; but rather is a Sacrament of our Redemption by Christ's death: insomuch that to such as rightly, worthily, and with faith, receive the same, the Bread which we break is a partaking of the Body of Christ; and likewise the Cup of Blessing is a partaking of the Blood of Christ.

Meditation
I cried unto thee, O Lord, and said : Thou art my hope, and my portion in the land of the living. Psalm 142. 6

BELIEF IN GOD THE CREATOR

I believe in God the Father Almighty, Maker of heaven and earth.
From the Apostles' Creed in 'Morning Prayer'

A General Thanksgiving
From 'Prayers and Thanksgivings'

ALMIGHTY God, Father of all mercies, we thine unworthy servants do give thee most humble and hearty thanks for all thy goodness and loving-kindness to us and to all men. We bless thee for our creation, preservation, and all the blessings of this life; but above all for thine inestimable love in the redemption of the world by our Lord Jesus Christ, for the means of grace, and for the hope of glory. And we beseech thee, give us that due sense of all thy mercies, that our hearts may be unfeignedly thankful, and that we shew forth thy praise, not only with our lips, but in our lives; by giving up ourselves to thy service, and by walking before thee in holiness and righteousness all our days; through Jesus Christ our Lord, to whom with thee and the Holy Ghost be all honour and glory, world without end. Amen.

Meditation
The heavens declare the glory of God : and the firmament sheweth his handywork.
Psalm 19. 1

COMFORT IN DANGER

And I said, O that I had wings like a dove : for then would I flee away, and be at rest. Psalm 55. 6

The Collect
From 'The Third Sunday After Trinity'

O LORD, we beseech thee mercifully to hear us; and grant that we, to whom thou hast given an hearty desire to pray, may by thy mighty aid be defended and comforted in all dangers and adversities; through Jesus Christ our Lord. Amen.

Psalm 55. *Exaudi, Deus*

A S for me, I will call upon God : and the Lord shall save me.
18. In the evening, and morning, and at noon-day will I pray, and that instantly : and he shall hear my voice.
19. It is he that hath delivered my soul in peace from the battle that was against me : for there were many with me ...
23. O cast thy burden upon the Lord, and he shall nourish thee : and shall not suffer the righteous to fall for ever.

Meditation
...Casting all your care upon him, for he careth for you. 1 St. Peter 5. 7

THE DILIGENT SEEKER

There is joy in the presence of the angels of God over one sinner that repenteth.

St. Luke 15. 10

The Gospel. *St. Luke 15. 1*
From 'The Third Sunday After Trinity'

THEN drew near unto him all the Publicans and sinners for to hear him. And the Pharisees and Scribes murmured, saying, This man receiveth sinners, and eateth with them. And he spake this parable unto them, saying, What man of you having an hundred sheep, if he lose one of them, doth not leave the ninety and nine in the wilderness, and go after that which is lost, until he find it? And when he hath found it, he layeth it on his shoulders, rejoicing. And when he cometh home, he calleth together his friends and neighbours, saying unto them, Rejoice with me, for I have found my sheep which was lost. I say unto you, that likewise joy shall be in heaven over one sinner that repenteth, more than over ninety and nine just persons, which need no repentance. Either what woman having ten pieces of silver, if she lose one piece, doth not light a candle, and sweep the house, and seek diligently till she find it? And when she hath found it, she calleth her friends and her neighbours together, saying, Rejoice with me, for I have found the piece which I had lost. Likewise, I say unto you, There is joy in the presence of the angels of God over one sinner that repenteth.

IN THE BREAKING OF THE BREAD

And it came to pass, as he sat at meat with them, he took bread, and blessed it, and brake, and gave to them. And their eyes were opened, and they knew him; and he vanished out of their sight. St. Luke 24. 30–31

From 'A Catechism'

WHY was the Sacrament of the Lord's Supper ordained?
Answer. For the continual remembrance of the sacrifice of the death of Christ, and of the benefits which we receive thereby.

Question. What is the outward part or sign of the Lord's Supper?

Answer. Bread and Wine, which the Lord hath commanded to be received.

Question. What is the inward part, or thing signified?

Answer. The Body and Blood of Christ, which are verily and indeed taken and received by the faithful in the Lord's Supper.

Question. What are the benefits whereof we are partakers thereby?

Answer. The strengthening and refreshing of our souls by the Body and Blood of Christ, as our bodies are by the Bread and Wine.

Question. What is required of them who come to the Lord's Supper?

Answer. To examine themselves, whether they repent them truly of their former sins, stedfastly purposing to lead a new life have a lively faith in God's mercy through Christ, with a thankful remembrance of his death; and be in charity with all men.

PSALMS OF PRAISE AND THANKSGIVING (15)

O come, let us sing unto the Lord : let us heartily rejoice in the strength of our salvation. Psalm 95. 1

Psalm 95. *Venite, exultemus*

O COME, let us sing unto the Lord : let us heartily rejoice in the strength of our salvation.

2. Let us come before his presence with thanksgiving : and shew ourselves glad in him with psalms.

3. For the Lord is a great God : and a great King above all gods.

4. In his hand are all the corners of the earth : and the strength of the hills is his also.

5. The sea is his, and he made it : and his hands prepared the dry land.

6. O come, let us worship and fall down : and kneel before the Lord our Maker.

7. For he is the Lord our God : and we are the people of his pasture, and the sheep of his hand.

8. To-day if ye will hear his voice, harden not your hearts : as in the provocation, and as in the day of temptation in the wilderness;

9. When your fathers tempted me : proved me, and saw my works.

10. Forty years long was I grieved with this generation, and said : It is a people that do err in their hearts, for they have not known my ways;

11. Unto whom I sware in my wrath : that they should not enter into my rest.

THE MESSIAH IN THE PSALMS (9)

He will be accused by false witnesses

False witnesses did rise up : they laid to my charge things that I knew not.

Psalm 35. 11

Psalm 35. *Judica, Domine*

PLEAD thou my cause, O Lord, with them that strive with me : and fight thou against them that fight against me.

2. Lay hand upon the shield and buckler : and stand up to help me.

3. Bring forth the spear, and stop the way against them that pursue me : say unto my soul, I am thy salvation.

4. Let them be confounded and put to shame, that seek after my soul : let them be turned back and brought to confusion, that imagine mischief for me.

5. Let them be as the dust before the wind : and the angel of the Lord scattering them.

6. Let their way be dark and slippery : and let the angel of the Lord persecute them.

7. For they have privily laid their net to destroy me without a cause : yea, even without a cause have they made a pit for my soul.

8. Let a sudden destruction come upon him unawares, and his net, that he hath laid privily, catch himself : that he may fall into his own mischief.

9. And, my soul, be joyful in the Lord : it shall rejoice in his salvation.

PSALMS OF PRAISE AND THANKSGIVING (16)
The Judge is coming

For he cometh, for he cometh to judge the earth : and with righteousness to judge the world, and the people with his truth. Psalm 96. 13

Psalm 96. *Cantate Domino*

O SING unto the Lord a new song : sing unto the Lord, all the whole earth.

2. Sing unto the Lord, and praise his Name : be telling of his salvation from day to day.

3. Declare his honour unto the heathen : and his wonders unto all people.

4. For the Lord is great, and cannot worthily be praised : he is more to be feared than all gods.

5. As for all the gods of the heathen, they are but idols : but it is the Lord that made the heavens.

6. Glory and worship are before him : power and honour are in his sanctuary.

7. Ascribe unto the Lord, O ye kindreds of the people : ascribe unto the Lord worship and power.

8. Ascribe unto the Lord the honour due unto his Name : bring presents, and come into his courts.

9. O worship the Lord in the beauty of holiness : let the whole earth stand in awe of him.

PSALMS OF PRAISE AND THANKSGIVING (17)

God loves his own people

O ye that love the Lord, see that ye hate the thing which is evil : the Lord preserveth the souls of his saints; he shall deliver them from the hand of the ungodly.

Psalm 97. 10

Psalm 97. *Dominus regnavit*

THE Lord is King, the earth may be glad thereof : yea, the multitude of the isles may be glad thereof.

2. Clouds and darkness are round about him : righteousness and judgement are the habitation of his seat.

3. There shall go a fire before him : and burn up his enemies on every side.

4. His lightnings gave shine unto the world : the earth saw it, and was afraid.

5. The hills melted like wax at the presence of the Lord : at the presence of the Lord of the whole earth.

6. The heavens have declared his righteousness : and all the people have seen his glory.

7. Confounded be all they that worship carved images, and that delight in vain gods : worship him, all ye gods.

8. Sion heard of it, and rejoiced : and the daughters of Judah were glad, because of thy judgements, O Lord.

9. For thou, Lord, art higher than all that are in the earth : thou art exalted far above all gods.

PRESENT SUFFERING AND FUTURE GLORY

I reckon that the sufferings of this present time are not worthy to be compared with the glory which shall be revealed in us. Romans 8. 18

The Collect
From 'The Fourth Sunday After Trinity'

O GOD, the protector of all that trust in thee, without whom nothing is strong, nothing is holy; Increase and multiply upon us thy mercy; that, thou being our ruler and guide, we may so pass through things temporal, that we finally lose not the things eternal: Grant this, O heavenly Father, for Jesus Christ's sake our Lord. Amen.

The Epistle. *Romans 8. 18*
From 'The Fourth Sunday After Trinity'

I RECKON that the sufferings of this present time are not worthy to be compared with the glory which shall be revealed in us. For the earnest expectation of the creature waiteth for the manifestation of the sons of God. For the creature was made subject to vanity, not willingly, but by reason of him who hath subjected the same in hope: because the creature itself also shall be delivered from the bondage of corruption into the glorious liberty of the children of God. For we know that the whole creation groaneth and travaileth in pain together until now. And not only they, but ourselves also, which have the first-fruits of the Spirit.

BE MERCIFUL

Blessed are the merciful: for they shall obtain mercy. St. Matthew 5. 7

The Gospel. *St. Luke 6. 36*
From 'The Fourth Sunday After Trinity'

BE ye therefore merciful, as your Father also is merciful. Judge not, and ye shall not be judged: condemn not, and ye shall not be condemned: forgive, and ye shall be forgiven: give, and it shall be given unto you; good measure, pressed down, and shaken together, and running over, shall men give into your bosom. For with the same measure that ye mete withal, it shall be measured to you again. And he spake a parable unto them, Can the blind lead the blind? shall they not both fall into the ditch? The disciple is not above his master; but every one that is perfect shall be as his master. And why beholdest thou the mote that is in thy brother's eye, but perceivest not the beam that is in thine own eye? Either how canst thou say to thy brother, Brother, let me pull out the mote that is in thine eye, when thou thyself beholdest not the beam that is in thine own eye? Thou hypocrite, cast out first the beam out of thine own eye, and then shalt thou see clearly to pull out the mote that is in thy brother's eye.

Meditation
But the merciful goodness of the Lord endureth for ever and ever upon them that fear him : and his righteousness upon children's children. Psalm 103. 17

EASTER DAY IS EVERY DAY

Christ being raised from the dead dieth no more. Romans 6. 9

Anthems
From 'Easter Day'

CHRIST our passover is sacrificed for us : therefore let us keep the feast; Not with the old leaven, nor with the leaven of malice and wickedness : but with the unleavened bread of sincerity and truth.

1 Corinthians 5. 7

CHRIST being raised from the dead dieth no more : death hath no more dominion over him. For in that he died, he died unto sin once : but in that he liveth, he liveth unto God. Likewise reckon ye also yourselves to be dead indeed unto sin : but alive unto God, through Jesus Christ our Lord.

Romans 6. 9

CHRIST is risen from the dead : and become the first-fruits of them that slept. For since by man came death : by man came also the resurrection of the dead. For as in Adam all die : even so in Christ shall all be made alive.

1 Corinthians 15. 20

Glory be to the Father, and to the Son : and to the Holy Ghost; As it was in the beginning, is now, and ever shall be : world without end. Amen.

'O LOVE THE LORD,
ALL YE HIS SAINTS'

For thou art my strong rock, and my castle : be thou also my guide, and lead me for thy Name's sake. Psalm 31. 4

From 'The Litany'

FROM all evil and mischief; from sin, from the crafts and assaults of the devil; from thy wrath, and from everlasting damnation.

Good Lord, deliver us.

From all blindness of heart; from pride, vainglory, and hypocrisy; from envy, hatred, and malice, and all uncharitableness,

Good Lord, deliver us.

From fornication, and all other deadly sin; and from all the deceits of the world, the flesh, and the devil,

Good Lord, deliver us.

From lightning and tempest; from plague, pestilence, and famine; from battle and murder, and from sudden death,

Good Lord, deliver us.

Meditation

I will be glad and rejoice in thy mercy : for thou hast considered my trouble, and hast known my soul in adversities. Psalm 31. 8

PSALMS OF PRAISE AND THANKSGIVING (18)

Shout for joy to the Lord

Praise the Lord upon the harp : sing to the harp with a psalm of thanksgiving. With trumpets also and shawms : O shew yourselves joyful before the Lord the King.

Psalm 98. 6–7

Psalm 98. *Cantate Domino*

O SING unto the Lord a new song : for he hath done marvellous things.

2. With his own right hand, and with his holy arm : hath he gotten himself the victory.

3. The Lord declared his salvation : his righteousness hath he openly shewed in the sight of the heathen.

4. He hath remembered his mercy and truth toward the house of Israel : and all the ends of the world have seen the salvation of our God.

5. Shew yourselves joyful unto the Lord, all ye lands : sing, rejoice, and give thanks.

6. Praise the Lord upon the harp : sing to the harp with a psalm of thanksgiving.

7. With trumpets also and shawms : O shew yourselves joyful before the Lord the King.

8. Let the sea make a noise, and all that therein is : the round world, and they that dwell therein.

9. Let the floods clap their hands, and let the hills be joyful together before the Lord : for he is come to judge the earth.

PSALMS OF PRAISE AND THANKSGIVING (19)
The Lord reigns and the Lord is good

The Lord is great in Sion : and high above all people. Psalm 99. 2

Psalm 99. *Dominus regnavit*

THE Lord is King, be the people never so unpatient : he sitteth between the cherubims, be the earth never so unquiet ...

3. They shall give thanks unto thy Name : which is great, wonderful, and holy.

4. The King's power loveth judgement; thou hast prepared equity : thou hast executed judgement and righteousness in Jacob.

5. O magnify the Lord our God : and fall down before his footstool, for he is holy.

6. Moses and Aaron among his priests, and Samuel among such as call upon his Name : these called upon the Lord, and he heard them.

7. He spake unto them out of the cloudy pillar : for they kept his testimonies, and the law that he gave them.

8. Thou heardest them, O Lord our God : thou forgavest them, O God, and punishedst their own inventions.

9. O magnify the Lord our God, and worship him upon his holy hill : for the Lord our God is holy.

Meditation
For the Lord is gracious, his mercy is everlasting : and his truth endureth from generation to generation. Psalm 100. 4

THE MESSIAH IN THE PSALMS (10)

He will be hated without a cause

O let not them that are mine enemies triumph over me ungodly : neither let them wink with their eyes that hate me without a cause. Psalm 35. 19

Psalm 35. *Judica, Domine*

WITH the flatterers were busy mockers : who gnashed upon me with their teeth.

17. Lord, how long wilt thou look upon this : O deliver my soul from the calamities which they bring on me, and my darling from the lions.

18. So will I give thee thanks in the great congregation : I will praise thee among much people …

20. And why? their communing is not for peace : but they imagine deceitful words against them that are quiet in the land.

21. They gaped upon me with their mouths, and said : Fie on thee, fie on thee, we saw it with our eyes.

22. This thou hast seen, O Lord : hold not thy tongue then, go not far from me, O Lord.

23. Awake, and stand up to judge my quarrel : avenge thou my cause, my God, and my Lord.

24. Judge me, O Lord my God, according to thy righteousness : and let them not triumph over me.

25. Let them not say in their hearts, There, there, so would we have it : neither let them say, We have devoured him.

COMPASSION FOR ONE ANOTHER

...having compassion one of another, love as brethren, be pitiful, be courteous.

1 St. Peter 3. 8

The Collect
From 'The Fifth Sunday After Trinity'

GRANT, O Lord, we beseech thee, that the course of this world may be so peacably ordered by thy governance, that thy Church may joyfully serve thee in all godly quietness; through Jesus Christ our Lord. Amen.

The Epistle. *1 St. Peter 3. 8*
From 'The Fifth Sunday After Trinity'

BE ye all of one mind, having compassion one of another, love as brethren, be pitiful, be courteous; not rendering evil for evil, or railing for railing: but contrariwise blessing; knowing that ye are thereunto called, that ye should inherit a blessing. For he that will love life, and see good days, let him refrain his tongue from evil, and his lips that they speak no guile: let him eschew evil, and do good; let him seek peace, and ensue it. For the eyes of the Lord are over the righteous, and his ears are open unto their prayers: but the face of the Lord is against them that do evil. And who is he that will harm you, if ye be followers of that which is good? But and if ye suffer for righteousness' sake, happy are ye: and be not afraid of their terror, neither be troubled; but sanctify the Lord God in your hearts.

24 July

LAUNCH OUT INTO THE DEEP

And Jesus said unto Simon, Fear not, from henceforth thou shalt catch men.

St. Luke 5. 10

The Gospel. *St. Luke 5. 1*
From 'The Fifth Sunday After Trinity'

IT came to pass that as the people pressed upon him to hear the word of God, he stood by the lake of Gennesareth and saw two ships standing by the lake: but the fishermen were gone out of them, and were washing their nets. And he entered into one of the ships, which was Simon's, and prayed him that he would thrust out a little from the land: and he sat down, and taught the people out of the ship. Now when he had left speaking, he said unto Simon, Launch out into the deep, and let down your nets for a draught. And Simon answering said unto him, Master, we have toiled all the night, and have taken nothing; nevertheless, at thy word I will let down the net. And when they had this done, they inclosed a great multitude of fishes, and their net brake. And they beckoned unto their partners which were in the other ship ... And they came, and filled both the ships, so that they began to sink. When Simon Peter saw it, he fell down at Jesus' knees, saying, Depart from me, for I am a sinful man, O Lord. For he was astonished, and all that were with him, at the draught of the fishes which they had taken; and so was also James, and John, the sons of Zebedee, which were partners with Simon. And Jesus said unto Simon, Fear not, from henceforth thou shalt catch men.

FAITHFUL UNTO DEATH

Herod the king stretched forth his hands to vex certain of the church. And he killed James the brother of John with the sword. Acts 12. 1–2

The Collect
From 'Saint James the Apostle'

GRANT, O merciful God, that as thine holy Apostle Saint James, leaving his father and all that he had, without delay was obedient unto the calling of thy Son Jesus Christ, and followed him; so we, forsaking all worldly and carnal affections, may be evermore ready to follow thy holy commandments; through Jesus Christ our Lord. Amen.

For the Epistle. *Acts 11. 27*
From 'Saint James the Apostle'

IN those days came prophets from Jerusalem unto Antioch. And there stood up one of them named Agabus, and signified by the Spirit, that there should be great dearth throughout all the world; which came to pass in the days of Claudius Caesar. Then the disciples, every man according to his ability, determined to send relief unto the brethren which dwelt in Judaea: which also they did, and sent it to the elders by the hands of Barnabas and Saul. Now about that time Herod the king stretched forth his hands to vex certain of the Church. And he killed James the brother of John with the sword. And because he saw it pleased the Jews, he proceeded further to take Peter also.

A MOTHER'S REQUEST

Grant that these my two sons may sit, the one on thy right hand, and the other on the left, in thy kingdom. St. Matthew 20. 21

The Gospel. *St. Matthew 20. 20*
From 'Saint James the Apostle'

THEN came to him the mother of Zebedee's children with her sons, worshipping him, and desiring a certain thing of him. And he said unto her, What wilt thou? She saith unto him, Grant that these my two sons may sit, the one on thy right hand, and the other on the left, in thy kingdom. But Jesus answered and said, Ye know not what ye ask. Are ye able to drink of the cup that I shall drink of, and to be baptized with the baptism that I am baptized with? They say unto him, We are able. And he saith unto them, Ye shall drink indeed of my cup, and be baptized with the baptism that I am baptized with: but to sit on my right hand, and on my left, is not mine to give; but it shall be given to them for whom it is prepared of my Father. And when the ten heard it, they were moved with indignation against the two brethren. But Jesus called them unto him, and said, Ye know that the princes of the Gentiles exercise dominion over them, and they that are great exercise authority upon them. But it shall not be so among you: but whosoever will be great among you, let him be your minister; and whosoever will be chief among you, let him be your servant: even as the Son of man came not to be ministered unto, but to minister, and to give his life a ransom for many.

PSALMS OF PRAISE AND THANKSGIVING (21)

The God who made everything

He sendeth the springs into the rivers : which run among the hills. Psalm 104. 10

Psalm 104. *Benedic, anima mea*

PRAISE the Lord, O my soul : O Lord my God, thou art become exceeding glorious; thou art clothed with majesty and honour.

2. Thou deckest thyself with light as it were with a garment : and spreadest out the heavens like a curtain.

3. Who layeth the beams of his chambers in the waters : and maketh the clouds his chariot, and walketh upon the wings of the wind.

4. He maketh his angels spirits : and his ministers a flaming fire.

5. He laid the foundations of the earth : that it never should move at any time.

6. Thou coveredst it with the deep like as with a garment : the waters stand in the hills.

7. At thy rebuke they flee : at the voice of thy thunder they are afraid.

8. They go up as high as the hills, and down to the valleys beneath : even unto the place which thou hast appointed for them.

9. Thou hast set them their bounds which they shall not pass : neither turn again to cover the earth ...

11. All beasts of the field drink thereof : and the wild asses quench their thirst.

12. Beside them shall the fowls of the air have their habitation : and sing among the branches.

PSALMS OF PRAISE AND THANKSGIVING (22)

God led his people out

What time as they went from one nation to another : from one kingdom to another people. Psalm 105. 13

Psalm 105. *Confitemini Domino*

O GIVE thanks unto the Lord, and call upon his Name : tell the people what things he hath done.

2. O let your songs be of him, and praise him : and let your talking be of all his wondrous works.

3. Rejoice in his holy Name : let the heart of them rejoice that seek the Lord.

4. Seek the Lord and his strength : seek his face evermore.

5. Remember the marvellous works that he hath done : his wonders, and the judgements of his mouth;

6. O ye seed of Abraham his servant : ye children of Jacob his chosen.

7. He is the Lord our God : his judgements are in all the world.

8. He hath been alway mindful of his covenant and promise : that he made to a thousand generations;

9. Even the covenant that he made with Abraham : and the oath that he sware unto Isaac;

10. And appointed the same unto Jacob for a law : and to Israel for an everlasting testament;

11. Saying, Unto thee will I give the land of Canaan : the lot of your inheritance.

INSTRUCTION FROM
GOD'S WORD (8)

Hold thou me up, and I shall be safe : yea, my delight shall be ever in thy statutes.
Psalm 119. 117

The Collect
From 'The Second Sunday in Advent'

BLESSED Lord, who hast caused all holy Scriptures to be written for our learning : Grant that we may in such wise hear them, read, mark, learn, and inwardly digest them, that by patience and comfort of thy holy Word, we may embrace and ever hold fast the blessed hope of everlasting life, which thou hast given us in our Saviour Jesus Christ. Amen.

Psalm 119. *Iniquos odio habui*

I HATE them that imagine evil things : but thy law do I love.
114. Thou art my defence and shield : and my trust is in thy word.
115. Away from me, ye wicked : I will keep the commandments of my God.
116. O stablish me according to thy word, that I may live : and let me not be disappointed of my hope.
117. Hold thou me up, and I shall be safe : yea, my delight shall be ever in thy statutes.
118. Thou hast trodden down all them that depart from thy statutes : for they imagine but deceit.

LOVING GOD ABOVE ALL THINGS

For he that is dead is freed from sin. Romans 6. 7

The Collect
From 'The Sixth Sunday After Trinity'

O GOD, who hast prepared for them that love thee such good things as pass man's understanding: Pour into our hearts such love toward thee, that we, loving thee above all things, may obtain thy promises, which exceed all that we can desire; through Jesus Christ our Lord. Amen.

From 'A Catechism'

WHAT dost thou chiefly learn by these Commandments?
Answer. I learn two things: my duty towards God, and my duty towards my Neighbour.

Question. What is thy duty towards God?

Answer. My duty towards God is to believe in him, to fear him, and to love him, with all my heart, with all my mind, with all my soul, and with all my strength; to worship him, to give him thanks, to put my whole trust in him, to call upon him, to honour his holy Name and his Word, and to serve him truly all the days of my life.

FIRST BE RECONCILED
TO THY BROTHER

Except your righteousness shall exceed the righteousness of the scribes and Pharisees,
ye shall in no case enter into the kingdom of heaven. St. Matthew 5. 20

The Gospel. *St. Matthew 5. 20*
From 'The Sixth Sunday After Trinity'

JESUS said unto his disciples, Except your righteousness shall exceed the righteousness of the Scribes and Pharisees, ye shall in no case enter into the kingdom of heaven. Ye have heard that it was said by them of old time, Thou shalt not kill: and whosoever shall kill, shall be in danger of the judgement. But I say unto you, that whosoever is angry with his brother without a cause shall be in danger of the judgement: and whosoever shall say to his brother, Raca, shall be in danger of the council: but whosoever shall say, Thou fool, shall be in danger of hell-fire. Therefore if thou bring thy gift to the altar, and there rememberest that thy brother hath ought against thee; leave there thy gift before the altar, and go thy way, first be reconciled to thy brother, and then come and offer thy gift. Agree with thine adversary quickly, whiles thou art in the way with him; lest at any time the adversary deliver thee to the judge, and the judge deliver thee to the officer, and thou be cast into prison. Verily I say unto thee, Thou shalt by no means come out thence, till thou hast paid the uttermost farthing.

PRESERVED IN BODY AND SOUL

O Lord our Governor, how excellent is thy Name in all the world! Psalm 8. 9

From 'The Order of Confirmation'

O ALMIGHTY Lord, and everlasting God, vouchsafe, we beseech thee, to direct, sanctify, and govern, both our hearts and bodies, in the ways of thy laws, and in the works of thy commandments; that through thy most mighty protection, both here and ever, we may be preserved in body and soul; through our Lord and Saviour Jesus Christ. Amen.

Psalm 8. *Domine, Dominus noster*

O LORD our Governor, how excellent is thy Name in all the world : thou that hast set thy glory above the heavens!

2. Out of the mouth of very babes and sucklings hast thou ordained strength, because of thine enemies : that thou mightest still the enemy and the avenger.

3. For I will consider thy heavens, even the works of thy fingers : the moon and the stars, which thou hast ordained.

4. What is man, that thou art mindful of him : and the son of man, that thou visitest him?

5. Thou madest him lower than the angels : to crown him with glory and worship.

PSALMS OF PRAISE AND THANKSGIVING (23)

God provided for his people

Then sent he Moses his servant : and Aaron whom he had chosen. Psalm 105. 26

Psalm 105. *Confitemini Domino*

ISRAEL also came into Egypt : and Jacob was a stranger in the land of Ham.

24. And he increased his people exceedingly : and made them stronger than their enemies;

25. Whose heart turned so, that they hated his people : and dealt untruly with his servants ...

27. And these shewed his tokens among them : and wonders in the land of Ham.

36. He brought them forth also with silver and gold : there was not one feeble person among their tribes.

37. Egypt was glad at their departing : for they were afraid of them.

38. He spread out a cloud to be a covering : and fire to give light in the night-season.

39. At their desire he brought quails : and he filled them with the bread of heaven.

40. He opened the rock of stone, and the waters flowed out : so that rivers ran in the dry places.

41. For why? he remembered his holy promise : and Abraham his servant.

42. And he brought forth his people with joy : and his chosen with gladness.

PSALMS OF PRAISE AND THANKSGIVING (25)

God who gives victory

Set up thyself, O God, above the heavens : and thy glory above all the earth.

Psalm 108. 5

Psalm 108. *Paratum cor meum*

O GOD, my heart is ready, my heart is ready : I will sing and give praise with the best member that I have.

2. Awake, thou lute, and harp : I myself will awake right early.

3. I will give thanks unto thee, O Lord, among the people : I will sing praises unto thee among the nations.

4. For thy mercy is greater than the heavens : and thy truth reacheth unto the clouds.

5. Set up thyself, O God, above the heavens : and thy glory above all the earth.

6. That thy beloved may be delivered : let thy right hand save them, and hear thou me.

7. God hath spoken in his holiness : I will rejoice therefore, and divide Sichem, and mete out the valley of Succoth.

8. Gilead is mine, and Manasses is mine : Ephraim also is the strength of my head.

9. Judah is my lawgiver, Moab is my wash-pot : over Edom will I cast out my shoe; upon Philistia will I triumph ...

12. O help us against the enemy : for vain is the help of man.

IN DEEP TROUBLE (5)

But let all those that seek thee be joyful and glad in thee : and let all such as delight in thy salvation say alway, The Lord be praised. Psalm 70. 4

Psalm 141. *Domine, clamavi*

LORD, I call upon thee, haste thee unto me : and consider my voice when I cry unto thee.

2. Let my prayer be set forth in thy sight as the incense : and let the lifting up of my hands be an evening sacrifice.

3. Set a watch, O Lord, before my mouth : and keep the door of my lips.

4. O let not mine heart be inclined to any evil thing : let me not be occupied in ungodly works with the men that work wickedness, lest I eat of such things as please them.

5. Let the righteous rather smite me friendly : and reprove me.

6. But let not their precious balms break my head : yea, I will pray yet against their wickedness.

7. Let their judges be overthrown in stony places : that they may hear my words, for they are sweet.

8. Our bones lie scattered before the pit : like as when one breaketh and heweth wood upon the earth.

9. But mine eyes look unto thee, O Lord God : in thee is my trust, O cast not out my soul.

10. Keep me from the snare that they have laid for me : and from the traps of the wicked doers.

EXPERIENCING GOD

O taste, and see, how gracious the Lord is. Psalm 34. 8

From 'The Litany'

BY the mystery of thy holy Incarnation; by thy holy Nativity and Circumcision; by thy Baptism, Fasting, and Temptation,
   Good Lord, deliver us.

By thine Agony and Bloody Sweat; by thy Cross and Passion; by thy precious Death and Burial; by thy glorious Resurrection and Ascension; and by the coming of the Holy Ghost,
   Good Lord, deliver us.

A Prayer of Saint Chrysostom
From 'Morning Prayer'

ALMIGHTY God, who hast given us grace at this time with one accord to make our common supplications unto thee; and dost promise, that when two or three are gathered together in thy Name thou wilt grant their requests: Fulfil now, O Lord, the desires and petitions of thy servants, as may be most expedient for them; granting us in this world knowledge of thy truth, and in the world to come life everlasting. Amen.

Meditation
O fear the Lord, ye that are his saints : for they that fear him lack nothing.
Psalm 34. 9

PSALMS OF PRAISE AND
THANKSGIVING (25)
God's deeds are very wonderful

He hath shewed his people the power of his works : that he may give them the heritage of the heathen. Psalm 111. 6

Psalm 111. *Confitebor tibi*

I WILL give thanks unto the Lord with my whole heart : secretly among the faithful, and in the congregation.

2. The works of the Lord are great : sought out of all them that have pleasure therein.

3. His work is worthy to be praised and had in honour : and his righteousness endureth for ever.

4. The merciful and gracious Lord hath so done his marvellous works : that they ought to be had in remembrance.

5. He hath given meat unto them that fear him : he shall ever be mindful of his covenant.

6. He hath shewed his people the power of his works : that he may give them the heritage of the heathen.

7. The works of his hands are verity and judgement : all his commandments are true.

8. They stand fast for ever and ever : and are done in truth and equity.

9. He sent redemption unto his people : he hath commanded his covenant for ever; holy and reverend is his Name.

10. The fear of the Lord is the beginning of wisdom : a good understanding have all they that do thereafter; the praise of it endureth for ever.

NOURISH US WITH
ALL GOODNESS

*But now being made free from sin, and become servants to God, ye have your fruit
unto holiness, and the end everlasting life.* Romans 6. 22

The Collect
From 'The Seventh Sunday After Trinity'

LORD of all power and might, who art the author and giver of all good
things: Graft in our hearts the love of thy name, increase in us true religion, nourish us with all goodness, and of thy great mercy keep us in the
same; through Jesus Christ our Lord. Amen.

The Epistle. *Romans 6. 19*
From 'The Seventh Sunday After Trinity'

I SPEAK after the manner of men, because of the infirmity of your flesh:
for as ye have yielded your members servants to uncleanness, and to
iniquity unto iniquity; even so now yield your members servants to righteousness, unto holiness. For when ye were the servants of sin, ye were free
from righteousness. What fruit had ye then in those things whereof ye are
now ashamed? for the end of those things is death. But now being made
free from sin, and become servants to God, ye have your fruit unto holiness, and the end everlasting life. For the wages of sin is death: but the gift
of God is eternal life, through Jesus Christ our Lord.

THE FEEDING OF THE
FOUR THOUSAND

Yea, the Lord shall shew loving-kindness : and our land shall give her increase.

Psalm 85. 12

The Gospel. *St. Mark 8. 1*
From 'The Seventh Sunday After Trinity'

IN those days the multitude being very great, and having nothing to eat, Jesus called his disciples unto him, and saith unto them, I have compassion on the multitude, because they have now been with me three days, and have nothing to eat: And if I send them away fasting to their own houses, they will faint by the way; for divers of them came from far. And his disciples answered him, From whence can a man satisfy these men with bread here in the wilderness? And he asked them, How many loaves have ye? And they said, Seven. And he commanded the people to sit down on the ground. And he took the seven loaves, and gave thanks, and brake, and gave to his disciples to set before them; and they did set them before the people. And they had a few small fishes; and he blessed, and commanded to set them also before them. So they did eat, and were filled: and they took up of the broken meat that was left seven baskets. And they that had eaten were about four thousand. And he sent them away.

Meditation
Behold, O God our defender : and look upon the face of thine anointed.

Psalm 84. 9

221

THE SICK

Peace be to this house, and to all that dwell in it.

From 'The Visitation of the Sick'

From 'The Visitation of the Sick'
Minister.

REMEMBER not, Lord, our iniquities, nor the iniquities of our fore-fathers: Spare us, good Lord, spare thy people, whom thou hast redeemed with thy most precious blood, and be not angry with us for ever.

Answer. Spare us, good Lord.

Then the Minister shall say,
Minister. Let us pray.
Lord, have mercy upon us.
Answer. Christ, have mercy upon us.
Minister: Lord, have mercy upon us.
O Lord, save thy servant ;
Answer. Which putteth *his* trust in thee.
Minister. Send *him* help from thy holy place;
Answer. And evermore mightily defend *him.*
Minister. Let the enemy have no advantage of *him*;
Answer. Nor the wicked approach to hurt *him.*
Minister. Be unto *him*, O Lord, a strong tower,
Answer. From the face of *his* enemy.

THE DYING

In all time of our tribulation; in all time of our wealth; in the hour of death, and in the day of judgement, Good Lord, deliver us. From 'The Litany'

From 'The Visitation of the Sick'

THE Almighty Lord, who is a most strong tower to all them that put their trust in him, to whom all things in heaven, in earth, and under the earth, do bow and obey, be now and evermore thy defence; and make thee know and feel, that there is none other Name under heaven given to man, in whom, and through whom, thou mayest receive health and salvation, but only the Name of our Lord Jesus Christ. Amen.

O ALMIGHTY God, with whom do live the spirits of just men made perfect, after they are delivered from their earthly prisons: We humbly commend the soul of this thy servant, our dear *brother*, into thy hands, as into the hands of a faithful Creator, and most merciful Saviour; most humbly beseeching thee that it may be precious in thy sight ... And teach us who survive, in this and other like daily spectacles of mortality, to see how frail and uncertain our own condition is; and so to number our days, that we may seriously apply our hearts to that holy and heavenly wisdom, whilst we live here, which may in the end bring us to life everlasting, through the merits of Jesus Christ, thine only Son our Lord. Amen.

PSALMS OF PRAISE AND THANKSGIVING (26)
Who is like the Lord our God?

Who is like unto the Lord our God, that hath his dwelling so high : and yet humbleth himself to behold the things that are in heaven and earth? Psalm 113. 5

Psalm 113. *Laudate, pueri*

PRAISE the Lord, ye servants : O praise the Name of the Lord.
2. Blessed be the Name of the Lord : from this time forth for evermore.
3. The Lord's Name is praised : from the rising up of the sun unto the going down of the same.
4. The Lord is high above all heathen : and his glory above the heavens.
5. Who is like unto the Lord our God, that hath his dwelling so high : and yet humbleth himself to behold the things that are in heaven and earth?
6. He taketh up the simple out of the dust : and lifteth the poor out of the mire;
7. That he may set him with the princes : even with the princes of his people.
8. He maketh the barren woman to keep house : and to be a joyful mother of children.

THE MESSIAH IN THE PSALMS (11)

He will be betrayed by a friend

Yea, even mine own familiar friend, whom I trusted : who did also eat of my bread, hath laid great wait for me. Psalm 41. 9

Psalm 41. *Beatus qui intelligit*

BLESSED is he that considereth the poor and needy : the Lord shall deliver him in the time of trouble.

2. The Lord preserve him, and keep him alive, that he may be blessed upon earth : and deliver not thou him into the will of his enemies.

3. The Lord comfort him, when he lieth sick upon his bed : make thou all his bed in his sickness.

4. I said, Lord, be merciful unto me : heal my soul, for I have sinned against thee.

5. Mine enemies speak evil of me : When shall he die, and his name perish?

6. And if he come to see me, he speaketh vanity : and his heart conceiveth falsehood within himself, and when he cometh forth he telleth it.

7. All mine enemies whisper together against me : even against me do they imagine this evil.

8. Let the sentence of guiltiness proceed against him : and now that he lieth, let him rise up no more.

9. Yea, even mine own familiar friend, whom I trusted : who did also eat of my bread, hath laid great wait for me.

13 August

GOD'S NEVER-FAILING PROVIDENCE

For ye have not received the spirit of bondage again to fear; but ye have received the spirit of adoption, whereby we cry, Abba, Father. Romans 8. 15

The Collect
From 'The Eighth Sunday After Trinity'

O GOD, whose never-failing providence ordereth all things both in heaven and earth: We humbly beseech thee to put away from us all hurtful things, and to give us those things which be profitable for us; through Jesus Christ our Lord. Amen.

The Epistle. *Romans 8. 12*
From 'The Eighth Sunday After Trinity'

BRETHREN, we are debtors, not to the flesh, to live after the flesh: for if ye live after the flesh, ye shall die; but if ye through the Spirit do mortify the deeds of the body, ye shall live. For as many as are led by the Spirit of God, they are the sons of God. For ye have not received the spirit of bondage again to fear; but ye have received the spirit of adoption, whereby we cry, Abba, Father. The Spirit itself beareth witness with our spirit, that we are the children of God: and if children, then heirs; heirs of God, and joint-heirs with Christ: if so be that we suffer with him, that we may be also glorified together.

GOOD FRUIT AND BAD FRUIT

They also shall bring forth more fruit in their age : and shall be fat and well-liking.
Psalm 92. 13

The Gospel. *St. Matthew 7. 15*
From 'The Eighth Sunday After Trinity'

BEWARE of false prophets, which come to you in sheep's clothing, but inwardly they are ravening wolves. Ye shall know them by their fruits. Do men gather grapes of thorns, or figs of thistles? Even so every good tree bringeth forth good fruit; but a corrupt tree bringeth forth evil fruit. A good tree cannot bring forth evil fruit, neither can a corrupt tree bring forth good fruit. Every tree that bringeth not forth good fruit is hewn down, and cast into the fire. Wherefore by their fruits ye shall know them. Not every one that saith unto me, Lord, Lord, shall enter into the kingdom of heaven; but he that doeth the will of my Father which is in heaven.

From the 'Articles of Religion'
XII. Of Good Works

ALBEIT that Good Works, which are the fruits of Faith, and follow after Justification, cannot put away our sins, and endure the severity of God's Judgement; yet are they pleasing and acceptable to God in Christ, and do spring out necessarily of a true and lively Faith; insomuch that by them a lively Faith may be as evidently known as a tree discerned by the fruit.

GOD RULES OVER THE CHURCH AND THE WORLD

All the ends of the world shall remember themselves, and be turned unto the Lord : and all the kindreds of the nations shall worship before him. Psalm 22. 27

A Collect
From 'The Accession Service'

O GOD, who providest for thy people by thy power, and rulest over them in love : Vouchsafe so to bless thy Servant our Queen, that under her this nation may be wisely governed, and thy Church may serve thee in all godly quietness; and grant that she being devoted to thee with her whole heart, and persevering in good works unto the end, may, by thy guidance, come to thine everlasting kingdom; through Jesus Christ thy Son our Lord, who liveth and reigneth with thee and the Holy Ghost, ever one God, world without end. Amen.

From 'The Litany'

WE sinners do beseech thee to hear us, O Lord God: and that it may please thee to rule and govern thy holy Church universal in the right way,

We beseech thee to hear us, good Lord.

That it may please thee to keep and strengthen in the true worshipping of thee, in righteousness and holiness of life, thy Servant *ELIZABETH*, our most gracious Queen and Governor,

We beseech thee to hear us, good Lord.

PRAYING FOR UNITY

Endeavouring to keep the unity of the Spirit in the bond of peace. Ephesians 4. 3

A Prayer for Unity
From 'The Accession Service'

O GOD the Father of our Lord Jesus Christ, our only Saviour, the Prince of Peace : Give us grace seriously to lay to heart the great dangers we are in by our unhappy divisions. Take away all hatred and prejudice, and whatsoever else may hinder us from godly union and concord : that, as there is but one Body, and one Spirit, and one hope of our calling, one Lord, one faith, one baptism, one God and Father of us all; so we may henceforth be all of one heart, and of one soul, united in one holy bond of truth and peace, of faith and charity, and may with one mind and one mouth glorify thee; through Jesus Christ our Lord. Amen.

From 'Holy Communion'

A LMIGHTY and everliving God, who by thy holy Apostle hast taught us to make prayers and supplications, and to give thanks, for all men: We humbly beseech thee most mercifully to receive these our prayers, which we offer unto thy Divine Majesty; beseeching thee to inspire continually the universal Church with the spirit of truth, unity, and concord: And grant, that all they that do confess thy holy Name may agree in the truth of thy holy Word, and live in unity, and godly love.

PSALMS OF PRAISE AND THANKSGIVING (27)

When the sea turned back

The sea saw that, and fled : Jordan was driven back. Psalm 114. 3

Psalm 77. *11 Voce mea ad Dominum*

I WILL remember the works of the Lord : and call to mind thy wonders of old time.

12. I will think also of all thy works : and my talking shall be of thy doings.

13. Thy way, O God, is holy : who is so great a God as our God?

14. Thou art the God that doeth wonders : and hast declared thy power among the people.

15. Thou hast mightily delivered thy people : even the sons of Jacob and Joseph.

16. The waters saw thee, O God, the waters saw thee, and were afraid : the depths also were troubled.

17. The clouds poured out water, the air thundered : and thine arrows went abroad.

18. The voice of thy thunder was heard round about : the lightnings shone upon the ground; the earth was moved, and shook withal.

19. Thy way is in the sea, and thy paths in the great waters : and thy foot-steps are not known.

20. Thou leddest thy people like sheep : by the hand of Moses and Aaron.

PRAYING FOR A SICK CHILD

O Lord, look down from heaven, behold, visit, and relieve this thy servant.
From 'The Visitation of the Sick'

From 'The Visitation of the Sick'

O ALMIGHTY God, and merciful Father, to whom alone belong the issues of life and death: Look down from heaven, we humbly beseech thee, with the eyes of mercy upon this child now lying upon the bed of sickness. Visit *him*, O Lord, with thy salvation; deliver *him* in thy good appointed time from *his* bodily pain, and save *his* soul for thy mercies' sake: hat, if it shall be thy pleasure to prolong *his* days here on earth, *he* may live to thee, and be an instrument of thy glory, by serving thee faithfully, and doing good in *his* generation; or else receive *him* into those heavenly habitations, where the souls of them that sleep in the Lord Jesus enjoy perpetual rest and felicity. Grant this, O Lord, for thy mercies' sake, in the same thy Son our Lord Jesus Christ, who liveth and reigneth with thee and the Holy Ghost, ever one God, world without end. Amen.

O UR Father which art in heaven, Hallowed be thy Name, Thy kingdom come, Thy will be done, in earth as it is in heaven. Give us this day our daily bread, And forgive us our trespasses, As we forgive them that trespass against us, And lead us not into temptation, But deliver us from evil. Amen.

PSALMS OF PRAISE AND THANKSGIVING (28)

God's actions

The Lord hath been mindful of us, and he shall bless us : even he shall bless the house of Israel, he shall bless the house of Aaron. Psalm 115. 12

Psalm 115. *Non nobis, Domine*

NOT unto us, O Lord, not unto us, but unto thy Name give the praise : for thy loving mercy and for thy truth's sake.

2. Wherefore shall the heathen say : Where is now their God?

3. As for our God, he is in heaven : he hath done whatsoever pleased him.

4. Their idols are silver and gold : even the work of men's hands.

5. They have mouths, and speak not : eyes have they, and see not.

6. They have ears, and hear not : noses have they, and smell not.

7. They have hands, and handle not; feet have they, and walk not : neither speak they through their throat.

8. They that make them are like unto them : and so are all such as put their trust in them.

9. But thou, house of Israel, trust thou in the Lord : he is their succour and defence.

10. Ye house of Aaron, put your trust in the Lord : he is their helper and defender.

11. Ye that fear the Lord, put your trust in the Lord : he is their helper and defender.

GOD IS FAITHFUL

Now these things were our examples. 1 Corinthians 10. 6

The Epistle. *1 Corinthians 10. 1*
From 'The Ninth Sunday After Trinity'

BRETHREN, I would not that ye should be ignorant, how that all our fathers were under the cloud, and all passed through the sea; and were all baptized unto Moses in the cloud, and in the sea; and did all eat the same spiritual meat, and did all drink the same spiritual drink: for they drank of that spiritual rock that followed them; and that rock was Christ. But with many of them God was not well pleased; for they were overthrown in the wilderness. Now these things were our examples, to the intent we should not lust after evil things, as they also lusted. Neither be ye idolaters, as were some of them; as it is written, The people sat down to eat and drink, and rose up to play. Neither let us commit fornication, as some of them committed, and fell in one day three and twenty thousand. Neither let us tempt Christ, as some of them also tempted, and were destroyed of serpents. Neither murmur ye, as some of them also murmured, and were destroyed of the destroyer. Now all these things happened unto them for ensamples: and they are written for our admonition, upon whom the ends of the world are come. Wherefore let him that thinketh he standeth take heed lest he fall. There hath no temptation taken you, but such as is common to man : but God is faithful, who will not suffer you to be tempted above that ye are able.

THE UNWISE CHILDREN OF LIGHT

Make to yourselves friends of the mammon of unrighteousness. St. Luke 16. 9

The Gospel. *St. Luke 16. 1*
From 'The Ninth Sunday After Trinity'

JESUS said unto his disciples, There was a certain rich man, which had a steward; and the same was accused unto him that he had wasted his goods. And he called him, and said unto him, How is it that I hear this of thee? Give an account of thy stewardship; for thou mayest be no longer steward. Then the steward said within himself, What shall I do? for my lord taketh away from me the stewardship: I cannot dig, to beg I am ashamed. I am resolved what to do, that, when I am put out of the stewardship, they may receive me into their houses. So he called every one of his lord's debtors unto him, and said unto the first, How much owest thou unto my lord? And he said, An hundred measures of oil. And he said unto him, Take thy bill, and sit down quickly, and write fifty. Then said he to another, And how much owest thou? And he said, An hundred measures of wheat. And he said unto him, Take thy bill, and write fourscore. And the lord commended the unjust steward, because he had done wisely : for the children of this world are in their generation wiser than the children of light. And I say unto you, Make to yourselves friends of the mammon of unrighteousness, that when ye fail, they may receive you into everlasting habitations.

'WE SPIRITUALLY EAT
THE FLESH OF CHRIST'

For then we spiritually eat the flesh of Christ, and drink his blood; then we dwell in Christ, and Christ in us; we are one with Christ, and Christ with us.

From 'Holy Communion'

From 'Holy Communion'

DEARLY beloved in the Lord, ye that mind to come to the holy Communion of the Body and Blood of our Saviour Christ, must consider how Saint Paul exhorteth all persons diligently to try and examine themselves, before they presume to eat of that Bread, and drink of that Cup. For as the benefit is great, if with a true penitent heart and lively faith we receive that holy Sacrament … so is the danger great, if we receive the same unworthily. For then we are guilty of the Body and Blood of Christ our Saviour; we eat and drink our own damnation, not considering the Lord's Body; we kindle God's wrath against us; we provoke him to plague us with divers diseases, and sundry kinds of death. Judge therefore yourselves, brethren, that ye be not judged of the Lord; repent you truly for your sins past; have a lively and stedfast faith in Christ our Saviour; amend your lives, and be in perfect charity with all men; so shall ye be meet partakers of those holy mysteries. And above all things ye must give most humble and hearty thanks to God, the Father, the Son, and the Holy Ghost, for the redemption of the world by the death and passion of our Saviour Christ, both God and man; who did humble himself, even to the death upon the Cross, for us miserable sinners.

PSALMS OF PRAISE AND THANKSGIVING (29)

Everyone is to praise God

O praise the Lord, all ye heathen : praise him, all ye nations. Psalm 117. 1

Psalm 116. *Dilexi, quoniam*

I AM well pleased : that the Lord hath heard the voice of my prayer;
2. That he hath inclined his ear unto me : therefore will I call upon him as long as I live.
3. The snares of death compassed me round about : and the pains of hell gat hold upon me.
4. I shall find trouble and heaviness, and I will call upon the Name of the Lord : O Lord, I beseech thee, deliver my soul.
5. Gracious is the Lord, and righteous : yea, our God is merciful.
6. The Lord preserveth the simple : I was in misery, and he helped me.
7. Turn again then unto thy rest, O my soul : for the Lord hath rewarded thee.
8. And why? thou hast delivered my soul from death : mine eyes from tears, and my feet from falling.
9. I will walk before the Lord : in the land of the living ...
12. I will receive the cup of salvation : and call upon the Name of the Lord.

ONE OF THE TWELVE

By the hands of the apostles were many signs and wonders wrought among the people. Acts 5. 12

The Collect
From 'Saint Bartholomew the Apostle'

O ALMIGHTY and everlasting God, who didst give to thine Apostle Bartholomew grace truly to believe and to preach thy Word: Grant, we beseech thee, unto thy Church, to love that Word which he believed, and both to preach and receive the same; through Jesus Christ our Lord. Amen.

For the Epistle. *Acts 5. 12*
From 'Saint Bartholomew the Apostle'

B Y the hands of the Apostles were many signs and wonders wrought among the people: (and they were all with one accord in Solomon's porch: and of the rest durst no man join himself to them: but the people magnified them: and believers were the more added to the Lord, multitudes both of men and women:) insomuch that they brought forth the sick into the streets, and laid them on beds and couches, that at the least the shadow of Peter passing by might overshadow some of them. There came also a multitude out of the cities round about unto Jerusalem, bringing sick folks, and them which were vexed with unclean spirits; and they were healed every one.

PRAYING FOR RULERS

King of kings, Lord of lords, the only Ruler of princes...

From 'Morning Prayer'

A Prayer for the Queen's Majesty
From 'Morning Prayer'

O LORD, our heavenly Father, high and mighty, King of kings, Lord of lords, the only Ruler of princes, who dost from thy throne behold all the dwellers upon earth: Most heartily we beseech thee with thy favour to behold our most gracious Sovereign Lady, Queen *ELIZABETH*; and so replenish her with the grace of thy Holy Spirit, that she may alway incline to thy will, and walk in thy way ... Amen.

From 'The Accession Service'

A LMIGHTY God, who rulest over all the kingdoms of the world, and dost order them according to thy good pleasure: We yield thee un-feigned thanks, for that thou wast pleased, *as on this day*, to set thy Servant our Sovereign Lady, Queen *ELIZABETH*, upon the Throne of this Realm. Let thy wisdom be her guide, and let thine arm strengthen her; let truth and justice, holiness and righteousness, peace and charity, abound in her days; direct all her counsels and endeavours to thy glory, and the wel-fare of her subjects; give us grace to obey her cheerfully for conscience sake, and let her always possess the hearts of her people ... through Jesus Christ our Lord. Amen.

PSALMS OF PRAISE AND THANKSGIVING (30)
The holy city

For there is the seat of judgement : even the seat of the house of David. O pray for the peace of Jerusalem : they shall prosper that love thee. Psalm 122. 5–6

Psalm 122. *Laetatus sum*

I WAS glad when they said unto me : We will go into the house of the Lord.

2. Our feet shall stand in thy gates : O Jerusalem.

3. Jerusalem is built as a city : that is at unity in itself.

4. For thither the tribes go up, even the tribes of the Lord : to testify unto Israel, to give thanks unto the Name of the Lord.

5. For there is the seat of judgement : even the seat of the house of David.

6. O pray for the peace of Jerusalem : they shall prosper that love thee.

7. Peace be within thy walls : and plenteousness within thy palaces.

8. For my brethren and companions' sakes : I will wish thee prosperity.

9. Yea, because of the house of the Lord our God : I will seek to do thee good.

Meditation
The hills stand about Jerusalem : even so standeth the Lord round about his people, from this time forth for evermore. Psalm 125. 2

SPIRITUAL GIFTS

When he ascended up on high, he led captivity captive, and gave gifts unto men.
Ephesians 4. 8

The Epistle. *1 Corinthians 12. 1*
From 'The Tenth Sunday After Trinity'

CONCERNING spiritual gifts, brethren, I would not have you ignorant. Ye know that ye were Gentiles, carried away unto these dumb
idols, even as ye were led. Wherefore I give you to understand, that no
man speaking by the Spirit of God calleth Jesus accursed: and that no man
can say that Jesus is the Lord, but by the Holy Ghost. Now there are diversities of gifts, but the same Spirit. And there are differences of administra-
tions, but the same Lord. And there are diversities of operations, but it is
the same God, who worketh all in all. But the manifestation of the Spirit is
given to every man to profit withal. For to one is given by the Spirit the
word of wisdom; to another the word of knowledge by the same Spirit; to
another faith by the same Spirit; to another the gifts of healing by the same
Spirit; to another the working of miracles; to another prophecy; to another
discerning of spirits; to another divers kinds of tongues; to another the in-
terpretation of tongues. But all these worketh that one and the self-same
Spirit, dividing to every man severally as he will.

'JERUSALEM, JERUSALEM'

Comfort ye, comfort ye my people, saith your God. Speak ye comfortably to Jerusalem, and cry unto her, that her warfare is accomplished, that her iniquity is pardoned. Isaiah 40. 1–2

The Gospel. *St. Luke 19. 41*
From 'The Tenth Sunday After Trinity'

AND when he was come near, he beheld the city, and wept over it, saying, If thou hadst known, even thou, at least in this thy day, the things which belong unto thy peace! but now they are hid from thine eyes. For the days shall come upon thee, that thine enemies shall cast a trench about thee, and compass thee round, and keep thee in on every side, and shall lay thee even with the ground, and thy children within thee; and they shall not leave in thee one stone upon another; because thou knewest not the time of thy visitation. And he went into the temple, and began to cast out them that sold therein, and them that bought, saying unto them, It is written, My house is the house of prayer: but ye have made it a den of thieves. And he taught daily in the temple.

Meditation
Keep me as the apple of an eye : hide me under the shadow of thy wings.

Psalm 17. 8

PSALMS OF PRAISE AND THANKSGIVING (31)

When Christians are united

Behold, how good and joyful a thing it is : brethren, to dwell together in unity!
                                                                            Psalm 133. 1

A Collect or Prayer for All Conditions of Men
From 'Prayers and Thanksgivings'

O GOD, the Creator and Preserver of all mankind, we humbly beseech thee for all sorts and conditions of men; that thou wouldest be pleased to make thy ways known unto them, thy saving health unto all nations. More especially we pray for the good estate of the Catholick Church; that it may be so guided and governed by thy good Spirit, that all who profess and call themselves Christians may be led into the way of truth, and hold the faith in unity of spirit, in the bond of peace, and in righteousness of life. Finally we commend to thy fatherly goodness all those, who are any ways afflicted or distressed, in mind, body, or estate; that it may please thee to comfort and relieve them, according to their several necessities, giving them patience under their sufferings, and a happy issue out of all their af- flictions. And this we beg for Jesus Christ his sake. Amen.

Meditation
And other sheep I have, which are not of this fold; them also I must bring, and they shall hear my voice; and there shall be one fold, and one shepherd.
                                                                            St. John 10. 16

PSALMS OF PRAISE AND THANKSGIVING (32)

'Come, bless the Lord'

Lift up your hands in the sanctuary : and praise the Lord. Psalm 134. 3

Psalm 134. *Ecce nunc*

BEHOLD now, praise the Lord : all ye servants of the Lord;
2. Ye that by night stand in the house of the Lord : even in the courts of the house of our God.
3. Lift up your hands in the sanctuary : and praise the Lord.
4. The Lord that made heaven and earth : give thee blessing out of Sion.

Te Deum Laudamus

From 'Morning Prayer'

WE praise thee, O God : we acknowledge thee to be the Lord.
All the earth doth worship thee : the Father everlasting.
To thee all Angels cry aloud : the heavens, and all the powers therein.
To thee Cherubin and Seraphin : continually do cry,
Holy, Holy, Holy : Lord God of Sabaoth;
Heaven and earth are full of the Majesty : of thy glory.
The glorious company of the Apostles : praise thee.
The goodly fellowship of the Prophets : praise thee.
The noble army of Martyrs : praise thee.
The holy Church throughout all the world : doth acknowledge thee ...

THE COMFORTABLE WORDS

Hear what comfortable words our Saviour Christ saith unto all that truly turn to him. Come unto me all that travail and are heavy laden, and I will refresh you. (St. Matthew 11. 28.) From 'Holy Communion'

From 'Holy Communion'

SO God loved the world, that he gave his only-begotten Son, to the end that all that believe in him should not perish, but have everlasting life.

St. John 3. 16.

Hear also what Saint Paul saith.

This is a true saying, and worthy of all men to be received, that Christ Jesus came into the world to save sinners.

1 Timothy 1. 15

From 'Holy Communion'

O ALMIGHTY Lord, and everlasting God, vouchsafe, we beseech thee, to direct, sanctify, and govern, both our hearts and bodies, in the ways of thy laws, and in the works of thy commandments; that through thy most mighty protection, both here and ever, we may be preserved in body and soul; through our Lord and Saviour Jesus Christ. Amen.

~

PRAYING FOR THE CLERGY

Withal praying also for us, that God would open unto us a door of utterance, to speak the mystery of Christ, for which I am also in bonds. Colossians 4. 3

From 'The Litany'

That it may please thee to illuminate all Bishops, Priests, and Deacons, with true knowledge and understanding of thy Word; and that both by their preaching and living they may set it forth, and shew it accordingly,

We beseech thee to hear us, good Lord.

A Prayer for the Clergy and People
From 'Morning Prayer'

ALMIGHTY and everlasting God, who alone workest great marvels: Send down upon our Bishops and Curates, and all Congregations committed to their charge, the healthful Spirit of thy grace; and that they may truly please thee, pour upon them the continual dew of thy blessing. Grant this, O Lord, for the honour of our Advocate and Mediator, Jesus Christ. Amen.

Meditation
Woe is unto me, if I preach not the gospel! 1 Corinthians 9. 16

INSTRUCTION FROM
GOD'S WORD (9)

When thy word goeth forth : it giveth light and understanding unto the simple.

Psalm 119. 130

The Collect
From 'The Second Sunday in Advent'

BLESSED Lord, who hast caused all holy Scriptures to be written for our learning : Grant that we may in such wise hear them, read, mark, learn, and inwardly digest them, that by patience and comfort of thy holy Word, we may embrace and ever hold fast the blessed hope of everlasting life, which thou hast given us in our Saviour Jesus Christ. Amen.

Psalm 119. *Mirabilia*

THY testimonies are wonderful : therefore doth my soul keep them.
130. When thy word goeth forth : it giveth light and understanding unto the simple.
131. I opened my mouth, and drew in my breath : for my delight was in thy commandments.
132. O look thou upon me, and be merciful unto me : as thou usest to do unto those that love thy Name.
133. Order my steps in thy word : and so shall no wickedness have dominion over me.

HEAVENLY TREASURE

Christ died for our sins according to the scriptures. 1 Corinthians 15. 3

The Epistle. *1 Corinthians 15. 1*
From 'The Eleventh Sunday After Trinity'

BRETHREN, I declare unto you the Gospel which I preached unto you, which also ye have received, and wherein ye stand: by which also ye are saved, if ye keep in memory what I preached unto you, unless ye have believed in vain. For I delivered unto you first of all, that which I also received, how that Christ died for our sins, according to the Scriptures; and that he was buried, and that he rose again the third day, according to the Scriptures: and that he was seen of Cephas; then of the twelve: after that, he was seen of above five hundred brethren at once; of whom the greater part remain unto this present, but some are fallen asleep: after that, he was seen of James; then of all the Apostles: and last of all he was seen of me also, as of one born out of due time. For I am the least of the Apostles, that am not meet to be called an Apostle, because I persecuted the Church of God. But by the grace of God I am what I am: and his grace which was bestowed upon me was not in vain; but I laboured more abundantly than they all; yet not I, but the grace of God which was with me. Therefore whether it were I or they, so we preach, and so ye believed.

TRUE PRAYER

*For if ye forgive men their trespasses, your heavenly Father will also forgive you :
But if ye forgive not men their trespasses, neither will your Father forgive your trespasses.* St. Matthew 6. 14–15

The Gospel. *Luke 18. 9*
From 'The Eleventh Sunday After Trinity'

JESUS spake this parable unto certain which trusted in themselves that
they were righteous, and despised others: Two men went up into the
temple to pray; the one a Pharisee, and the other a publican. The Pharisee
stood and prayed thus with himself, God, I thank thee that I am not as
other men are, extortioners, unjust, adulterers, or even as this Publican. I
fast twice in the week, I give tithes of all that I possess. And the Publican,
standing afar off, would not lift up so much as his eyes unto heaven, but
smote upon his breast, saying, God be merciful to me a sinner. I tell you,
this man went down to his house justified rather than the other: for every
one that exalteth himself shall be abased; and he that humbleth himself shall
be exalted.

Meditation
The Lord is my strength : and he is the wholesome defence of his Anointed.

Psalm 28. 9

THE LITANY (1)

O holy, blessed, and glorious Trinity, three Persons and one God : have mercy upon us miserable sinners. From 'The Litany'

From 'The Litany'

O GOD the Father of heaven : have mercy upon us miserable sinners.
O God the Father of heaven : have mercy upon us miserable sinners.

O God the Son, Redeemer of the world : have mercy upon us miserable sinners.

O God the Son, Redeemer of the world : have mercy upon us miserable sinners.

O God the Holy Ghost, proceeding from the Father and the Son : have mercy upon us miserable sinners.

O God the Holy Ghost, proceeding from the Father and the Son : have mercy upon us miserable sinners.

O holy, blessed, and glorious Trinity, three Persons and one God : have mercy upon us miserable sinners.

O holy, blessed, and glorious Trinity, three Persons and one God : have mercy upon us miserable sinners.

Remember not, Lord, our offences, nor the offences of our forefathers; neither take thou vengeance of our sins: spare us, good Lord, spare thy people, whom thou hast redeemed with thy most precious blood, and be not angry with us for ever.

THE LITANY (2)

In all time of our tribulation; in all time of our wealth; in the hour of death, and in the day of judgement, Good Lord, deliver us. From 'The Litany'

From 'The Litany'

WE sinners do beseech thee to hear us, O Lord God: and that it may please thee to rule and govern thy holy Church universal in the right way,

We beseech thee to hear us, good Lord.

That it may please thee to keep and strengthen in the true worshipping of thee, in righteousness and holiness of life, thy Servant *ELIZABETH*, our most gracious Queen and Governor;

We beseech thee to hear us, good Lord.

That it may please thee to rule her heart in thy faith, fear, and love, and that she may evermore have affiance in thee, and ever seek thy honour and glory,

We beseech thee to hear us, good Lord.

That it may please thee to be her defender and keeper, giving her the victory over all her enemies,

We beseech thee to hear us, good Lord.

That it may please thee to bless and preserve *Elizabeth* the Queen Mother, *Philip* Duke of *Edinburgh*, *Charles* Prince of *Wales*, and all the Royal Family,

We beseech thee to hear us, good Lord.

THE LITANY (3)

That it may please thee to give us an heart to love and dread thee, and diligently to live after thy commandments, we beseech thee to hear us, good Lord.

From 'The Litany'

From 'The Litany'

THAT it may please thee to give to all thy people increase of grace, to hear meekly thy Word, and to receive it with pure affection, and to bring forth the fruits of the Spirit,

We beseech thee to hear us, good Lord.

That it may please thee to bring into the way of truth all such as have erred, and are deceived,

We beseech thee to hear us, good Lord.

That it may please thee to strengthen such as do stand; and to comfort and help the weak-hearted; and to raise up them that fall; and finally to beat down Satan under our feet,

We beseech thee to hear us, good Lord.

That it may please thee to succour, help, and comfort, all that are in danger, necessity, and tribulation,

We beseech thee to hear us, good Lord.

That it may please thee to preserve all that travel by land or by water, all women labouring of child, all sick persons, and young children; and to shew thy pity upon all prisoners and captives,

We beseech thee to hear us, good Lord.

THE LITANY (4)

That it may please thee to give us true repentance; to forgive us all our sins, negligences, and ignorances ; and to endue us with the grace of thy Holy Spirit, to amend our lives according to thy holy Word; We beseech thee to hear us, good Lord.

From 'The Litany'

From 'The Litany'
SON of God : we beseech thee to hear us.
Son of God : we beseech thee to hear us.
  O Lamb of God : that takest away the sins of the world;
  Grant us thy peace.
  O Lamb of God : that takest away the sins of the world;
  Have mercy upon us.
  O Christ, hear us.
  O Christ, hear us.
Lord, have mercy upon us.
Lord, have mercy upon us.
Christ, have mercy upon us.
Christ, have mercy upon us.
Lord, have mercy upon us.
Lord, have mercy upon us.

THE LITANY (5)

O God, we have heard with our ears, and our fathers have declared unto us, the noble works that thou didst in their days, and in the old time before them.

From 'The Litany'

From 'The Litany'

O LORD, arise, help us, and deliver us for thine honour.
Glory be to the Father, and to the Son : and to the Holy Ghost;
As it was in the beginning, is now, and ever shall be : world without end. Amen.

From our enemies defend us, O Christ.
Graciously look upon our afflictions.
Pitifully behold the sorrows of our hearts.
Mercifully forgive the sins of thy people.
Favourably with mercy hear our prayers.
O Son of David, have mercy upon us.
Both now and ever vouchsafe to hear us, O Christ.
Graciously hear us, O Christ; graciously hear us, O Lord Christ.
O Lord, let thy mercy be shewed upon us;
As we do put our trust in thee.

MINISTERS OF THE
NEW COVENANT

But the merciful goodness of the Lord endureth for ever and ever upon them that fear him : and his righteousness upon children's children; Even upon such as keep his covenant. Psalm 103. 17–18

The Collect
From 'The Twelfth Sunday After Trinity'

ALMIGHTY and everlasting God, who art always more ready to hear than we to pray, and art wont to give more than either we desire or deserve: Pour down upon us the abundance of thy mercy; forgiving us those things whereof our conscience is afraid, and giving us those good things which we are not worthy to ask, but through the merits and mediation of Jesus Christ, thy Son, our Lord. Amen.

The Epistle. *2 Corinthians 3. 4*
From 'The Twelfth Sunday After Trinity'

SUCH trust have we through Christ to Godward: not that we are sufficient of ourselves to think any thing as of ourselves; but our sufficiency is of God; who also hath made us able ministers of the new testament; not of the letter, but of the spirit: for the letter killeth, but the spirit giveth life. But if the ministration of death written and engraven in stones, was glorious, so that the children of Israel could not stedfastly behold the face of Moses for the glory of his countenance, which glory was to be done away; how shall not the ministration of the spirit be rather glorious?

EPHPHATHA, 'BE OPENED'

Praise the Lord, O my soul : and forget not all his benefits; who forgiveth all thy sin : and healeth all thine infirmities. Psalm 103. 2–3

The Gospel. *St. Mark 7. 31*
From 'The Twelfth Sunday After Trinity'

JESUS, departing from the coasts of Tyre and Sidon, came unto the sea of Galilee, through the midst of the coasts of Decapolis. And they bring unto him one that was deaf, and had an impediment in his speech; and they beseech him to put his hand upon him. And he took him aside from the multitude, and put his fingers into his ears, and he spit, and touched his tongue; and looking up to heaven, he sighed, and saith unto him, *Ephphatha*, that is, Be opened. And straightway his ears were opened, and the string of his tongue was loosed, and he spake plain. And he charged them that they should tell no man: but the more he charged them, so much the more a great deal they published it; and were beyond measure astonished, saying, He hath done all things well; he maketh both the deaf to hear, and the dumb to speak.

Meditation
God anointed Jesus of Nazareth with the Holy Ghost, and with power; who went about doing good, and healing all that were oppressed of the devil: for God was with him. Acts 10. 38

GOD'S LAW

Thou shalt have none other gods but me. Exodus 20. 3

The Ten Commandments

GOD spake these words, and said; I am the Lord thy God: Thou shalt have none other gods but me.

Minister. Thou shalt not make to thyself any graven image, nor the likeness of any thing that is in heaven above, or in the earth beneath, or in the water under the earth. Thou shalt not bow down to them, nor worship them. For I the Lord thy God am a jealous God, and visit the sins of the fathers upon the children unto the third and fourth generation of them that hate me, and shew mercy unto thousands in them that love me and keep my commandments.

Thou shalt not take the Name of the Lord thy God in vain: for the Lord will not hold him guiltless, that taketh his Name in vain.

Remember that thou keep holy the Sabbath-day. Six days shalt thou labour, and do all that thou hast to do; but the seventh day is the Sabbath of the Lord thy God. In it thou shalt do no manner of work, thou, and thy son, and thy daughter, thy man-servant, and thy maid-servant, thy cattle, and the stranger that is within thy gates. For in six days the Lord made heaven and earth, the sea, and all that in them is, and rested the seventh day: wherefore the Lord blessed the seventh day, and hallowed it.

People. Lord, have mercy upon us, and incline our hearts to keep this law.

THOU SHALT NOT ...

Thou shalt not bear false witness against thy neighbour. Exodus 20. 16

The Ten Commandments

HONOUR thy father and thy mother; that thy days may be long in the land which the Lord thy God giveth thee.

People. Lord, have mercy upon us, and incline our hearts to keep this law.

Minister. Thou shalt do no murder.

People. Lord, have mercy upon us, and incline our hearts to keep this law.

Minister. Thou shalt not commit adultery.

People. Lord, have mercy upon us, and incline our hearts to keep this law.

Minister. Thou shalt not steal.

People. Lord, have mercy upon us, and incline our hearts to keep this law.

Minister. Thou shalt not bear false witness against thy neighbour.

People. Lord, have mercy upon us, and incline our hearts to keep this law.

Minister. Thou shalt not covet thy neighbour's house, thou shalt not covet thy neighbour's wife, nor his servant, nor his maid, nor his ox, nor his ass, nor any thing that is his.

THE GOD OF ALL COMFORT

Blessed be God, even the Father of our Lord Jesus Christ, the Father of mercies, and God of all comfort. 2 Corinthians 1. 3

From 'The Visitation of the Sick'

O BLESSED Lord, the Father of mercies, and the God of all comforts: We beseech thee, look down in pity and compassion upon this thy afflicted servant. Thou writest bitter things against *him*, and makest *him* to possess *his* former iniquities; thy wrath lieth hard upon *him*, and *his* soul is full of trouble: but, O merciful God, who hast written thy holy Word for our learning, that we, through patience and comfort of thy holy Scriptures, might have hope; give *him* a right understanding of *himself*, and of thy threats and promises; that *he* may neither cast away *his* confidence in thee, nor place it any where but in thee. Give *him* strength against all *his* temptations, and heal all *his* distempers. Break not the bruised reed, nor quench the smoking flax. Shut not up thy tender mercies in displeasure; but make *him* to hear of joy and gladness, that the bones which thou hast broken may rejoice. Deliver *him* from fear of the enemy, and lift up the light of thy countenance upon *him*, and give *him* peace, through the merits and mediation of Jesus Christ our Lord. Amen.

Meditation
O give me the comfort of thy help again. Psalm 51. 12

INESTIMABLE LOVE

They shall give thanks unto thy Name : which is great, wonderful, and holy.
Psalm 99. 3

A General Thanksgiving
From 'Thanksgivings'

ALMIGHTY God, Father of all mercies, we thine unworthy servants do give thee most humble and hearty thanks for all thy goodness and loving-kindness to us and to all men. We bless thee for our creation, preservation, and all the blessings of this life; but above all for thine inestimable love in the redemption of the world by our Lord Jesus Christ, for the means of grace, and for the hope of glory. And we beseech thee, give us that due sense of all thy mercies, that our hearts may be unfeignedly thankful, and that we shew forth thy praise, not only with our lips, but in our lives; by giving up ourselves to thy service, and by walking before thee in holiness and righteousness all our days; through Jesus Christ our Lord, to whom with thee and the Holy Ghost be all honour and glory, world without end. Amen.

Meditation
O magnify the Lord our God, and worship him upon his holy hill : for the Lord our God is holy. Psalm 99. 9

PSALMS OF PRAISE AND THANKSGIVING (33)

Our Lord is above all gods

For the Lord will ... be gracious unto his servants. Psalm 135. 14

Psalm 135. *Laudate Nomen*

O PRAISE the Lord, laud ye the Name of the Lord : praise it, O ye servants of the Lord;

2. Ye that stand in the house of the Lord : in the courts of the house of our God.

3. O praise the Lord, for the Lord is gracious : O sing praises unto his Name, for it is lovely.

4. For why? the Lord hath chosen Jacob unto himself : and Israel for his own possession.

5. For I know that the Lord is great : and that our Lord is above all gods.

6. Whatsoever the Lord pleased, that did he in heaven and in earth : and in the sea, and in all deep places.

7. He bringeth forth the clouds from the ends of the world : and sendeth forth lightnings with the rain, bringing the winds out of his treasuries.

8. He smote the first-born of Egypt : both of man and beast.

9. He hath sent tokens and wonders into the midst of thee, O thou land of Egypt : upon Pharaoh, and all his servants ...

12. And gave their land to be an heritage : even an heritage unto Israel his people.

13. Thy Name, O Lord, endureth for ever : so doth thy memorial, O Lord, from one generation to another.

THE LAW AND THE PROMISE

But the Scripture hath concluded all under sin, that the promise by faith of Jesus Christ might be given to them that believe. Galatians 3. 22

The Epistle. *Galatians 3. 16*
From 'The Thirteenth Sunday After Trinity'

TO Abraham and his seed were the promises made. He saith not, And to seeds, as of many; but as of one, And to thy seed, which is Christ. And this I say, that the covenant that was confirmed before of God in Christ, the law, which was four hundred and thirty years after, cannot disannul, that it should make the promise of none effect. For if the inheritance be of the law, it is no more of promise; but God gave it to Abraham by promise. Wherefore then serveth the law? It was added because of transgressions, till the seed should come, to whom the promise was made; and it was ordained by angels in the hand of a mediator. Now a mediator is not a mediator of one; but God is one. Is the law then against the promises of God? God forbid: for if there had been a law given which could have given life, verily righteousness should have been by the law. But the Scripture hath concluded all under sin, that the promise by faith of Jesus Christ might be given to them that believe.

Meditation
Let the poor and needy give praise unto thy Name. Psalm 74. 22

'A CERTAIN SAMARITAN'

Whatsoever ye would that men should do unto you, even so do unto them; for this is the Law and the Prophets. St. Matthew 7. 12

The Gospel. *St. Luke 10. 25*
From 'The Thirteenth Sunday After Trinity'

AND behold, a certain Lawyer stood up, and tempted him, saying, Master, what shall I do to inherit eternal life? He said unto him, What is written in the law? how readest thou? And he answering said, Thou shalt love the Lord thy God with all thy heart, and with all thy soul, and with all thy strength, and with all thy mind; and thy neighbour as thyself. And he said unto him, Thou hast answered right; this do, and thou shalt live. But he … said unto Jesus, And who is my neighbour? And Jesus answering said, A certain man went down from Jerusalem to Jericho, and fell among thieves, which stripped him of his raiment, and wounded him, and departed, leaving him half dead. And by chance there came down a certain Priest that way, and, when he saw him, he passed by on the other side. And likewise a Levite, when he was at the place, came and looked on him, and passed by on the other side. But a certain Samaritan, as he journeyed, came where he was; and, when he saw him, he had compassion on him, and went to him, and bound up his wounds … and brought him to an inn, and took care of him. Which now of these three, thinkest thou, was neighbour unto him that fell among the thieves? And he said, He that shewed mercy on him. Then said Jesus unto him, Go, and do thou likewise.

LIFE AFTER DEATH

I am the resurrection and the life, saith the Lord. St. John 11. 25

Psalm 39. *Dixi, Custodiam*
I SAID, I will take heed to my ways : that I offend not in my tongue.
2. I will keep my mouth as it were with a bridle : while the ungodly is in my sight.
3. I held my tongue, and spake nothing : I kept silence, yea, even from good words; but it was pain and grief to me.
4. My heart was hot within me, and while I was thus musing the fire kindled : and at the last I spake with my tongue;
5. Lord, let me know mine end, and the number of my days : that I may be certified how long I have to live.
6. Behold, thou hast made my days as it were a span long : and mine age is even as nothing in respect of thee; and verily every man living is altogether vanity.
7. For man walketh in a vain shadow, and disquieteth himself in vain : he heapeth up riches, and cannot tell who shall gather them.
8. And now, Lord, what is my hope : truly my hope is even in thee.

Meditation
I know that my Redeemer liveth. Job 19. 25

PSALMS OF PRAISE AND THANKSGIVING (34)
God's love endures for ever

Who led his people through the wilderness : for his mercy endureth for ever.

Psalm 136. 16

Psalm 136. *Confitemini*

O GIVE thanks unto the Lord, for he is gracious : and his mercy endureth for ever.

2. O give thanks unto the God of all gods : for his mercy endureth for ever.

3. O thank the Lord of all lords : for his mercy endureth for ever.

4. Who only doeth great wonders : for his mercy endureth for ever.

5. Who by his excellent wisdom made the heavens : for his mercy endureth for ever.

6. Who laid out the earth above the waters : for his mercy endureth for ever.

7. Who hath made great lights : for his mercy endureth for ever;

8. The sun to rule the day : for his mercy endureth for ever;

9. The moon and the stars to govern the night : for his mercy endureth for ever.

10. Who smote Egypt with their first-born : for his mercy endureth for ever;

11. And brought out Israel from among them : for his mercy endureth for ever;

12. With a mighty hand, and stretched out arm : for his mercy endureth for ever.

MATTHEW THE TAX-COLLECTOR

He [Matthew] arose, and followed him [Jesus]. St. Matthew 9. 9

The Collect
From 'Saint Matthew the Apostle'

O ALMIGHTY God, who by thy blessed Son didst call Matthew from the receipt of custom to be an Apostle and Evangelist: Grant us grace to forsake all covetous desires and inordinate love of riches, and to follow the same thy Son Jesus Christ, who liveth and reigneth with thee and the Holy Ghost, one God, world without end. Amen.

The Epistle. *2 Corinthians 4. 1*
From 'Saint Matthew the Apostle'

THEREFORE seeing we have this ministry, as we have received mercy, we faint not; but have renounced the hidden things of dishonesty, not walking in craftiness, nor handling the word of God deceitfully, but by manifestation of the truth commending ourselves to every man's conscience in the sight of God. But if our Gospel be hid, it is hid to them that are lost: in whom the God of this world hath blinded the minds of them which believe not, lest the light of the glorious Gospel of Christ, who is the image of God, should shine unto them ... For God, who commanded the light to shine out of darkness, hath shined in our hearts, to give the light of the knowledge of the glory of God, in the face of Jesus Christ.

PSALMS OF PRAISE AND
THANKSGIVING (35)
God is faithful to all his promises

The Lord is gracious and merciful : long-suffering, and of great goodness.

Psalm 145. 8

Psalm 145. *Exaltabo te, Deus*

I WILL magnify thee, O God, my King : and I will praise thy Name for ever and ever.

2. Every day will I give thanks unto thee : and praise thy Name for ever and ever.

3. Great is the Lord, and marvellous worthy to be praised : there is no end of his greatness.

4. One generation shall praise thy works unto another : and declare thy power.

5. As for me, I will be talking of thy worship : thy glory, thy praise, and wondrous works;

6. So that men shall speak of thy marvellous acts : and I will also tell of thy greatness.

7. The memorial of thine abundant kindness shall be shewed : and men shall sing of thy righteousness.

8. The Lord is gracious and merciful : long-suffering, and of great goodness.

9. The Lord is loving unto every man : and his mercy is over all his works.

THE MESSIAH IN THE PSALMS (12)

'His throne will be for ever'

Thy seat, O God, endureth for ever : the sceptre of thy kingdom is a right sceptre.

Psalm 45. 7

Psalm 45. *Eructavit cor meum*

MY heart is inditing of a good matter : I speak of the things which I have made unto the King.

2. My tongue is the pen : of a ready writer.

3. Thou art fairer than the children of men : full of grace are thy lips, because God hath blessed thee for ever.

4. Gird thee with thy sword upon thy thigh, O thou most Mighty : according to thy worship and renown.

5. Good luck have thou with thine honour : ride on, because of the word of truth, of meekness, and righteousness; and thy right hand shall teach thee terrible things.

6. Thy arrows are very sharp, and the people shall be subdued unto thee : even in the midst among the King's enemies.

7. Thy seat, O God, endureth for ever : the sceptre of thy kingdom is a right sceptre.

8. Thou hast loved righteousness, and hated iniquity : wherefore God, even thy God, hath anointed thee with the oil of gladness above thy fellows.

THE FRUIT OF THE SPIRIT

But the fruit of the Spirit is love, joy, peace, long-suffering, gentleness, goodness, faith, meekness, temperance. Galatians 5. 22–23

The Collect
From 'The Fourteenth Sunday After Trinity'

ALMIGHTY and everlasting God, give unto us the increase of faith, hope, and charity; and, that we may obtain that which thou dost promise, make us to love that which thou dost command; through Jesus Christ our Lord. Amen.

The Epistle. *Galatians 5. 16*
From 'The Fourteenth Sunday After Trinity'

I SAY then, Walk in the Spirit, and ye shall not fulfil the lust of the flesh. For the flesh lusteth against the Spirit, and the Spirit against the flesh; and these are contrary the one to the other; so that ye cannot do the things that ye would. But if ye be led by the Spirit, ye are not under the law. Now the works of the flesh are manifest, which are these; adultery, fornication, uncleanness, lasciviousness, idolatry, witchcraft, hatred, variance, emulations, wrath, strife, seditions, heresies, envyings, murders, drunkenness, revellings, and such like: of the which I tell you before, as I have also told you in time past, that they who do such things shall not inherit the kingdom of God. But the fruit of the Spirit is love, joy, peace, long-suffering, gentleness, goodness, faith, meekness, temperance: against such there is no law.

THE GRATEFUL SAMARITAN

O sing unto the Lord with thanksgiving : sing praises upon the harp unto our God.

Psalm 147. 7

The Gospel. *St. Luke 17. 11*
From 'The Fourteenth Sunday After Trinity'

AND it came to pass, as Jesus went to Jerusalem, that he passed through the midst of Samaria and Galilee. And as he entered into a certain village, there met him ten men that were lepers, which stood afar off: and they lifted up their voices, and said, Jesus, Master, have mercy on us. And when he saw them, he said unto them, Go, shew yourselves unto the priests. And it came to pass, that, as they went, they were cleansed. And one of them, when he saw that he was healed, turned back, and with a loud voice glorified God, and fell down on his face at his feet, giving him thanks; and he was a Samaritan. And Jesus answering said, Were there not ten cleansed? but where are the nine? There are not found that returned to give glory to God, save this stranger. And he said unto him, Arise, go thy way, thy faith hath made thee whole.

Meditation
I will thank thee, for thou hast heard me : and art become my salvation.

Psalm 118. 21

I BELIEVE

I believe in the Holy Ghost, The Lord and giver of life. From the Creed

The Creed

IBELIEVE in one God the Father Almighty, Maker of heaven and earth, And of all things visible and invisible:

And in one Lord Jesus Christ, the only-begotten Son of God, Begotten of his Father before all worlds, God of God, Light of Light, Very God of very God, Begotten, not made, Being of one substance with the Father, By whom all things were made: Who for us men and for our salvation came down from heaven, And was incarnate by the Holy Ghost of the Virgin Mary, And was made man, And was crucified also for us under Pontius Pilate. He suffered and was buried, And the third day he rose again according to the Scriptures, And ascended into heaven, And sitteth on the right hand of the Father. And he shall come again with glory to judge both the quick and dead; Whose kingdom shall have no end.

And I believe in the Holy Ghost, The Lord and giver of life, Who proceedeth from the Father and the Son, Who with the Father and the Son together is worshipped and glorified, Who spake by the Prophets. And I believe one Catholick and Apostolick Church. I acknowledge one Baptism for the remission of sins. And I look for the Resurrection of the dead, And the life of the world to come. Amen.

PSALMS OF PRAISE AND THANKSGIVING (36)

The Lord is a righteous God

The Lord is righteous in all his ways : and holy in all his works. Psalm 145. 17

Psalm 145. *Exaltabo te, Deus*

ALL thy works praise thee, O Lord : and thy saints give thanks unto thee.

11. They shew the glory of thy kingdom : and talk of thy power;

12. That thy power, thy glory, and mightiness of thy kingdom : might be known unto men.

13. Thy kingdom is an everlasting kingdom : and thy dominion endureth throughout all ages.

14. The Lord upholdeth all such as fall : and lifteth up all those that are down.

15. The eyes of all wait upon thee, O Lord : and thou givest them their meat in due season …

18. The Lord is nigh unto all them that call upon him : yea, all such as call upon him faithfully.

19. He will fulfil the desire of them that fear him : he also will hear their cry, and will help them.

20. The Lord preserveth all them that love him : but scattereth abroad all the ungodly.

21. My mouth shall speak the praise of the Lord : and let all flesh give thanks unto his holy Name for ever and ever.

PSALMS OF PRAISE AND
THANKSGIVING (37)
'How wonderful is our God'

The Lord careth for the strangers, he defendeth the fatherless and widow : as for the way of the ungodly, he turneth it upside down. Psalm 146. 9

Psalm 146. *Lauda, anima mea*

PRAISE the Lord, O my soul : while I live will I praise the Lord : yea, as long as I have any being, I will sing praises unto my God.

2. O put not your trust in princes, nor in any child of man : for there is no help in them.

3. For when the breath of man goeth forth, he shall turn again to his earth : and then all his thoughts perish.

4. Blessed is he that hath the God of Jacob for his help : and whose hope is in the Lord his God;

5. Who made heaven and earth, the sea, and all that therein is : who keepeth his promise for ever;

6. Who helpeth them to right that suffer wrong : who feedeth the hungry.

7. The Lord looseth men out of prison : the Lord giveth sight to the blind.

8. The Lord helpeth them that are fallen : the Lord careth for the righteous.

9. The Lord careth for the strangers, he defendeth the fatherless and widow : as for the way of the ungodly, he turneth it upside down.

10. The Lord thy God, O Sion, shall be King for evermore : and throughout all generations.

WAR IN HEAVEN

Michael and his angels fought against the dragon. Revelation 12. 7

The Collect
From 'Saint Michael and All Angels'

OEVERLASTING God, who hast ordained and constituted the services of Angels and men in a wonderful order: Mercifully grant, that as thy holy Angels alway do thee service in heaven, so by thy appointment they may succour and defend us on earth; through Jesus Christ our Lord. Amen.

For the Epistle. *Revelation 12. 7*
From 'Saint Michael and All Angels'

THERE was war in heaven: Michael and his angels fought against the dragon; and the dragon fought and his angels, and prevailed not, neither was their place found any more in heaven. And the great dragon was cast out, that old serpent, called the devil and Satan, which deceiveth the whole world; he was cast out into the earth, and his angels were cast out with him. And I heard a loud voice saying in heaven, Now is come salvation, and strength, and the kingdom of our God, and the power of his Christ : for the accuser of our brethren is cast down, which accused them before our God day and night. And they overcame him by the blood of the Lamb, and by the word of their testimony; and they loved not their lives unto the death. Therefore rejoice, ye heavens, and ye that dwell in them.

ANGELIC OVERSIGHT

In heaven their angels do always behold the face of my Father which is in heaven.
St. Matthew 18. 10

The Gospel. *St. Matthew 18. 1*
From 'Saint Michael and All Angels'

A T the same time came the disciples unto Jesus, saying, Who is the greatest in the kingdom of heaven? And Jesus called a little child unto him, and set him in the midst of them, And said, Verily I say unto you, Except ye be converted, and become as little children, ye shall not enter into the kingdom of heaven. Whosoever therefore shall humble himself as this little child, the same is greatest in the kingdom of heaven. And whoso shall receive one such little child in my name receiveth me. But whoso shall offend one of these little ones which believe in me, it were better for him that a millstone were hanged about his neck, and that he were drowned in the depth of the sea. Woe unto the world because of offences: for it must needs be that offences come: but woe to that man by whom the offence cometh. Wherefore if thy hand or thy foot offend thee, cut them off, and cast them from thee: it is better for thee to enter into life halt or maimed, rather than having two hands or two feet to be cast into everlasting fire … Take heed that ye despise not one of these little ones; for I say unto you, that in heaven their angels do always behold the face of my Father which is in heaven.

GLORYING IN CHRIST

God forbid that I should glory, save in the cross of our Lord Jesus Christ.

Galatians 6. 14

The Collect
From 'The Fifteenth Sunday After Trinity'

KEEP, we beseech thee, O Lord, thy Church with thy perpetual mercy: and, because the frailty of man without thee cannot but fall, keep us ever by thy help from all things hurtful, and lead us to all things profitable to our salvation; through Jesus Christ our Lord. Amen.

The Epistle. *Galatians 6. 11*
From 'The Fifteenth Sunday After Trinity'

YE see how large a letter I have written unto you with mine own hand. As many as desire to make a fair shew in the flesh, they constrain you to be circumcised; only lest they should suffer persecution for the cross of Christ. For neither they themselves who are circumcised keep the law; but desire to have you circumcised, that they may glory in your flesh. But God forbid that I should glory, save in the cross of our Lord Jesus Christ, by whom the world is crucified unto me, and I unto the world. For in Christ Jesus neither circumcision availeth any thing, nor uncircumcision, but a new creature. And as many as walk according to this rule, peace be on them, and mercy, and upon the Israel of God. From henceforth let no man trouble me: for I bear in my body the marks of the Lord Jesus.

TWO MASTERS

For the love of money is the root of all evil. 1 Timothy 6. 10

The Gospel. *St. Matthew 6. 24*
From 'The Fifteenth Sunday After Trinity'

NO man can serve two masters: for either he will hate the one, and love the other; or else he will hold to the one, and despise the other. Ye cannot serve God and Mammon. Therefore I say unto you, Take no thought for your life, what ye shall eat, or what ye shall drink; nor yet for your body, what ye shall put on. Is not the life more than meat, and the body than raiment? Behold the fowls of the air; for they sow not, neither do they reap, nor gather into barns; yet your heavenly Father feedeth them. Are ye not much better than they? Which of you by taking thought can add one cubit unto his stature? And why take ye thought for raiment? Consider the lilies of the field, how they grow: they toil not, neither do they spin: and yet I say unto you, that even Solomon in all his glory was not arrayed like one of these. Wherefore, if God so clothe the grass of the field, which to-day is, and to-morrow is cast into the oven; shall he not much more clothe you, O ye of little faith? Therefore take no thought, saying, What shall we eat? or, What shall we drink? or, Wherewithal shall we be clothed? (For after all these things do the Gentiles seek:) for your heavenly Father knoweth that ye have need of all these things. But seek ye first the kingdom of God, and his righteousness; and all these things shall be added unto you.

PERSECUTED FOR CHRIST'S SAKE

Of the Jews five times received I forty stripes save one; thrice was I beaten with rods; once was I stoned... 2 Corinthians 11. 24–25

Psalm 7. *Domine, Deus meus*

O LORD my God, in thee have I put my trust : save me from all them that persecute me, and deliver me;

2. Lest he devour my soul, like a lion, and tear it in pieces : while there is none to help.

3. O Lord my God, if I have done any such thing : or if there be any wickedness in my hands;

4. If I have rewarded evil unto him that dealt friendly with me : yea, I have delivered him that without any cause is mine enemy;

5. Then let mine enemy persecute my soul, and take me : yea, let him tread my life down upon the earth, and lay mine honour in the dust.

6. Stand up, O Lord, in thy wrath, and lift up thyself, because of the indignation of mine enemies : arise up for me in the judgement that thou hast commanded.

7. And so shall the congregation of the people come about thee : for their sakes therefore lift up thyself again.

8. The Lord shall judge the people; give sentence with me, O Lord : according to my righteousness, and according to the innocency that is in me.

9. O let the wickedness of the ungodly come to an end : but guide thou the just.

PSALMS OF PRAISE AND THANKSGIVING (38)

He heals the broken-hearted

He healeth those that are broken in heart : and giveth medicine to heal their sickness. Psalm 147. 3

Psalm 147. *Laudate Dominum*

O PRAISE the Lord, for it is a good thing to sing praises unto our God : yea, a joyful and pleasant thing it is to be thankful.

2. The Lord doth build up Jerusalem : and gather together the out-casts of Israel.

3. He healeth those that are broken in heart : and giveth medicine to heal their sickness.

4. He telleth the number of the stars : and calleth them all by their names.

5. Great is our Lord, and great is his power : yea, and his wisdom is infinite.

6. The Lord setteth up the meek : and bringeth the ungodly down to the ground.

7. O sing unto the Lord with thanksgiving : sing praises upon the harp unto our God;

8. Who covereth the heaven with clouds, and prepareth rain for the earth : and maketh the grass to grow upon the mountains, and herb for the use of men;

9. Who giveth fodder unto the cattle : and feedeth the young ravens that call upon him.

THE MESSIAH IN THE PSALMS (13)
He will ascend to God's right hand

Thou art gone up on high, thou hast led captivity captive, and received gifts for men : yea, even for thine enemies, that the Lord God might dwell among them.

Psalm 68. 18

Psalm 68. *Exurgat Deus*

PRAISED be the Lord daily : even the God who helpeth us, and poureth his benefits upon us.

20. He is our God, even the God of whom cometh salvation : God is the Lord, by whom we escape death.

21. God shall wound the head of his enemies : and the hairy scalp of such a one as goeth on still in his wickedness.

22. The Lord hath said, I will bring my people again, as I did from Basan : mine own will I bring again, as I did sometime from the deep of the sea.

23. That thy foot may be dipped in the blood of thine enemies : and that the tongue of thy dogs may be red through the same.

24. It is well seen, O God, how thou goest : how thou, my God and King, goest in the sanctuary.

25. The singers go before, the minstrels follow after : in the midst are the damsels playing with the timbrels.

26. Give thanks, O Israel, unto God the Lord in the congregations : from the ground of the heart.

THE RESURRECTION LIFE

I know that my Redeemer liveth, and that he shall stand at the latter day upon the earth. And though after my skin worms destroy this body, yet in my flesh shall I see God: whom I shall see for myself, and mine eyes shall behold, and not another.

Job 19. 25–27

Psalm 90. *Domine, refugium*

L ORD, thou hast been our refuge : from one generation to another.

2. Before the mountains were brought forth, or ever the earth and the world were made : thou art God from everlasting, and world without end.

3. Thou turnest man to destruction : again thou sayest, Come again, ye children of men.

4. For a thousand years in thy sight are but as yesterday seeing that is past : as a watch in the night.

5. As soon as thou scatterest them they are even as a sleep : and fade away suddenly like the grass.

6. In the morning it is green, and groweth up : but in the evening it is cut down, dried up, and withered.

7. For we consume away in thy displeasure : and are afraid at thy wrathful indignation.

8. Thou hast set our misdeeds before thee : and our secret sins in the light of thy countenance.

DO GOOD

Zacchaeus stood forth, and said unto the Lord, Behold, Lord, the half of my goods I give to the poor; and if I have done any wrong to any man, I restore four-fold.

St. Luke 19. 8

Sentences
From 'Holy Communion'

WHO goeth a warfare at any time of his own cost? who planteth a vineyard, and eateth not of the fruit thereof? or who feedeth a flock, and eateth not of the milk of the flock? 1 Corinthians 9

If we have sown unto you spiritual things, is it a great matter if we shall reap your worldly things? 1 Corinthians 9

Do ye not know that they who minister about holy things live of the sacrifice; and they who wait at the altar are partakers with the altar? Even so hath the Lord also ordained, that they who preach the Gospel should live of the Gospel. 1 Corinthians 9

He that soweth little shall reap little; and he that soweth plenteously shall reap plenteously. Let every man do according as he is disposed in his heart, not grudging, or of necessity; for God loveth a cheerful giver.

2 Corinthians 9

While we have time, let us do good unto all men; and specially unto them that are of the household of faith. Galatians 6

ROOTED AND GROUNDED
IN DIVINE LOVE

... to know the love of Christ, which passeth knowledge. Ephesians 3. 19

The Collect
From 'The Sixteenth Sunday After Trinity'

O LORD, we besseth thee, let thy continual pity cleanse and defend thy Church; and, because it cannot continue in safety without thy succour, preserve it evermore by thy help and goodness; through Jesus Christ our Lord. Amen.

The Epistle. *Ephesians 3. 13*
From 'The Sixteenth Sunday After Trinity'

I DESIRE that ye faint not at my tribulations for you, which is your glory. For this cause I bow my knees unto the Father of our Lord Jesus Christ, of whom the whole family in heaven and earth is named, that he would grant you, according to the riches of his glory, to be strengthened with might by his Spirit in the inner man; that Christ may dwell in your hearts by faith; that ye, being rooted and grounded in love, may be able to comprehend with all saints, what is the breadth, and length, and depth, and height; and to know the love of Christ, which passeth knowledge, that ye might be filled with all the fulness of God. Now unto him that is able to do exceeding abundantly above all that we ask or think, according to the power that worketh in us, unto him be glory in the Church by Christ Jesus throughout all ages, world without end. Amen.

A BEREFT WIDOW

I am the resurrection and the life, saith the Lord: he that believeth in me, though he were dead, yet shall he live: and whosoever liveth and believeth in me shall never die. St. John 11. 25–26

The Gospel. *St. Luke 7. 11*
From 'The Sixteenth Sunday After Trinity'

AND it came to pass the day after, that Jesus went into a city called Nain; and many of his disciples went with him, and much people. Now when he came nigh to the gate of the city, behold, there was a dead man carried out, the only son of his mother, and she was a widow; and much people of the city was with her. And when the Lord saw her, he had compassion on her, and said unto her, Weep not. And he came and touched the bier; and they that bare him stood still: and he said, Young man, I say unto thee, Arise. And he that was dead sat up, and began to speak: and he delivered him to his mother. And there came a fear on all, and they glorified God, saying, that a great Prophet is risen up among us, and, that God hath visited his people. And this rumour of him went forth throughout all Judaea, and throughout all the region round about.

Meditation
Comfort the soul of thy servant : for unto thee, O Lord, do I lift up my soul.

Psalm 86. 4

LUKE'S ACCOUNT OF
CHRIST'S PASSION (1)

Behold the Lamb of God, which taketh away the sin of the world. St. John 1. 29

The Gospel. *St. Luke 22. 1–13*
From 'Wednesday Before Easter'

NOW the feast of unleavened bread drew nigh, which is called the
Passover. And the chief priests and scribes sought how they might kill
him; for they feared the people. Then entered Satan into Judas surnamed
Iscariot, being of the number of the twelve. And he went his way, and
communed with the chief priests and captains, how he might betray him
unto them. And they were glad, and covenanted to give him money. And
he promised, and sought opportunity to betray him unto them in the ab-
sence of the multitude. Then came the day of unleavened bread, when the
passover must be killed. And he sent Peter and John, saying, Go and prepare us the passover, that we may eat. And they said unto him, Where wilt
thou that we prepare? And he said unto them, Behold, when ye are entered into the city, there shall a man meet you, bearing a pitcher of water;
follow him into the house where he entereth in. And ye shall say unto the
goodman of the house, The Master saith unto thee, Where is the guest-
chamber, where I shall eat the passover with my disciples? And he shall
shew you a large upper-room furnished : there make ready. And they
went, and found as he had said unto them: and they made ready the
passover.

LUKE'S ACCOUNT OF CHRIST'S PASSION (2)

And he took bread, and gave thanks, and brake it, and gave unto them, saying, This is my body which is given for you. St. Luke 22. 19

The Gospel. *St. Luke 22. 14–23*
From 'Wednesday Before Easter'

A ND when the hour was come he sat down, and the twelve Apostles with him. And he said unto them, With desire I have desired to eat this passover with you before I suffer: for I say unto you, I will not any more eat thereof, until it be fulfilled in the Kingdom of God. And he took the cup, and gave thanks, and said, Take this, and divide it among yourselves. For I say unto you, I will not drink of the fruit of the vine, until the Kingdom of God shall come. And he took bread, and gave thanks, and brake it, and gave unto them, saying, This is my body, which is given for you: this do in remembrance of me. Likewise also the cup after supper, saying, This cup is the new testament in my blood, which is shed for you. But behold, the hand of him that betrayeth me is with me on the table. And truly the Son of Man goeth as it was determined: but woe unto that man by whom he is betrayed. And they began to inquire among themselves, which of them it was that should do this thing.

Meditation
This do in remembrance of me. St. Luke 22. 19

LUKE'S ACCOUNT OF
CHRIST'S PASSION (3)

He humbled himself, and became obedient unto death, even the death of the cross.

Philippians 2. 8

The Gospel. *St. Luke 22. 24*
From 'Wednesday before Easter'

AND there was also a strife among them, which of them should be accounted the greatest. And he said unto them, The kings of the Gentiles exercise lordship over them, and they that exercise authority upon them are called benefactors. But ye shall not be so: but he that is greatest among you, let him be as the younger; and he that is chief, as he that doth serve. For whether is greater, he that sitteth at meat, or he that serveth? is not he that sitteth at meat? but I am among you as he that serveth. Ye are they which have continued with me in my temptations. And I appoint unto you a kingdom, as my Father hath appointed unto me; that ye may eat and drink at my table in my kingdom, and sit on thrones, judging the twelve tribes of Israel. And the Lord said, Simon, Simon, behold, Satan hath desired to have you, that he may sift you as wheat: but I have prayed for thee, that thy faith fail not; and when thou art converted, strengthen thy brethren. And he said unto him, Lord, I am ready to go with thee both into prison and to death. And he said, I tell thee, Peter, the cock shall not crow this day, before that thou shalt thrice deny that thou knowest me.

LUKE'S ACCOUNT OF
CHRIST'S PASSION (4)

… he became the author of eternal salvation unto all them that obey him.

Hebrews 5. 9

The Gospel. *St. Luke 22. 35*
From 'Wednesday Before Easter'

AND he said unto them, When I sent you without purse, and scrip, and shoes, lacked ye any thing? And they said, Nothing. Then said he unto them, But now, he that hath a purse, let him take it, and likewise his scrip: and he that hath no sword, let him sell his garment, and buy one. For I say unto you, That this that is written must yet be accomplished in me, And he was reckoned among the transgressors: for the things concerning me have an end. And they said, Lord, behold, here are two swords. And he said unto them, It is enough. And he came out, and went, as he was wont, to the mount of Olives, and his disciples also followed him. And when he was at the place, he said unto them, Pray, that ye enter not into temptation. And he was withdrawn from them about a stone's cast, and kneeled down, and prayed, saying, Father, if thou be willing, remove this cup from me: nevertheless, not my will, but thine be done. And there appeared an angel unto him from heaven, strengthening him. And being in an agony, he prayed more earnestly; and his sweat was as it were great drops of blood falling down to the ground. And when he rose up from prayer, and was come to his disciples, he found them sleeping for sorrow, and said unto them, Why sleep ye? rise and pray, lest ye enter into temptation.

LUKE'S ACCOUNT OF CHRIST'S PASSION (5)

Yea, even mine own familiar friend, whom I trusted : who did also eat of my bread, hath laid great wait for me. Psalm 41. 9

The Gospel. *St. Luke 22. 47*
From 'Wednesday Before Easter'

AND immediately, while he yet spake, behold, a multitude, and he that was called Judas, one of the twelve, went before them, and drew near unto Jesus to kiss him. But Jesus said unto him, Judas, betrayest thou the Son of Man with a kiss? When they who were about him saw what would follow, they said unto him, Lord, shall we smite with the sword? And one of them smote the servant of the high priest, and cut off his right ear. And Jesus answered and said, Suffer ye thus far. And he touched his ear, and healed him. Then Jesus said unto the chief priests, and captains of the temple, and the elders who were come to him, Be ye come out as against a thief, with swords and staves? When I was daily with you in the temple, ye stretched forth no hands against me: but this is your hour, and the power of darkness. Then took they him, and led him, and brought him into the high priest's house: and Peter followed afar off.

Meditation

Behold, we go up to Jerusalem; and the Son of man shall be betrayed unto the chief priests and unto the scribes, and they shall condemn him to death.

St. Matthew 20. 18

288

THE UNITY OF THE SPIRIT

Neither pray I for these alone, but for them also which shall believe on me through their word; that they all may be one; as thou, Father, art in me, and I in thee, that they also may be one in us. St. John 17. 20–21

The Collect
From 'The Seventeenth Sunday after Trinity'

LORD, we pray thee that thy grace may always prevent and follow us, and make us continually to be given to all good works; through Jesus Christ our Lord. Amen.

The Epistle. *Ephesians 4. 1*
From 'The Seventeenth Sunday after Trinity'

I THEREFORE the prisoner of the Lord beseech you, that ye walk worthy of the vocation wherewith ye are called, with all lowliness and meekness, with long-suffering, forbearing one another in love; endeavouring to keep the unity of the Spirit in the bond of peace. There is one body, and one Spirit, even as ye are called in one hope of your calling; one Lord, one faith, one baptism, one God and Father of all, who is above all, and through all, and in you all.

Meditation
Behold, how good and joyful a thing it is: brethren, to dwell together in unity!

Psalm 133. 1

IS IT LAWFUL TO HEAL
ON THE SABBATH-DAY?

The Son of Man is Lord also of the sabbath. St. Luke 6. 5

The Gospel. *St. Luke 14. 1*
From 'The Seventeenth Sunday after Trinity'

IT came to pass, as Jesus went into the house of one of the chief Pharisees to eat bread on the sabbath-day, that they watched him. And behold, there was a certain man before him which had the dropsy. And Jesus answering spake unto the Lawyers and Pharisees, saying, Is it lawful to heal on the sabbath-day? And they held their peace. And he took him, and healed him, and let him go; and answered them, saying, Which of you shall have an ass, or an ox, fallen into a pit, and will not straightway pull him out on the sabbath day? And they could not answer him again to these things. And he put forth a parable to those which were bidden, when he marked how they chose out the chief rooms; saying unto them, When thou art bidden of any man to a wedding, sit not down in the highest room; lest a more honourable man than thou be bidden of him; and he that bade thee and him come and say to thee, Give this man place; and thou begin with shame to take the lowest room. But when thou art bidden, go and sit down in the lowest room; that, when he that bade thee cometh, he may say unto thee, Friend, go up higher: then shalt thou have worship in the presence of them that sit at meat with thee. For whosoever exalteth himself shall be abased; and he that humbleth himself shall be exalted.

PRAYERS FROM
'HOLY COMMUNION'

… be ready to give, and glad to distribute… 1 Timothy 6. 18

A Prayer for the Church

ALMIGHTY and everliving God, who by thy holy Apostle hast taught us to make prayers and supplications, and to give thanks for all men: We humbly beseech thee most mercifully to receive these our prayers, which we offer unto thy Divine Majesty; beseeching thee to inspire continually the universal Church with the spirit of truth, unity, and concord: And grant, that all they that do confess thy holy Name may agree in the truth of thy holy Word, and live in unity, and godly love. We beseech thee also to save and defend all Christian Kings, Princes, and Governors; and specially thy servant *ELIZABETH* our Queen; that under her we may be godly and quietly governed: And grant unto her whole Council, and to all that are put in authority under her, that they may truly and indifferently minister justice, to the punishment of wickedness and vice, and to the maintenance of thy true religion, and virtue. Give grace, O heavenly Father, to all Bishops and Curates, that they may both by their life and doctrine set forth thy true and lively Word, and rightly and duly administer thy holy Sacraments And to all thy people give thy heavenly grace; and especially to this congregation here present; that, with meek heart and due reverence, they may hear, and receive thy holy Word; truly serving thee in holiness and righteousness all the days of their life. Grant this, O Father, for Jesus Christ's sake, our only Mediator and Advocate. Amen.

A PHYSICIAN OF THE SOUL

Luke, the beloved physician, and Demas, greet you. Colossians 4. 14

The Epistle. *2 Timothy 4. 5*
From 'Saint Luke the Evangelist'

WATCH thou in all things, endure afflictions, do the work of an Evangelist, make full proof of thy ministry. For I am now ready to be offered, and the time of my departure is at hand. I have fought a good fight, I have finished my course, I have kept the faith. Henceforth there is laid up for me a crown of righteousness, which the Lord, the righteous Judge, shall give me at that day: and not to me only, but unto all them also that love his appearing. Do thy diligence to come shortly unto me: for Demas hath forsaken me, having loved this present world, and is departed unto Thessalonica; Crescens to Galatia, Titus unto Dalmatia. Only Luke is with me. Take Mark and bring him with thee: for he is profitable to me for the ministry. And Tychicus have I sent to Ephesus. The cloke that I left at Troas with Carpus, when thou comest, bring with thee and the books, but especially the parchments. Alexander the copper-smith did me much evil: the Lord reward him according to his works. Of whom be thou ware also, for he hath greatly withstood our words.

Meditation
Only Luke is with me. 2 Timothy 4. 11

THE ACCURATE HISTORIAN

It seemed good to me also, having had perfect understanding of all things from the very first, to write unto thee in order, most excellent Theophilus, that thou mightest know the certainty of those things, wherein thou hast been instructed.

St. Luke 1. 3–4

The Gospel. *St. Luke 10. 1*
From 'Saint Luke the Evangelist'

THE Lord appointed other seventy also, and sent them two and two before his face into every city and place whither he himself would come. Therefore said he unto them, The harvest truly is great, but the labourers are few; pray ye therefore the Lord of the harvest, that he would send forth labourers into his harvest. Go your ways; behold, I send you forth as lambs among wolves. Carry neither purse, nor scrip, nor shoes: and salute no man by the way. And into whatsoever house ye enter, first say, Peace be to this house. And if the son of peace be there, your peace shall rest upon it: if not, it shall turn to you again. And in the same house remain, eating and drinking such things as they give: for the labourer is worthy of his hire.

Meditation
My soul doth magnify the Lord: and my spirit hath rejoiced in God my Saviour.

St. Luke 1. 46–47

OUR LAST HOUR

Behold, I shew you a mystery. 1 Corinthians 15. 51

1 Corinthians 15. 48–58
From 'The Burial of the Dead'

AS is the earthy, such are they that are earthy: and as is the heavenly, such are they also that are heavenly. And as we have borne the image of the earthy, we shall also bear the image of the heavenly. Now this I say, brethren, that flesh and blood cannot inherit the kingdom of God; neither doth corruption inherit incorruption. Behold, I shew you a mystery: We shall not all sleep, but we shall all be changed, in a moment, in the twinkling of an eye, at the last trump: for the trumpet shall sound, and the dead shall be raised incorruptible, and we shall be changed. For this corruptible must put on incorruption, and this mortal must put on immortality. So when this corruptible shall have put on incorruption, and this mortal shall have put on immortality; then shall be brought to pass the saying that is written, Death is swallowed up in victory. O death, where is thy sting? O grave, where is thy victory? The sting of death is sin; and the strength of sin is the law. But thanks be to God, which giveth us the victory through our Lord Jesus Christ. Therefore, my beloved brethren, be ye stedfast, unmoveable, always abounding in the work of the Lord, forasmuch as ye know that your labour is not in vain in the Lord.

CELEBRATING A BIRTH

Forasmuch as it hath pleased Almighty God of his goodness to give you safe deliverance, and hath preserved you in the great danger of Child-birth : you shall therefore give hearty thanks unto God, and say... From 'The Churching of Women'

Psalm 116. *Dilexi quoniam*
From 'The Churching of Women'

I AM well pleased : that the Lord hath heard the voice of my prayer;
That he hath inclined his ear unto me : therefore will I call upon him as long as I live.

The snares of death compassed me round about : and the pains of hell gat hold upon me.

I found trouble and heaviness, and I called upon the name of the Lord : O Lord, I beseech thee, deliver my soul.

Gracious is the Lord, and righteous : yea, our God is merciful.

The Lord preserveth the simple : I was in misery, and he helped me.

Turn again then unto thy rest, O my soul : for the Lord hath rewarded thee.

And why? thou hast delivered my soul from death : mine eyes from tears, and my feet from falling.

I will walk before the Lord : in the land of the living.

THE WORLD, THE FLESH AND THE DEVIL

I sent to know your faith, lest by some means the tempter have tempted you, and our labour be in vain. 1 Thessalonians 3. 5

The Collect
From 'The Eighteenth Sunday After Trinity'

LORD, we beseech thee, grant thy people grace to withstand the temp-tations of the world, the flesh, and the devil, and with pure hearts and minds to follow thee the only God; through Jesus Christ our Lord. Amen.

The Epistle. *1 Corinthians 1. 4*
From 'The Eighteenth Sunday after Trinity'

I THANK my God always on your behalf, for the grace of God which is given you by Jesus Christ; that in every thing ye are enriched by him, in all utterance, and in all knowledge; even as the testimony of Christ was confirmed in you: so that ye come behind in no gift; waiting for the coming of our Lord Jesus Christ, who shall also confirm you unto the end, that ye may be blameless in the day of our Lord Jesus Christ.

Meditation
Be sober, be vigilant; because your adversary the devil, as a roaring lion, walketh about, seeking whom he may devour: whom resist, stedfast in the faith.

1 St. Peter 5. 8–9

THE GREAT COMMANDMENT

Thou shalt love the Lord thy God with all thy heart, and with all thy soul, and with all thy mind. St. Matthew 22. 37

The Gospel. *St. Matthew 22. 34*
From 'The Eighteenth Sunday after Trinity'

WHEN the Pharisees had heard that Jesus had put the Sadducees to silence, they were gathered together. Then one of them, who was a lawyer, asked him a question, tempting him, and saying, Master, which is the great commandment in the law? Jesus said unto him, Thou shalt love the Lord thy God with all thy heart, and with all thy soul, and with all thy mind. This is the first and great commandment. And the second is like unto it, Thou shalt love thy neighbour as thyself. On these two command-ments hang all the law and the prophets. While the Pharisees were gathered together, Jesus asked them, saying, What think ye of Christ? whose son is he? They say unto him, The son of David. He saith unto them, How then doth David in spirit call him Lord, saying, The LORD said unto my Lord, Sit thou on my right hand, till I make thine enemies thy foot-stool? If David then call him Lord, how is he his son? And no man was able to answer him a word neither durst any man from that day forth ask him any more questions.

LUKE'S ACCOUNT OF CHRIST'S PASSION (6)

And Peter said, Man, I know not what thou sayest. St. Luke 22. 60

The Collect
From 'The Sunday Next Before Easter'

ALMIGHTY and everlasting God, who, of thy tender love towards mankind, hast sent thy Son our Saviour Jesus Christ, to take upon him our flesh, and to suffer death upon the cross, that all mankind should follow the example of his great humility: Mercifully grant, that we may both follow the example of his patience, and also be made partakers of his resurrection; through the same Jesus Christ our Lord. Amen.

The Gospel. *St. Luke 22. 54*
From 'Wednesday Before Easter'

AND Peter followed afar off. And when they had kindled a fire in the midst of the hall, and were set down together, Peter sat down among them. But a certain maid beheld him, as he sat by the fire, and earnestly looked upon him, and said, This man was also with him. And he denied him, saying, Woman, I know him not. And after a little while another saw him, and said, Thou art also of them. And Peter said, Man, I am not. And about the space of one hour after another, confidently affirmed, saying, Of a truth this fellow also was with him; for he is a Galilaean. And Peter said, Man, I know not what thou sayest. And immediately, while he yet spake, the cock crew.

LUKE'S ACCOUNT OF
CHRIST'S PASSION (7)

And the men that held Jesus mocked him, and smote him. St. Luke 22. 63

The Collect
From 'The Sunday Next Before Easter'

A LMIGHTY and everlasting God, who, of thy tender love towards
mankind, hast sent thy Son our Saviour Jesus Christ, to take upon him
our flesh, and to suffer death upon the cross, that all mankind should follow
the example of his great humility: Mercifully grant, that we may both follow the example of his patience, and also be made partakers of his resurrection; through the same Jesus Christ our Lord. Amen.

The Gospel. *St. Luke 22. 63–71*
From 'Wednesday Before Easter'

A ND the men that held Jesus mocked him, and smote him. And when
they had blindfolded him, they struck him on the face, and asked him,
saying, Prophesy, who is it that smote thee? And many other things blas-
phemously spake they against him. And as soon as it was day, the elders of
the people and the chief priests and the scribes came together, and led him
into their council, saying, Art thou the Christ? tell us. And he said unto
them, If I tell you, ye will not believe: and if I also ask you, ye will not
answer me, nor let me go. Hereafter shall the Son of Man sit on the right
hand of the power of God. Then said they all, Art thou then the Son of
God? And he said unto them, Ye say that I am.

LUKE'S ACCOUNT OF
CHRIST'S PASSION (8)

And Pilate asked him, saying, Art thou the King of the Jews? St. Luke 23. 3

The Gospel. *St. Luke 23. 1–12*
From 'Thursday Before Easter'

THE whole multitude of them arose, and led him unto Pilate. And they began to accuse him, saying, We found this fellow perverting the nation, and forbidding to give tribute to Caesar, saying, That he himself is Christ a King. And Pilate asked him, saying, Art thou the King of the Jews? And he answered him, and said, Thou sayest it. Then said Pilate to the chief priests and to the people, I find no fault in this man. And they were the more fierce, saying, He stirreth up the people, teaching throughout all Jewry, beginning from Galilee to this place. When Pilate heard of Galilee, he asked whether the man were a Galilaean. And as soon as he knew that he belonged unto Herod's jurisdiction, he sent him to Herod, who himself also was at Jerusalem at that time. And when Herod saw Jesus he was exceeding glad; for he was desirous to see him of a long season, because he had heard many things of him; and he hoped to have seen some miracle done by him. Then he questioned with him in many words; but he answered him nothing. And the chief priests and scribes stood and vehemently accused him. And Herod with his men of war set him at nought, and mocked him, and arrayed him in a gorgeous robe, and sent him again to Pilate. And the same day Pilate and Herod were made friends together; for before they were at enmity between themselves.

SERVANTS OF JESUS CHRIST

But ye, beloved, building up yourselves on your most holy faith, praying in the Holy Ghost. St. Jude 20

The Epistle. *St. Jude 1*
From 'Saint Simon and Saint Jude, Apostles'

JUDE, the servant of Jesus Christ, and brother of James, to them that are sanctified by God the Father, and preserved in Jesus Christ, and called: Mercy unto you, and peace, and love, be multiplied. Beloved, when I gave all diligence to write unto you of the common salvation, it was needful for me to write unto you, and exhort you, that ye should earnestly contend for the faith which was once delivered unto the saints. For there are certain men crept in unawares, who were before of old ordained to this condemnation; ungodly men, turning the grace of our God into lasciviousness, and denying the only Lord God and our Lord Jesus Christ. I will therefore put you in remembrance, though ye once knew this, how that the Lord, having saved the people out of the land of Egypt, afterward destroyed them that believed not. And the angels which kept not their first estate, but left their own habitation, he hath reserved in everlasting chains under darkness unto the judgement of the great day. Even as Sodom and Gomorrha, and the cities about them, in like manner giving themselves over to fornication, and going after strange flesh, are set forth for an example, suffering the vengeance of eternal fire. Likewise also these filthy dreamers defile the flesh, despise dominion, and speak evil of dignities.

GOD'S PROTECTING POWER

Now unto him that is able to keep you from falling, and to present you faultless before the presence of his glory with exceeding joy... St. Jude 24

The Gospel. *St. John 15. 17*
From 'Saint Simon and Saint Jude, Apostles'

THESE things I command you, that ye love one another. If the world hate you, ye know that it hated me before it hated you. If ye were of the world, the world would love his own: but because ye are not of the world, but I have chosen you out of the world, therefore the world hateth you. Remember the word that I said unto you, The servant is not greater than the lord: if they have persecuted me, they will also persecute you; if they have kept my saying, they will keep yours also. But all these things will they do unto you for my name's sake, because they know not him that sent me. If I had not come and spoken unto them, they had not had sin: but now they have no cloke for their sin. He that hateth me hateth my Father also. If I had not done among them the works which none other man did, they had not had sin; but now have they both seen and hated both me and my Father. But this cometh to pass, that the word might be fulfilled that is written in their law, They hated me without a cause. But when the Comforter is come, whom I will send unto you from the Father, even the Spirit of truth, which proceedeth from the Father, he shall testify of me: and ye also shall bear witness, because ye have been with me from the beginning.

LIVING AS CHILDREN OF LIGHT

Be ye angry and sin not: let not the sun go down upon your wrath.

Ephesians 4. 26

The Epistle. *Ephesians 4. 17*
From 'The Nineteenth Sunday After Trinity'

THIS I say therefore, and testify in the Lord, that ye henceforth walk not as other Gentiles walk, in the vanity of their mind; having the understanding darkened, being alienated from the life of God through the ignorance that is in them, because of the blindness of their heart: who being past feeling, have given themselves over unto lasciviousness, to work all uncleanness with greediness. But ye have not so learned Christ; if so be that ye have heard him, and have been taught by him, as the truth is in Jesus: that ye put off, concerning the former conversation, the old man, which is corrupt according to the deceitful lusts; and be renewed in the spirit of your mind; and that ye put on the new man, which after God is created in righteousness and true holiness. Wherefore, putting away lying, speak every man truth with his neighbour: for we are members one of another. Be ye angry and sin not: let not the sun go down upon your wrath: neither give place to the devil. Let him that stole steal no more; but rather let him labour, working with his hands the thing which is good, that he may have to give to him that needeth. Let no corrupt communication proceed out of your mouth, but that which is good to the use of edifying, that it may minister grace unto the hearers.

POWER TO FORGIVE SINS

In whom we have redemption through his blood, the forgiveness of sins, according to the riches of his grace. Ephesians 1. 7

The Collect
From 'The Nineteenth Sunday After Trinity'

O GOD, forasmuch as without thee we are not able to please thee; Mercifully grant, that thy Holy Spirit may in all things direct and rule our hearts; through Jesus Christ our Lord. Amen.

The Gospel. *St. Matthew 9. 1*
From 'The Nineteenth Sunday After Trinity'

JESUS entered into a ship, and passed over, and came into his own city. And behold, they brought to him a man sick of the palsy, lying on a bed. And Jesus, seeing their faith, said unto the sick of the palsy, Son, be of good cheer; thy sins be forgiven thee. And behold, certain of the Scribes said within themselves, This man blasphemeth. And Jesus knowing their thoughts, said, Wherefore think ye evil in your hearts? For whether is easier, to say, Thy sins be forgiven thee; or to say, Arise, and walk? But that ye may know that the Son of man hath power on earth to forgive sins, (then saith he to the sick of the palsy,) Arise, take up thy bed, and go unto thine house. And he arose, and departed to his house. But when the multitude saw it, they marvelled, and glorified God, who had given such power unto men.

INSTRUCTION FROM
GOD'S WORD (10)

Early in the morning do I cry unto thee : for in thy word is my trust.

Psalm 119. 147

The Collect
From 'The Second Sunday in Advent'

BLESSED Lord, who hast caused all holy Scriptures to be written for our learning: Grant that we may in such wise hear them, read, mark, learn, and inwardly digest them, that by patience and comfort of thy holy Word, we may embrace and ever hold fast the blessed hope of everlasting life, which thou hast given us in our Saviour Jesus Christ. Amen.

Psalm 119. *Clamavi in toto corde meo*

I CALL with my whole heart : hear me, O Lord, I will keep thy statutes.
146. Yea, even unto thee do I call : help me, and I shall keep thy testimonies.
147. Early in the morning do I cry unto thee : for in thy word is my trust.
148. Mine eyes prevent the night-watches : that I might be occupied in thy words.
149. Hear my voice, O Lord, according unto thy loving-kindness : quicken me, according as thou are wont.
150. They draw nigh that of malice persecute me : and are far from thy law.

~

A GREAT MULTITUDE

After this I beheld, and lo, a great multitude, which no man could number, of all nations, and kindreds, and people, and tongues, stood before the throne, and before the Lamb, clothed with white robes, and palms in their hands.

Revelation 7. 9–10

For the Epistle. *Revelation 7. 2*
From 'All Saints' Day'

AND I saw another angel ascending from the east, having the seal of the living God; and he cried with a loud voice to the four angels, to whom it was given to hurt the earth, and the sea, saying, Hurt not the earth, neither the sea, nor the trees, till we have sealed the servants of our God in their foreheads. And I heard the number of them which were sealed; and there were sealed an hundred and forty and four thousand, of all the tribes of the children of Israel...

After this I beheld, and lo, a great multitude, which no man could number, of all nations, and kindreds, and people, and tongues, stood before the throne, and before the Lamb, clothed with white robes, and palms in their hands; and cried with a loud voice, saying, Salvation to our God which sitteth upon the throne, and unto the Lamb. And all the angels stood round about the throne, and about the elders, and the four beasts, and fell before the throne on their faces, and worshipped God, saying, Amen; Blessing, and glory, and wisdom, and thanksgiving, and honour, and power, and might, be unto our God for ever and ever. Amen.

CONTRITION (2)

Praised be the Lord : for he hath heard the voice of my humble petitions.

Psalm 28. 7

Psalm 88. *Domine Deus*

O LORD God of my salvation, I have cried day and night before thee :
O let my prayer enter into thy presence, incline thine ear unto my
calling.

2. For my soul is full of trouble : and my life draweth nigh unto hell.

3. I am counted as one of them that go down into the pit : and I have
been even as a man that hath no strength.

4. Free among the dead, like unto them that are wounded, and lie in the
grave : who are out of remembrance, and are cut away from thy hand.

5. Thou hast laid me in the lowest pit : in a place of darkness, and in the
deep.

6. Thine indignation lieth hard upon me : and thou hast vexed me with all
thy storms.

7. Thou hast put away mine acquaintance far from me : and made me to
be abhorred of them.

8. I am so fast in prison : that I cannot get forth.

9. My sight faileth for very trouble : Lord, I have called daily upon thee, I
have stretched forth my hands unto thee.

LUKE'S ACCOUNT OF CHRIST'S PASSION (9)

But they cried, saying, Crucify him, crucify him. St. Luke 23.21

The Gospel. *St. Luke 23. 13*
From 'Thursday Before Easter'

AND Pilate, when he had called together the chief priests and the rulers and the people, said unto them, Ye have brought this man unto me, as one that perverteth the people: and behold, I, having examined him before you, have found no fault in this man touching those things whereof ye accuse him: No, nor yet Herod: for I sent you to him; and lo, nothing worthy of death is done unto him. I will therefore chastise him, and release him. For of necessity he must release one unto them at the feast. And they cried out all at once, saying, Away with this man, and release unto us Barabbas: (who for a certain sedition made in the city, and for murder, was cast into prison.) Pilate therefore, willing to release Jesus, spake again to them. But they cried, saying, Crucify him, crucify him. And he said unto them the third time, Why, what evil hath he done? I have found no cause of death in him: I will therefore chastise him, and let him go. And they were instant with loud voices, requiring that he might be crucified, and the voices of them and of the chief priests prevailed. And Pilate gave sentence that it should be as they required. And he released unto them him that for sedition and murder was cast into prison, whom they had desired; but he delivered Jesus to their will.

LUKE'S ACCOUNT OF
CHRIST'S PASSION (10)

And when they were come to the place which is called Calvary, there they crucified him. St. Luke 23. 33

The Collect
From 'The Sunday Next Before Easter'

ALMIGHTY and everlasting God, who, of thy tender love towards mankind, hast sent thy Son our Saviour Jesus Christ, to take upon him our flesh, and to suffer death upon the cross, that all mankind should follow the example of his great humility: Mercifully grant, that we may both follow the example of his patience, and also be made partakers of his resurrection; through the same Jesus Christ our Lord. Amen.

The Gospel. *St. Luke 23. 26–30*
From 'Thursday Before Easter'

AND as they led him away, they laid hold upon one Simon a Cyrenian, coming out of the country, and on him they laid the cross, that he might bear it after Jesus. And there followed him a great company of people, and of women, which also bewailed and lamented him. But Jesus, turning unto them, said, Daughters of Jerusalem, weep not for me, but weep for yourselves, and for your children. For behold, the days are coming, in the which they shall say, Blessed are the barren, and the wombs that never bare, and the paps which never gave suck. Then shall they begin to say to the mountains, Fall on us; and to the hills, Cover us.

'BE FILLED WITH THE SPIRIT'

... singing and making melody in your heart to the Lord. Ephesians 5. 19

The Collect
From 'The Twentieth Sunday After Trinity'
O ALMIGHTY and most merciful God, of thy bountiful goodness keep us, we beseech thee, from all things that may hurt us ; that we, being ready both in body and soul, may cheerfully accomplish those things that thou wouldest have done; through Jesus Christ our Lord. Amen.

The Epistle. *Ephesians 5. 15*
From 'The Twentieth Sunday After Trinity'
SEE then that ye walk circumspectly, not as fools, but as wise, redeeming the time, because the days are evil. Wherefore be ye not unwise, but understanding what the will of the Lord is. And be not drunk with wine, wherein is excess; but be filled with the Spirit; speaking to yourselves in psalms and hymns and spiritual songs, singing and making melody in your heart to the Lord; giving thanks always for all things unto God and the Father, in the name of our Lord Jesus Christ; submitting yourselves one to another in the fear of God.

Meditation
Let us come before his presence with thanksgiving : and shew ourselves glad in him with psalms. Psalm 95. 2

GOD'S GRACIOUS INVITATION

Come unto me, all ye that labour and are heavy laden, and I will give you rest.
St. Matthew 11. 28

The Gospel. *St. Matthew 22. 1*
From 'The Twentieth Sunday After Trinity'

JESUS said, The kingdom of heaven is like unto a certain king, who made a marriage for his son; and sent forth his servants to call them that were bidden to the wedding; and they would not come. Again, he sent forth other servants, saying, Tell them which are bidden, Behold, I have prepared my dinner; my oxen and my fatlings are killed, and all things are ready; come unto the marriage. But they made light of it, and went their ways, one to his farm, another to his merchandise: and the remnant took his servants, and entreated them spitefully, and slew them. But when the king heard thereof, he was wroth: and he sent forth his armies, and destroyed those murderers, and burnt up their city. Then saith he to his servants, The wedding is ready, but they who were bidden were not worthy. Go ye therefore into the high-ways, and as many as ye shall find bid to the marriage. So those servants went out into the high-ways, and gathered together all, as many as they found, both bad and good; and the wedding was furnished with guests. And when the king came in to see the guests, he saw there a man which had not on a wedding-garment. And he saith unto him, Friend, how camest thou in hither, not having a wedding-garment? And he was speechless.

LUKE'S ACCOUNT OF
CHRIST'S PASSION (11)

And a superscription also was written over him in letters of Greek, and Latin, and Hebrew, THIS IS THE KING OF THE JEWS. St. Luke 23. 38

The Collect
From 'The Sunday Next Before Easter'

ALMIGHTY and everlasting God, who, of thy tender love towards mankind, hast sent thy Son, our Saviour Jesus Christ, to take upon him our flesh, and to suffer death upon the cross, that all mankind should follow the example of his great humility: Mercifully grant, that we may both follow the example of his patience, and also be made partakers of his resurrection; through the same Jesus Christ our Lord. Amen.

The Gospel. St. Luke 23. 36
From 'Thursday Before Easter'

AND the soldiers also mocked him, coming to him, and offering him vinegar, and saying, If thou be the King of the Jews, save thyself ... And one of the malefactors, which were hanged, railed on him, saying, If thou be Christ, save thyself and us. But the other answering rebuked him, saying, Dost not thou fear God, seeing thou art in the same condemnation? And we indeed justly; for we receive the due reward of our deeds; but this man hath done nothing amiss. And he said unto Jesus, Lord, remember me when thou comest into thy kingdom. And Jesus said unto him, Verily I say unto thee, To-day shalt thou be with me in paradise.

LUKE'S ACCOUNT OF
CHRIST'S PASSION (12)

Father, into thy hands I commend my spirit. St. Luke 23. 46

The Collect
From 'The Sunday Next Before Easter'

ALMIGHTY and everlasting God, who, of thy tender love towards mankind, hast sent thy Son our Saviour Jesus Christ, to take upon him our flesh, and to suffer death upon the cross, that all mankind should follow the example of his great humility: Mercifully grant, that we may both follow the example of his patience, and also be made partakers of his resurrection: through the same Jesus Christ our Lord. Amen.

The Gospel. St. Luke 23. 44
From 'Thursday Before Easter'

AND it was about the sixth hour and there was a darkness over all the earth until the ninth hour. And the sun was darkened, and the vail of the temple was rent in the midst. And when Jesus had cried with a loud voice, he said, Father, into thy hands I commend my spirit: and having said thus, he gave up the ghost. Now when the centurion saw what was done, he glorified God, saying, Certainly this was a righteous man. And all the people that came together to that sight, beholding the things that were done, smote their breasts and returned. And all his acquaintance, and the women that followed him from Galilee, stood afar off, beholding these things.

THE MESSIAH IN THE PSALMS (14)
Zeal for God's house will consume him

For the zeal of thine house hath even eaten me : and the rebukes of them that rebuked thee are fallen upon me. Psalm 69. 9

Psalm 69. *Salvum me fac*

SAVE me, O God : for the waters are come in, even unto my soul.

2. I stick fast in the deep mire, where no ground is : I am come into deep waters, so that the floods run over me.

3. I am weary of crying; my throat is dry : my sight faileth me for waiting so long upon my God.

4. They that hate me without a cause are more than the hairs of my head : they that are mine enemies, and would destroy me guiltless, are mighty.

5. I paid them the things that I never took : God, thou knowest my simpleness, and my faults are not hid from thee.

6. Let not them that trust in thee, O Lord God of hosts, be ashamed for my cause : let not those that seek thee be confounded through me, O Lord God of Israel.

7. And why? for thy sake have I suffered reproof : shame hath covered my face.

8. I am become a stranger unto my brethren : even an alien unto my mother's children.

9. For the zeal of thine house hath even eaten me : and the rebukes of them that rebuked thee are fallen upon me.

PRAYERS FROM
'HOLY COMMUNION' (6)

Christ Jesus came into the world to save sinners. 1 Timothy 1. 15

L IFT up your hearts.
Answer. We lift them up unto the Lord.
   Priest. Let us give thanks unto our Lord God.
   Answer. It is meet and right so to do.
   Priest. It is very meet, right, and our bounden duty, that we should at all times, and in all places, give thanks unto thee, O Lord, Holy Father, Almighty, Everlasting God.

Therefore with Angels and Archangels, and with all the company of heaven, we laud and magnify thy glorious Name; evermore praising thee, and saying: Holy, holy, holy, Lord God of hosts, heaven and earth are full of thy glory: Glory be to thee, O Lord most High. Amen.

G LORY be to God on high, and in earth peace, good will towards men. We praise thee, we bless thee, we worship thee, we glorify thee, we give thanks to thee for thy great glory, O Lord God, heavenly King, God the Father Almighty.

O Lord, the only, begotten Son, Jesus Christ; O Lord God, Lamb of God, Son of the Father, that takest away the sins of the world, have mercy upon us. Thou that takest away the sins of the world, have mercy upon us. Thou that takest away the sins of the world, receive our prayer. Thou that sittest at the right hand of God the Father, have mercy upon us.

REMEMBRANCE DAY

Behold, I shew you a mystery : We shall not all sleep, but we shall all be changed, in a moment, in the twinkling of an eye, at the last trump.

1 Corinthians 15. 51–52

1 Corinthians 15. 40
From 'The Burial of the Dead'

THERE are also celestial bodies, and bodies terrestrial; but the glory of the celestial is one, and the glory of the terrestrial is another. There is one glory of the sun, and another glory of the moon, and another glory of the stars; for one star differeth from another star in glory. So also is the resurrection of the dead. It is sown in corruption; it is raised in incorruption; it is sown in dishonour; it is raised in glory: it is sown in weakness; it is raised in power: it is sown a natural body; it is raised a spiritual body. There is a natural body, and there is a spiritual body. And so it is written, The first man Adam was made a living soul; the last Adam was made a quickening spirit. Howbeit, that was not first which is spiritual, but that which is natural; and afterward that which is spiritual. The first man is of the earth, earthy: the second man is the Lord from heaven. As is the earthy, such are they that are earthy: and as is the heavenly, such are they also that are heavenly. And as we have borne the image of the earthy, we shall also bear the image of the heavenly. Now this I say, brethren, that flesh and blood cannot inherit the kingdom of God; neither doth corruption inherit incorruption.

GOD'S ARMOUR

The Lord is my strength and my shield. Psalm 28. 8

The Collect
From 'The Twenty-First Sunday After Trinity'

GRANT, we beseech thee, merciful Lord, to thy faithful people pardon and peace; that they may be cleansed from all their sins, and serve thee with a quiet mind; through Jesus Christ our Lord. Amen.

The Epistle. *Ephesians 6. 10*
From 'The Twenty-First Sunday After Trinity'

MY brethren, be strong in the Lord, and in the power of his might. Put on the whole armour of God, that ye may be able to stand against the wiles of the devil. For we wrestle not against flesh and blood, but against principalities, against powers, against the rulers of the darkness of this world, against spiritual wickedness in high places. Wherefore take unto you the whole armour of God, that ye may be able to withstand in the evil day, and, having done all, to stand. Stand therefore, having your loins girt about with truth and having on the breast–plate of righteousness; and your feet shod with the preparation of the Gospel of peace; above all, taking the shield of faith, wherewith ye shall be able to quench all the fiery darts of the wicked: and take the helmet of salvation, and the sword of the Spirit, which is the word of God.

'THY SON LIVETH'

Blessed is he that considereth the poor and needy : the Lord shall deliver him in the time of trouble. Psalm 41. 1

The Gospel. *St. John 4. 46*
From 'The Twenty-First Sunday After Trinity'

THERE was a certain nobleman, whose son was sick at Capernaum. When he heard that Jesus was come out of Judaea into Galilee, he went unto him, and besought him that he would come down and heal his son; for he was at the point of death. Then said Jesus unto him, Except ye see signs and wonders, ye will not believe. The nobleman saith unto him, Sir, come down ere my child die. Jesus saith unto him, Go thy way, thy son liveth. And the man believed the word that Jesus had spoken unto him, and he went his way. And as he was now going down, his servants met him, and told him, saying, Thy son liveth. Then inquired he of them the hour when he began to amend: and they said unto him, Yesterday at the seventh hour the fever left him. So the father knew that it was at the same hour, in the which Jesus said unto him, Thy son liveth; and himself believed, and his whole house. This is again the second miracle that Jesus did, when he was come out of Judaea into Galilee.

OPPRESSED BY SIN

Against thee only have I sinned, and done this evil in thy sight. Psalm 51. 4

From 'A Commination'

LORD, have mercy upon us.
Christ, have mercy upon us.
Lord, have mercy upon us.

OUR Father which art in heaven, Hallowed be thy Name, Thy kingdom come, Thy will be done, in earth as it is in heaven. Give us this day our daily bread, And forgive us our trespasses, As we forgive them that trespass against us, And lead us not into temptation; But deliver us from evil. Amen.

Minister. O Lord, save thy servants;
Answer. That put their trust in thee.
Minister. Send unto them help from above.
Answer. And evermore mightily defend them.
Minister. Help us, O God our Saviour.
Answer. And for the glory of thy Name deliver us; be merciful unto us sinners, for thy Name's sake.
Minister. O Lord, hear our prayer.
Answer. And let our cry come unto thee.

UNITY

That they all may be one; as thou, Father, art in me, and I in thee, that they also may be one in us: that the world may believe that thou hast sent me.

St. John 17. 21

A Prayer for Unity
From 'The Accession Service'

O GOD the Father of our Lord Jesus Christ, our only Saviour, the Prince of Peace: Give us grace seriously to lay to heart the great dangers we are in by our unhappy divisions. Take away all hatred and prejudice, and whatsoever else may hinder us from godly union and concord: that, as there is but one Body, and one Spirit, and one hope of our calling, one Lord, one faith, one baptism, one God and Father of us all; so we may henceforth be all of one heart, and of one soul, united in one holy bond of truth and peace, of faith and charity, and may with one mind and one mouth glorify thee; through Jesus Christ our Lord. Amen

Meditation

And the glory which thou gavest me I have given them; that they may be one, even as we are one: I in them, and thou in me, that they may be made perfect in one; and that the world may know that thou hast sent me. St. John 17. 21–22

LIVING IN GOD'S PRESENCE

Lord, who shall dwell in thy tabernacle : or who shall rest upon thy holy hill?

Psalm 15. 1

From 'Evening Prayer'

O LORD, shew thy mercy upon us.
Answer. And grant us thy salvation.
Priest. O Lord, save the Queen.
Answer. And mercifully hear us when we call upon thee.
Priest. Endue thy Ministers with righteousness.
Answer. And make thy chosen people joyful.
Priest. O Lord, save thy people.
Answer. And bless thine inheritance.
Priest. Give peace in our time, O Lord.

The Second Collect

From 'Evening Prayer'

O GOD, from whom all holy desires, all good counsels, and all just works do proceed: Give unto thy servants that peace which the world cannot give; that both our hearts may be set to obey thy commandments, and also that by thee we being defended from the fear of our enemies may pass our time in rest and quietness; through the merits of Jesus Christ our Saviour. Amen.

PSALMS OF PRAISE AND THANKSGIVING (39)

His name alone is exalted

He shall exalt the horn of his people : all his saints shall praise him : even the children of Israel, even the people that serveth him. Psalm 148. 13

Psalm 148. *Laudate Dominum*

O PRAISE the Lord of heaven : praise him in the height.

2. Praise him, all ye angels of his : praise him, all his host.

3. Praise him, sun and moon : praise him, all ye stars and light.

4. Praise him, all ye heavens : and ye waters that are above the heavens.

5. Let them praise the Name of the Lord : for he spake the word, and they were made; he commanded, and they were created.

6. He hath made them fast for ever and ever : he hath given them a law which shall not be broken.

7. Praise the Lord upon the earth : ye dragons, and all deeps;

8. Fire and hail, snow and vapours : wind and storm, fulfilling his word;

9. Mountains and all hills : fruitful trees and all cedars;

10. Beasts and all cattle : worms and feathered fowls ;

11. Kings of the earth and all people : princes and all judges of the world;

12. Young men and maidens, old men and children, praise the Name of the Lord : for his Name only is excellent, and his praise above heaven and earth.

13. He shall exalt the horn of his people : all his saints shall praise him : even the children of Israel, even the people that serveth him.

THE MESSIAH IN THE PSALMS (15)

He will be given vinegar and gall to drink

They gave me gall to eat : and when I was thirsty they gave me vinegar to drink.
                                                                Psalm 69. 22

Psalm 69. *Salvum me fac*

HEAR me, O Lord, for thy loving-indness is comfortable : turn thee unto me according to the multitude of thy mercies.

18. And hide not thy face from thy servant, for I am in trouble : O haste thee, and hear me.

19. Draw nigh unto my soul, and save it : O deliver me, because of mine enemies.

20. Thou hast known my reproof, my shame, and my dishonour : mine adversaries are all in thy sight.

21. Thy rebuke hath broken my heart; I am full of heaviness : I looked for some to have pity on me, but there was no man, neither found I any to comfort me.

22. They gave me gall to eat : and when I was thirsty they gave me vinegar to drink…

30. As for me, when I am poor and in heaviness : thy help, O God, shall lift me up.

31. I will praise the Name of God with a song : and magnify it with thanksgiving …

33. The humble shall consider this, and be glad : seek ye after God, and your soul shall live.

PRAYING FOR OTHERS

For this cause we also, since the day we heard it, do not cease to pray for you, and to desire that ye might be filled with the knowledge of his will in all wisdom and spiritual understanding. Colossians 1. 9

The Epistle. *Philippians 1. 3*
From 'The Twenty-Second Sunday After Trinity'

ITHANK my God upon every remembrance of you, always in every prayer of mine for you all making request with joy, for your fellowship in the Gospel from the first day until now; being confident of this very thing, that he who hath begun a good work in you will perform it until the day of Jesus Christ; even as it is meet for me to think this of you all, because I have you in my heart, inasmuch as both in my bonds, and in the defence and confirmation of the Gospel, ye all are partakers of my grace. For God is my record, how greatly I long after you all in the bowels of Jesus Christ. And this I pray, that your love may abound yet more and more in knowledge and in all judgement: that ye may approve things that are excellent; that ye may be sincere, and without offence, till the day of Christ: being filled with the fruits of righteousness, which are by Jesus Christ unto the glory and praise of God.

Meditation

We give thanks to God always for you all, making mention of you in our prayers.

1 Thessalonians 1. 2

TILL SEVEN TIMES?

...Forgive men their trespasses ... St. Matthew 6. 14

The Gospel. *St. Matthew 18. 21*
From 'The Twenty-Second Sunday After Trinity'

PETER said unto Jesus, Lord, how oft shall my brother sin against me, and I forgive him? till seven times? Jesus saith unto him, I say not unto thee, until seven times; but, until seventy times seven. Therefore is the kingdom of heaven likened unto a certain king, which would take account of his servants. And when he had begun to reckon, one was brought unto him, which owed him ten thousand talents. But forasmuch as he had not to pay, his Lord commanded him to be sold, and his wife, and children, and all that he had, and payment to be made. The servant therefore fell down and worshipped him, saying, Lord, have patience with me, and I will pay thee all. Then the Lord of that servant was moved with compassion, and loosed him, and forgave him the debt. But the same servant went out, and found one of his fellow-servants, which owed him an hundred pence; and he laid hands on him, and took him by the throat, saying, Pay me that thou owest. And his fellow-servant fell down at his feet, and besought him, saying, Have patience with me, and I will pay thee all. And he would not; but went and cast him into prison, till he should pay the debt ... Then his Lord, after that he had called him, said unto him, O thou wicked servant, I forgave thee all that debt, because thou desiredst me: shouldest not thou also have had compassion on thy fellow-servant, even as I had pity on thee?

PRAYER

In the evening, and morning, and at noon-day will I pray, and that instantly : and he shall hear my voice. Psalm 55. 18

Psalm 55. *Exaudi, Deus*

A S for me, I will call upon God : and the Lord shall save me.
18. In the evening, and morning, and at noon-day will I pray, and that instantly : and he shall hear my voice.
19. It is he that hath delivered my soul in peace from the battle that was against me : for there were many with me.
20. Yea, even God, that endureth for ever, shall hear me, and bring them down : for they will not turn, nor fear God.
21. He laid his hands upon such as be at peace with him : and he brake his covenant.

The Lord's Prayer
From 'Morning Prayer'

O UR Father which art in heaven, Hallowed be thy Name. Thy king-dom come, Thy will be done, in earth as it is in heaven. Give us this day our daily bread, And forgive us our trespasses, As we forgive them that trespass against us, And lead us not into temptation, But deliver us from evil. Amen.

PSALMS OF PRAISE AND THANKSGIVING (40)

God's pleasure in his people

For the Lord hath pleasure in his people : and helpeth the meek-hearted.

Psalm 149. 4

Psalm 149. *Cantate Domino*

O SING unto the Lord a new song : let the congregation of saints praise him.

2. Let Israel rejoice in him that made him : and let the children of Sion be joyful in their King.

3. Let them praise his Name in the dance : let them sing praises unto him with tabret and harp.

4. For the Lord hath pleasure in his people : and helpeth the meek-hearted.

5. Let the saints be joyful with glory : let them rejoice in their beds.

6. Let the praises of God be in their mouth : and a two-edged sword in their hands;

7. To be avenged of the heathen : and to rebuke the people;

8. To bind their kings in chains : and their nobles with links of iron;

9. That they may be avenged of them, as it is written : Such honour have all his saints.

Meditation

Let them be glad and rejoice, that favour my righteous dealing : yea, let them say alway, Blessed be the Lord, who hath pleasure in the prosperity of his servant.

Psalm 35. 27

PRAYERS FROM
'HOLY COMMUNION'

Direct, sanctify, and govern, both our hearts and bodies, in the ways of thy laws.
From 'Holy Communion'

Collects from 'Holy Communion'

ASSIST us mercifully, O Lord, in these our supplications and prayers, and dispose the way of thy servants towards the attainment of everlasting salvation; that, among all the changes and chances of this mortal life, they may ever be defended by thy most gracious and ready help; through Jesus Christ our Lord. Amen.

O ALMIGHTY Lord, and everlasting God, vouchsafe, we beseech thee, to direct, sanctify, and govern, both our hearts and bodies, in the ways of thy laws, and in the works of thy commandments; that through thy most mighty protection, both here and ever, we may be preserved in body and soul; through our Lord and Saviour Jesus Christ. Amen.

GRANT, we beseech thee, Almighty God, that the words, which we have heard this day with our outward ears, may through thy grace be so grafted inwardly in our hearts, that they may bring forth in us the fruit of good living, to the honour and praise of thy Name; through Jesus Christ our Lord. Amen.

THE MESSIAH IN THE PSALMS (16)

He will pray for his enemies

Thus have they rewarded me evil for good : and hatred for my good will.

Psalm 109. 4

Psalm 109. *Deus, laudem*

HOLD not thy tongue, O God of my praise : for the mouth of the ungodly, yea, the mouth of the deceitful is opened upon me.

2. And they have spoken against me with false tongues : they compassed me about also with words of hatred, and fought against me without a cause.

3. For the love that I had unto them, lo, they take now my contrary part : but I give myself unto prayer.

4. Thus have they rewarded me evil for good : and hatred for my good will.

5. Set thou an ungodly man to be ruler over him : and let Satan stand at his right hand.

6. When sentence is given upon him, let him be condemned : and let his prayer be turned into sin.

Meditation

And there were also two other, malefactors, led with him to be put to death. And when they were come to the place which is called Calvary, there they crucified him; and the malefactors, one on the right hand, and the other on the left. Then said Jesus, Father, forgive them; for they know not what they do. St. Luke 23. 32–34

A BABY'S SAFE ARRIVAL

Except the Lord build the house : their labour is but lost that build it.

Psalm 127. 1

From 'The Churching of Women'

O ALMIGHTY God, we give thee humble thanks for that thou hast vouchsafed to deliver this woman thy servant from the great pain and peril of child-birth: Grant, we beseech thee, most merciful Father, that she through thy help may both faithfully live and walk according to thy will, in this life present; and also may be partaker of everlasting glory in the life to come; through Jesus Christ our Lord. Amen.

Psalm 127. *Nisi Dominus*

E XCEPT the Lord build the house : their labour is but lost that build it.

2. Except the Lord keep the city : the watchman waketh but in vain.

3. It is but lost labour that ye haste to rise up early, and so late take rest, and eat the bread of carefulness : for so he giveth his beloved sleep.

4. Lo, children and the fruit of the womb : are an heritage and gift that cometh of the Lord.

5. Like as the arrows in the hand of the giant : even so are the young children.

6. Happy is the man that hath his quiver full of them : they shall not be ashamed when they speak with their enemies in the gate.

A TRANSFORMED BODY

Who shall change our vile body, that it may be fashioned like unto his glorious body. Philippians 3. 21

The Collect
From 'The Twenty-Third Sunday After Trinity'

O GOD, our refuge and strength, who art the author of all godliness: Be ready, we beseech thee, to hear the devout prayers of thy Church; and grant that those things which we ask faithfully we may obtain effectually; through Jesus Christ our Lord. Amen.

The Epistle. *Philippians 3. 17*
From 'The Twenty-Third Sunday After Trinity'

BRETHREN, be followers together of me, and mark them which walk so as ye have us for an ensample. (For many walk, of whom I have told you often, and now tell you even weeping, that they are the enemies of the cross of Christ; whose end is destruction, whose god is their belly, and whose glory is in their shame, who mind earthly things.) For our conversation is in heaven; from whence also we look for the Saviour, the Lord Jesus Christ; who shall change our vile body, that it may be fashioned like unto his glorious body, according to the working whereby he is able even to subdue all things unto himself.

WICKED MOTIVES PERCEIVED

Render therefore unto Caesar the things which are Caesar's; and unto God the things that are God's. St. Matthew 22. 21

The Gospel. *St. Matthew 22. 15*
From 'The Twenty-Third Sunday After Trinity'

THEN went the Pharisees, and took counsel how they might entangle him in his talk. And they sent out unto him their disciples, with the Herodians, saying, Master, we know that thou art true, and teachest the way of God in truth, neither carest thou for any man : for thou regardest not the person of men. Tell us therefore, what thinkest thou? Is it lawful to give tribute unto Caesar, or not? But Jesus perceived their wickedness, and said, Why tempt ye me, ye hypocrites? shew me the tribute-money. And they brought unto him a penny. And he saith unto them, Whose is this image and superscription? They say unto him, Caesar's. Then saith he unto them, Render therefore unto Caesar the things which are Caesar's; and unto God the things that are God's. When they had heard these words, they marvelled, and left him, and went their way.

Meditation
The Lord shall make good his loving-kindness toward me : yea, thy mercy, O Lord, endureth for ever; despise not then the works of thine own hands. Psalm 138. 8

THE MESSIAH IN THE PSALMS (17)

His betrayer's office will be fulfilled by another

Let his days be few : and let another take his office. Psalm 109. 7

Psalm 109. *Deus, laudem*

L ET his days be few : and let another take his office.
8. Let his children be fatherless : and his wife a widow.
9. Let his children be vagabonds, and beg their bread : let them seek it also out of desolate places.
10. Let the extortioner consume all that he hath : and let the stranger spoil his labour.
11. Let there be no man to pity him : nor to have compassion upon his fatherless children.
12. Let his posterity be destroyed : and in the next generation let his name be clean put out.
13. Let the wickedness of his fathers be had in remembrance in the sight of the Lord : and let not the sin of his mother be done away.
14. Let them always be before the Lord : that he may root out the memorial of them from off the earth;

Meditation

For it is written in the book of Psalms, Let his habitation be desolate, and let no man dwell therein; and, His bishoprick let another take. Acts 1. 20

INSTRUCTION FROM GOD'S WORD (11)

Seven times a day do I praise thee : because of thy righteous judgements.

Psalm 119. 164

The Collect
From 'The Second Sunday in Advent'

BLESSED Lord, who hast caused all holy Scriptures to be written for our learning : Grant that we may in such wise hear them, read, mark, learn, and inwardly digest them, that by patience and comfort of thy holy Word, we may embrace and ever hold fast the blessed hope of everlasting life, which thou hast given us in our Saviour Jesus Christ. Amen.

Psalm 119. *Principes persecuti sunt*

PRINCES have persecuted me without a cause : but my heart standeth in awe of thy word.

162. I am as glad of thy word : as one that findeth great spoils.

163. As for lies, I hate and abhor them : but thy law do I love.

164. Seven times a day do I praise thee : because of thy righteous judgements.

165. Great is the peace that they have who love thy law : and they are not offended at it.

166. Lord, I have looked for thy saving health : and done after thy commandments.

167. My soul hath kept thy testimonies : and loved them exceedingly.

ISRAEL'S UNBELIEF

How beautiful are the feet of them that preach the Gospel of peace, and bring glad tidings of good things! Romans 10. 15

The Epistle. *Romans 10. 9*
From 'Saint Andrew's Day'

IF thou shalt confess with thy mouth the Lord Jesus, and shalt believe in thine heart that God hath raised him from the dead, thou shalt be saved. For with the heart man believeth unto righteousness, and with the mouth confession is made unto salvation. For the Scripture saith, Whosoever believeth on him shall not be ashamed. For there is no difference between the Jew and the Greek: for the same Lord over all is rich unto all that call upon him. For whosoever shall call upon the name of the Lord shall be saved. How then shall they call on him, in whom they have not believed? And how shall they believe in him, of whom they have not heard? And how shall they hear without a preacher? And how shall they preach, except they be sent? As it is written, How beautiful are the feet of them that preach the Gospel of peace, and bring glad tidings of good things! But they have not all obeyed the Gospel. For Esaias saith, Lord, who hath believed our report? So then faith cometh by hearing, and hearing by the word of God.

CALLED BY GOD

Follow me; and I will make you fishers of men. And they straightway left their nets, and followed him. St. Matthew 4. 19–20

The Collect
From 'Saint Andrew's Day'

ALMIGHTY God, who didst give such grace unto thy holy Apostle Saint Andrew, that he readily obeyed the calling of thy Son Jesus Christ, and followed him without delay: Grant unto us all, that we, being called by thy holy word, may forthwith give up ourselves obediently to fulfil thy holy commandments; through the same Jesus Christ our Lord. Amen.

The Gospel. *St. Matthew 4. 18*
From 'Saint Andrew's Day'

JESUS, walking by the sea of Galilee, saw two brethren, Simon called Peter, and Andrew his brother, casting a net into the sea, (for they were fishers;) and he saith unto them, Follow me and I will make you fishers of men. And they straightway left their nets, and followed him. And going on from thence he saw other two brethren, James the son of Zebedee, and John his brother, in a ship with Zebedee their father, mending their nets; and he called them. And they immediately left the ship and their father, and followed him.

THE MESSIAH IN THE PSALMS (18)
His enemies will be made subject to him

The Lord said unto my Lord : Sit thou on my right hand, until I make thine enemies thy footstool. Psalm 110. 1

Psalm 110. *Dixit Dominus*

THE Lord said unto my Lord : Sit thou on my right hand, until I make thine enemies thy footstool.

2. The Lord shall send the rod of thy power out of Sion : be thou ruler, even in the midst among thine enemies.

3. In the day of thy power shall the people offer thee free-will offerings with an holy worship : the dew of thy birth is as the womb of the morning.

4. The Lord sware, and will not repent : Thou art a priest for ever after the order of Melchisedech.

5. The Lord upon thy right hand : shall wound even kings in the day of his wrath.

Meditation
While the Pharisees were gathered together, Jesus asked them, saying, What think ye of Christ? whose son is he? They say unto him, The son of David. He saith unto them, How then doth David in spirit call him Lord, saying, The LORD said unto my Lord, Sit thou on my right hand, till I make thine enemies thy foot-stool? If David then call him Lord, how is he his son? St. Matthew 22. 41–45

THE ARMOUR OF LIGHT

The night is far spent, the day is at hand; let us therefore cast off the works of dark-ness, and let us put on the armour of light. Let us walk honestly as in the day.

Romans 13. 12

The Collect
From 'The First Sunday in Advent'

A LMIGHTY God, give us grace that we may cast away the works of darkness, and put upon us the armour of light, now in the time of this mortal life, in which thy Son Jesus Christ came to visit us in great humility; that in the last day, when he shall come again in his glorious Majesty to judge both the quick and the dead, we may rise to the life immortal; through him who liveth and reigneth with thee and the Holy Ghost, now and for ever. Amen.

The Epistle. *Romans 13. 8*
From 'The First Sunday in Advent'

O WE no man any thing, but to love one another: for he that loveth another hath fulfilled the law. For this, Thou shalt not commit adultery, Thou shalt not kill, Thou shalt not steal, Thou shalt not bear false witness, Thou shalt not covet; and if there be any other commandment, it is briefly comprehended in this saying, namely, Thou shalt love thy neighbour as thyself. Love worketh no ill to his neighbour; therefore love is the fulfilling of the law.

ENTERING JERUSALEM

Tell ye the daughter of Sion, Behold, thy King cometh unto thee, meek, and sitting upon an ass, and a colt the foal of an ass. St. Matthew 21. 5

The Gospel. *St. Matthew 21. 1*
From 'The First Sunday of Advent'

WHEN they drew nigh unto Jerusalem, and were come to Bethphage, unto the mount of Olives, then sent Jesus two disciples, saying unto them, Go into the village over against you, and straightway ye shall find an ass tied, and a colt with her: loose them, and bring them unto me. And if any man say ought unto you, ye shall say, The Lord hath need of them; and straightway he will send them. All this was done, that it might be fulfilled which was spoken by the prophet, saying, Tell ye the daughter of Sion, Behold, thy King cometh unto thee, meek, and sitting upon an ass, and a colt the foal of an ass. And the disciples went, and did as Jesus commanded them; and brought the ass, and the colt, and put on them their clothes, and they set him thereon. And a very great multitude spread their garments in the way; others cut down branches from the trees, and strawed them in the way. And the multitudes that went before, and that followed, cried, saying, Hosanna to the son of David; Blessed is he that cometh in the Name of the Lord; Hosanna in the Highest. And when he was come into Jerusalem, all the city was moved, saying, Who is this? And the multitude said, This is Jesus the prophet of Nazareth of Galilee.

THE MESSIAH IN THE PSALMS (19)

He will be the chief cornerstone

The same stone which the builders refused : is become the head-stone in the corner.
                                                                    Psalm 118. 22

Psalm 118. *Confitemini Domino*

O GIVE thanks unto the Lord, for he is gracious : because his mercy endureth for ever.

2. Let Israel now confess that he is gracious : and that his mercy endureth for ever.

3. Let the house of Aaron now confess : that his mercy endureth for ever.

4. Yea, let them now that fear the Lord confess : that his mercy endureth for ever.

5. I called upon the Lord in trouble : and the Lord heard me at large.

6. The Lord is on my side : I will not fear what man doeth unto me.

7. The Lord taketh my part with them that help me : therefore shall I see my desire upon mine enemies.

8. It is better to trust in the Lord : than to put any confidence in man.

9. It is better to trust in the Lord : than to put any confidence in princes.

Meditation

Jesus saith unto them, Did ye never read in the scriptures, The stone which the builders rejected, the same is become the head of the corner: this is the Lord's doing, and it is marvellous in our eyes? St. Matthew 21. 42

GOVERNMENTS

I exhort therefore, that, first of all, supplications, prayers, intercessions, and giving of thanks, be made for all men; for kings ... 1 Timothy 2. 1–2

The Collect
From the Communion in 'The Accession Service'

O GOD, who providest for thy people by thy power, and rulest over them in love: Vouchsafe so to bless thy Servant our Queen, that under her this nation may be wisely governed, and thy Church may serve thee in all godly quietness; and grant that she being devoted to thee with her whole heart, and persevering in good works unto the end, may, by thy guidance, come to thine everlasting kingdom; through Jesus Christ thy Son our Lord, who liveth and reigneth with thee and the Holy Ghost, ever one God, world without end. Amen.

The Gospel. *St. Matthew 22. 16*
From the Communion in 'The Accession Service'

A ND they sent out unto him their disciples ... Is it lawful to give tribute unto Ceasar, or not? But Jesus perceived their wickedness, and said, Why tempt ye me, ye hypocrites? shew me the tribute-money ... Then saith he unto them, Render therefore unto Caesar the things which are Caesar's; and unto God the things that are God's. When they had heard these words, they marvelled, and left him, and went their way.

'PRAISE THE LORD'

Let every thing that hath breath : praise the Lord. Psalm 150. 6

Psalm 149. *Cantate Domino*

O SING unto the Lord a new song : let the congregation of saints praise him.

2. Let Israel rejoice in him that made him : and let the children of Sion be joyful in their King.

3. Let them praise his Name in the dance : let them sing praises unto him with tabret and harp.

4. For the Lord hath pleasure in his people : and helpeth the meek-hearted.

5. Let the saints be joyful with glory : let them rejoice in their beds.

6. Let the praises of God be in their mouth : and a two-edged sword in their hands;

7. To be avenged of the heathen : and to rebuke the people;

8. To bind their kings in chains : and their nobles with links of iron.

9. That they may be avenged of them, as it is written : Such honour have all his saints.

Meditation
O sing unto the Lord a new song : let the congregation of saints praise him.

Psalm 149. 1

THE MESSIAH IN THE PSALMS (20)

He will come in the name of the Lord

Blessed be he that cometh in the Name of the Lord : we have wished you good luck, ye that are of the house of the Lord. Psalm 118. 26

Psalm 118. *Confitemini Domino*

THE right hand of the Lord hath the pre-eminence : the right hand of the Lord bringeth mighty things to pass.

17. I shall not die, but live : and declare the works of the Lord.

18. The Lord hath chastened and corrected me : but he hath not given me over unto death.

19. Open me the gates of righteousness : that I may go into them, and give thanks unto the Lord.

20. This is the gate of the Lord : the righteous shall enter into it.

21. I will thank thee, for thou hast heard me : and art become my salvation.

22. The same stone which the builders refused : is become the head-stone in the comer.

23. This is the Lord's doing : and it is marvellous in our eyes.

24. This is the day which the Lord hath made : we will rejoice and be glad in it.

25. Help me now, O Lord : O Lord, send us now prosperity.

26. Blessed be he that cometh in the Name of the Lord : we have wished you good luck, ye that are of the house of the Lord.

TE DEUM LAUDAMUS

Heaven and earth are full of the Majesty : of thy glory.

From 'Te Deum Laudamus'

Te Deum Laudamus
From 'Morning Prayer'

WE praise thee, O God : we acknowledge thee to be the Lord.
　　All the earth doth worship thee : the Father everlasting.
　To thee all Angels cry aloud : the heavens, and all the powers therein.
　To thee Cherubin and Seraphin : continually do cry,
　Holy, Holy, Holy : Lord God of Sabaoth;
　Heaven and earth are full of the Majesty : of thy glory.
　The glorious company of the Apostles : praise thee.
　The goodly fellowship of the Prophets : praise thee.
　The noble army of Martyrs : praise thee.
　The holy Church throughout all the world : doth acknowledge thee;
　The Father : of an infinite Majesty;
　Thine honourable, true : and only Son;
　Also the Holy Ghost : the Comforter.
　Thou art the King of Glory : O Christ.
　Thou art the everlasting Son : of the Father.
　When thou tookest upon thee to deliver man : thou didst not abhor the
Virgin's womb.

'READ, MARK, LEARN, AND INWARDLY DIGEST'

Thy words have I hid within my heart : that I should not sin against thee.

Psalm 119. 11

The Epistle. *Romans 15. 4*
From 'The Second Sunday in Advent'

WHATSOEVER things were written aforetime were written for our learning that we through patience and comfort of the Scriptures might have hope. Now the God of patience and consolation grant you to be like-minded one towards another according to Christ Jesus: that ye may with one mind and one mouth glorify God, even the Father of our Lord Jesus Christ. Wherefore receive ye one another, as Christ also received us, to the glory of God. Now I say, that Jesus Christ was a minister of the circumcision for the truth of God, to confirm the promises made unto the fathers; and that the Gentiles might glorify God for his mercy; as it is written, For this cause I will confess to thee among the Gentiles, and sing unto thy Name. And again he saith, Rejoice, ye Gentiles, with his people. And again, Praise the Lord, all ye Gentiles, and laud him, all ye people. And again, Esaias saith, There shall be a root of Jesse, and he that shall rise to reign over the Gentiles, in him shall the Gentiles trust. Now the God of hope fill you with all joy and peace in believing, that ye may abound in hope, through the power of the Holy Ghost.

SIGNS

Verily I say unto you, This generation shall not pass away, till all be fulfilled.
St. Luke 21. 32

The Gospel. *St. Luke 21. 25*
From 'The Second Sunday in Advent'

AND there shall be signs in the sun, and in the moon, and in the stars; and upon the earth distress of nations, with perplexity; the sea and the waves roaring; men's hearts failing them for fear, and for looking after those things which are coming on the earth: for the powers of heaven shall be shaken. And then shall they see the Son of Man coming in a cloud with power and great glory. And when these things begin to come to pass, then look up, and lift up your heads; for your redemption draweth nigh. And he spake to them a parable; Behold the fig-tree, and all the trees; when they now shoot forth, ye see and know of your own selves that summer is now nigh at hand. So likewise ye, when ye see these things come to pass, know ye that the kingdom of God is nigh at hand. Verily I say unto you, This generation shall not pass away, till all be fulfilled: heaven and earth shall pass away; but my words shall not pass away.

Meditation
It is not for you to know the times or the seasons, which the Father hath put in his own power. Acts 1. 7

THE POOR IN SPIRIT
AND THEY THAT MOURN

Jesus, seeing the multitudes, went up into a mountain; and when he was set, his disciples came unto him. And he opened his mouth, and taught them, saying, Blessed are the poor in spirit: for theirs is the kingdom of heaven. Blessed are they that mourn: for they shall be comforted. St. Matthew 5. 1–4

Psalm 51. *Miserere mei, Deus*

HAVE mercy upon me, O God, after thy great goodness : according to the multitude of thy mercies do away mine offences.

2. Wash me throughly from my wickedness : and cleanse me from my sin.

3. For I acknowledge my faults : and my sin is ever before me.

4. Against thee only have I sinned, and done this evil in thy sight : that thou mightest be justified in thy saying, and clear when thou art judged.

5. Behold, I was shapen in wickedness : and in sin hath my mother conceived me.

6. But lo, thou requirest truth in the inward parts : and shalt make me to understand wisdom secretly.

7. Thou shalt purge me with hyssop, and I shall be clean : thou shalt wash me, and I shall be whiter than snow.

8. Thou shalt make me hear of joy and gladness : that the bones which thou hast broken may rejoice.

9. Turn thy face from my sins : and put out all my misdeeds.

10. Make me a clean heart, O God : and renew a right spirit within me.

THE MEEK AND THOSE WHO HUNGER AND THIRST AFTER RIGHTEOUSNESS

Blessed are the meek: for they shall inherit the earth. Blessed are they which do hunger and thirst after righteousness: for they shall be filled. St. Matthew 5. 5–6

Psalm 19. *Caeli enarrant*

THE heavens declare the glory of God : and the firmament sheweth his handy-work.

2. One day telleth another : and one night certifieth another.

3. There is neither speech nor language : but their voices are heard among them.

4. Their sound is gone out into all lands : and their words into the ends of the world.

5. In them hath he set a tabernacle for the sun : which cometh forth as a bridegroom out of his chamber, and rejoiceth as a giant to run his course.

6. It goeth forth from the uttermost part of the heaven, and runneth about unto the end of it again : and there is nothing hid from the heat thereof.

7. The law of the Lord is an undefiled law, converting the soul : the testimony of the Lord is sure, and giveth wisdom unto the simple.

8. The statutes of the Lord are right, and rejoice the heart : the commandment of the Lord is pure, and giveth light unto the eyes.

9. The fear of the Lord is clean, and endureth for ever : the judgements of the Lord are true, and righteous altogether.

THE MERCIFUL AND
THE PURE IN HEART

*Blessed are the merciful: for they shall obtain mercy. Blessed are the pure in heart :
for they shall see God.* St. Matthew 5. 7–8

Psalm 85. *Benedixisti, Domine*

LORD, thou art become gracious unto thy land : thou hast turned away
the captivity of Jacob.

2. Thou hast forgiven the offence of thy people : and covered all their sins.

3. Thou hast taken away all thy displeasure : and turned thyself from thy
wrathful indignation.

4. Turn us then, O God our Saviour : and let thine anger cease from us.

5. Wilt thou be displeased at us for ever : and wilt thou stretch out thy
wrath from one generation to another?

6. Wilt thou not turn again, and quicken us : that thy people may rejoice
in thee?

7. Shew us thy mercy, O Lord : and grant us thy salvation.

8. I will hearken what the Lord God will say concerning me : for he shall
speak peace unto his people, and to his saints, that they turn not again.

9. For his salvation is nigh them that fear him : that glory may dwell in our
land.

Meditation

*Help us, O God of our salvation, for the glory of thy Name : O deliver us, and be
merciful unto our sins, for thy Name's sake.* Psalm 79. 9

THE PEACEMAKERS

Blessed are the peace-makers : for they shall be called the children of God.
St. Matthew 5. 9

Psalm 85. *Benedixisti, Domine*

10. MERCY and truth are met together : righteousness and peace have kissed each other.

11. Truth shall flourish out of the earth : and righteousness hath looked down from heaven.

12. Yea, the Lord shall shew loving-kindness : and our land shall give her increase.

13. Righteousness shall go before him : and HE shall direct his going in the way.

Psalm 86. *Inclina, Domine*

BOW down thine ear, O Lord, and hear me : for I am poor, and in misery.

2. Preserve thou my soul, for I am holy : my God, save thy servant that putteth his trust in thee.

3. Be merciful unto me, O Lord : for I will call daily upon thee.

4. Comfort the soul of thy servant : for unto thee, O Lord, do I lift up my soul.

5. For thou, Lord, art good and gracious : and of great mercy unto all them that call upon thee.

THE PERSECUTED

Blessed are they which are persecuted for righteousness' sake: for theirs is the kingdom of heaven. Blessed are ye, when men shall revile you, and persecute you, and shall say all manner of evil against you falsely, for my sake. Rejoice, and be exceeding glad: for great is your reward in heaven: for so persecuted they the prophets which were before you. St. Matthew 5. 10–12

Psalm 56. *Miserere mei, Deus*

BE merciful unto me, O God, for man goeth about to devour me : he is daily fighting, and troubling me.

2. Mine enemies are daily in hand to swallow me up : for they be many that fight against me, O thou most Highest.

3. Nevertheless, though I am sometime afraid : yet put I my trust in thee.

4. I will praise God, because of his word : I have put my trust in God, and will not fear what flesh can do unto me.

5. They daily mistake my words : all that they imagine is to do me evil.

6. They hold all together, and keep themselves close : and mark my steps, when they lay wait for my soul.

7. Shall they escape for their wickedness : thou, O God, in thy displeasure shalt cast them down.

8. Thou tellest my flittings; put my tears into thy bottle : are not these things noted in thy book?

9. Whensoever I call upon thee, then shall mine enemies be put to flight : this I know; for God is on my side.

FAITHFUL MINISTERS

Moreover, it is required in stewards, that a man be found faithful.

1 Corinthians 4. 2

The Gospel. *St. Matthew 11. 2*
From 'The Third Sunday in Advent'

NOW when John had heard in the prison the works of Christ, he sent two of his disciples, and said unto him, Art thou he that should come, or do we look for another? Jesus answered and said unto them, Go and shew John again those things which ye do hear and see : the blind receive their sight, and the lame walk, the lepers are cleansed, and the deaf hear, the dead are raised up, and the poor have the Gospel preached to them. And blessed is he whosoever shall not be offended in me. And as they departed, Jesus began to say unto the multitudes concerning John, What went ye out into the wilderness to see? a reed shaken with the wind? But what went ye out for to see? a man clothed in soft raiment? behold, they that wear soft clothing are in kings' houses. But what went ye out for to see? a prophet? yea, I say unto you, and more than a prophet. For this is he of whom it is written, Behold, I send my messenger before thy face, which shall prepare thy way before thee.

Meditation
And blessed is he whosoever shall not be offended in me. St. Matthew 11. 6

PSALMS OF PRAISE AND THANKSGIVING (41)

Let everything praise the Lord

Let every thing that hath breath : praise the Lord. Psalm 150. 6

Psalm 103. *Benedic, anima mea*

YEA, like as a father pitieth his own children : even so is the Lord merciful unto them that fear him.

14. For he knoweth whereof we are made : he remembereth that we are but dust.

15. The days of man are but as grass : for he flourisheth as a flower of the field.

16. For as soon as the wind goeth over it, it is gone : and the place thereof shall know it no more.

17. But the merciful goodness of the Lord endureth for ever and ever upon them that fear him : and his righteousness upon children's children;

18. Even upon such as keep his covenant : and think upon his commandments to do them.

19. The Lord hath prepared his seat in heaven : and his kingdom ruleth over all.

20. O praise the Lord, ye angels of his, ye that excel in strength : ye that fulfil his commandment, and hearken unto the voice of his words.

21. O praise the Lord, all ye his hosts : ye servants of his that do his pleasure.

22. O speak good of the Lord, all ye works of his, in all places of his dominion : praise thou the Lord, O my soul.

GOD OUR SAVIOUR

Righteousness shall go before him : and shall direct his going in the way.

Psalm 85. 13

Psalm 85. *Benedixisti, Domine*

L ORD, thou art become gracious unto thy land : thou hast turned away the captivity of Jacob.

2. Thou hast forgiven the offence of thy people : and covered all their sins.

3. Thou hast taken away all thy displeasure : and turned thyself from thy wrathful indignation.

4. Turn us then, O God our Saviour : and let thine anger cease from us.

5. Wilt thou be displeased at us for ever : and wilt thou stretch out thy wrath from one generation to another?

6. Wilt thou not turn again, and quicken us : that thy people may rejoice in thee?

7. Shew us thy mercy, O Lord : and grant us thy salvation.

8. I will hearken what the Lord God will say concerning me: for he shall speak peace unto his people, and to his saints, that they turn not again.

9. For his salvation is nigh them that fear him : that glory may dwell in our land.

10. Mercy and truth are met together : righteousness and peace have kissed each other.

PREPARING FOR CHRISTMAS

In the beginning was the Word, and the Word was with God, and the Word was God. St. John 1. 1

The Gospel. *St. John 1. 1*
From 'Christmas Day'

IN the beginning was the Word, and the Word was with God, and the Word was God. The same was in the beginning with God. All things were made by him; and without him was not any thing made that was made. In him was life; and the life was the light of men. And the light shineth in darkness; and the darkness comprehended it not. There was a man sent from God, whose name was John. The same came for a witness, to bear witness of the light, that all men through him might believe. He was not that light, but was sent to bear witness of that light. That was the true light, which lighteth every man that cometh into the world. He was in the world, and the world was made by him, and the world knew him not. He came unto his own, and his own received him not. But as many as received him, to them gave he power to become the sons of God, even to them that believe on his Name: which were born, not of blood, nor of the will of the flesh, nor of the will of man, but of God. And the Word was made flesh, and dwelt among us (and we beheld his glory, the glory as of the only-begotten of the Father) full of grace and truth.

SAINT THOMAS THE APOSTLE

And Thomas answered and said unto him, My Lord, and my God
St. John 20. 28

The Collect
From 'Saint Thomas the Apostle'

ALMIGHTY and everliving God, who for the more confirmation of the faith didst suffer thy holy Apostle Thomas to be doubtful in thy Son's resurrection ; Grant us so perfectly, and without all doubt, to believe in thy Son Jesus Christ, that our faith in thy sight may never be reproved. Hear us, O Lord, through the same Jesus Christ, to whom, with thee and the Holy Ghost, be all honour and glory, now and fore evermore. Amen.

The Gospel. *St. John 20. 24*
From 'Saint Thomas the Apostle'

THOMAS, one of the twelve, called Didymus, was not with them when Jesus came. The other disciples therefore said unto him, We have seen the Lord. But he said unto them, Except I shall see in his hands the print of the nails, and put my finger into the print of the nails, and thrust my hand into his side, I will not believe. And after eight days again his disciples were within, and Thomas with them: then came Jesus, the doors being shut, and stood in the midst, and said, Peace be unto you. Then saith he to Thomas, Reach hither thy finger, and behold my hands; and reach hither thy hand, and thrust it into my side.

HE SENT HIS ONLY SON
INTO THE WORLD

Sing and rejoice, O daughter of Zion : for, lo, I come, and I will dwell in the midst of thee, saith the Lord. Zechariah 2. 10

The Epistle. *1 St. John 4. 7*
From 'The First Sunday After Trinity'

BELOVED, let us love one another : for love is of God; and every one that loveth is born of God, and knoweth God. He that loveth not knoweth not God; for God is love. In this was manifested the love of God towards us, because that God sent his only-begotten Son into the world, that we might live through him. Herein is love, not that we loved God, but that he loved us, and sent his Son to be the propitiation for our sins. Beloved, if God so loved us, we ought also to love one another. No man hath seen God at any time. If we love one another, God dwelleth in us, and his love is perfected in us. Hereby know we that we dwell in him, and he in us; because he hath given us of his Spirit. And we have seen, and do testify, that the Father sent the Son to be the Saviour of the world. Whosoever shall confess that Jesus is the Son of God, God dwelleth in him, and he in God. And we have known and believed the love that God hath to us. God is love; and he that dwelleth in love dwelleth in God, and God in him. Herein is our love made perfect, that we may have boldness in the day of judgement; because as he is, so are we in this world. There is no fear in love; but perfect love casteth out fear; because fear hath torment: he that feareth is not made perfect in love. We love him, because he first loved us.

THE EVE OF CHRISTMAS EVE

God ... hath in these last days spoken unto us by his Son. Hebrews 1. 1–2

The Collect
From 'The First Sunday in Advent'

ALMIGHTY God, give us grace that we may cast away the works of darkness, and put upon us the armour of light, now in the time of this mortal life, in which thy Son Jesus Christ came to visit us in great humility; that in the last day, when he shall come again in his glorious Majesty, to judge both the quick and the dead, we may rise to the life immortal; through him who liveth and reigneth with thee and the Holy Ghost, now and ever. Amen.

The Epistle. *Philippians 4. 4*
From 'The Fourth Sunday in Advent'

REJOICE in the Lord alway: and again I say, Rejoice. Let your moderation be known unto all men. The Lord is at hand. Be careful for nothing: but in every thing, by prayer and supplication with thanksgiving, let your requests be made known unto God. And the peace of God, which passeth all understanding, shall keep your hearts and minds through Christ Jesus.

HELP FROM THE LORD

The Lord is at hand. Philippians 4. 5

The Collect
From 'The Fourth Sunday in Advent'

O LORD, raise up (we pray thee) thy power, and come among us, and with great might succour us ; that whereas, through our sins and wickedness, we are sore let and hindered in running the race that is set before us, thy bountiful grace and mercy may speedily help and deliver us; through the satisfaction of thy Son our Lord, to whom with thee and the Holy Ghost be honour and glory, world without end. Amen.

The Gospel. *St. John 1. 19*
From 'The Fourth Sunday in Advent'

T HIS is the record of John, when the Jews sent Priests and Levites from Jerusalem to ask him, Who art thou? And he confessed, and denied not; but confessed, I am not the Christ. And they asked him, What then? Art thou Elias? And he saith, I am not. Art thou that Prophet? And he answered, No. Then said they unto him, Who art thou? that we may give an answer to them that sent us. What sayest thou of thyself? He said, I am the voice of one crying in the wilderness, Make straight the way of the Lord, as said the prophet Esaias … I baptize with water: but there standeth one among you, whom ye know not: he it is who coming after me is preferred before me, whose shoe's latchet I am not worthy to unloose.

CHRISTMAS DAY

And she brought forth her firstborn son, and wrapped him in swaddling clothes, and laid him in a manger; because there was no room for them in the inn.

St. Luke 2. 7

The Epistle. *Hebrews 1. 1–12*
From 'Christmas Day'

GOD, who at sundry times and in divers manners spake in time past unto the fathers by the prophets, hath in these last days spoken unto us by his Son, whom he hath appointed heir of all things, by whom also he made the worlds; who being the brightness of his glory, and the express image of his person, and upholding all things by the word of his power, when he had by himself purged our sins, sat down on the right hand of the Majesty on high; being made so much better than the angels, as he hath by inheritance obtained a more excellent name than they. For unto which of the angels said he at any time, Thou art my Son, this day have I begotten thee? And again, I will be to him a Father, and he shall be to me a Son? And again, when he bringeth in the first-begotten into the world, he saith, And let all the angels of God worship him. And of the angels he saith, Who maketh his angels spirits, and his ministers a flame of fire. But unto the Son he saith, Thy throne, O God, is for ever and ever; a sceptre of righteousness is the sceptre of thy kingdom: Thou hast loved righteousness, and hated iniquity; therefore God, even thy God, hath anointed thee with the oil of gladness above thy fellows.

STEPHEN, THE FIRST
CHRISTIAN MARTYR

And they stoned Stephen, calling upon God, and saying, Lord Jesus, receive my spirit. Acts 7. 59

The Collect
From 'Saint Stephen's Day'

GRANT, O Lord, that in all our sufferings here upon earth for the testimony of thy truth, we may stedfastly look up to heaven, and by faith behold the glory that shall be revealed; and, being filled with the Holy Ghost, may learn to love and bless our persecutors, by the example of thy first Martyr Saint Stephen, who prayed for his murderers to thee, O blessed Jesus, who standest at the right hand of God to succour all those that suffer for thee, our only Mediator and Advocate. Amen.

For the Epistle. *Acts 7. 55*
From 'Saint Stephen's Day'

STEPHEN, being full of the Holy Ghost, looked up stedfastly into heaven, and saw the glory of God, and Jesus standing on the right hand of God, and said, Behold, I see the heavens opened, and the Son of Man standing on the right hand of God. Then they cried out with a loud voice, and stopped their ears, and ran upon him with one accord, and cast him out of the city, and stoned him: and the witnesses laid down their clothes at a young man's feet, whose name was Saul ... And he kneeled down, and cried with a loud voice, Lord, lay not this sin to their charge.

THE DISCIPLE WHOM
JESUS LOVED

That which we have seen and heard declare we unto you, that ye also may have fellowship with us; and truly our fellowship is with the Father, and with his Son Jesus Christ. 1 St. John 1. 3

The Epistle. *1 St. John 1. 1*
From 'Saint John the Evangelist's Day'

THAT which was from the beginning, which we have heard, which we have seen with our eyes, which we have looked upon, and our hands have handled, of the word of life; (for the life was manifested, and we have seen it, and bear witness, and shew unto you that eternal life, which was with the Father, and was manifested unto us;) That which we have seen and heard declare we unto you, that ye also may have fellowship with us; and truly our fellowship is with the Father, and with his Son Jesus Christ. And these things write we unto you, that your joy may be full. This then is the message which we have heard of him, and declare unto you, That God is light, and in him is no darkness at all. If we say that we have fellowship with him, and walk in darkness, we lie, and do not the truth: but if we walk in the light, as he is in the light, we have fellowship one with another, and the blood of Jesus Christ his Son cleanseth us from all sin. If we say that we have no sin, we deceive ourselves, and the truth is not in us. If we confess our sins, he is faithful and just to forgive us our sins, and to cleanse us from all unrighteousness. If we say that we have not sinned, we make him a liar, and his word is not in us.

INNOCENTS' DAY

Herod will seek the young child to destroy him. St. Matthew 2. 13

The Collect
From 'The Innocents' Day'

O ALMIGHTY God, who out of the mouths of babes and sucklings hast ordained strength, and madest infants to glorify thee by their deaths; Mortify and kill all vices in us, and so strengthen us by thy grace, that by the innocency of our lives, and constancy of our faith even unto death, we may glorify thy holy Name; through Jesus Christ our Lord. Amen.

The Gospel. *St. Matthew 2. 13*
From 'The Innocents' Day'

T HE Angel of the Lord appeareth to Joseph in a dream, saying, Arise, and take the young child, and his mother, and flee into Egypt, and be thou there until I bring thee word; for Herod will seek the young child to destroy him. When he arose, he took the young child and his mother by night, and departed into Egypt, and was there until the death of Herod; that it might be fulfilled which was spoken of the Lord by the prophet, saying, Out of Egypt have I called my Son. Then Herod, when he saw that he was mocked of the wise men, was exceeding wroth; and sent forth, and slew all the children that were in Bethlehem, and in all the coasts thereof, from two years old and under.

REMEMBERING CHRISTMAS

And she shall bring forth a Son, and thou shalt call his name JESUS; for he shall save his people from their sins. St. Matthew 1. 21

The Collect
From 'Christmas-Day'

ALMIGHTY God, who hast given us thy only-begotten Son to take our nature upon him, and as at this time to be born of a pure Virgin: Grant that we being regenerate, and made thy children by adoption and grace, may daily be renewed by thy Holy Spirit; through the same our Lord Jesus Christ, who liveth and reigneth with thee and the same Spirit, ever one God, world without end. Amen.

Psalm 89. *Misericordias Domini*

MY song shall be alway of the loving-kindness of the Lord : with my mouth will I ever be shewing thy truth from one generation to another.

2. For I have said, Mercy shall be set up for ever : thy truth shalt thou stablish in the heavens.

3. I have made a covenant with my chosen : I have sworn unto David my servant:

4. Thy seed will I stablish for ever : and set up thy throne from one generation to another.

DAILY RENEWED BY
THE HOLY SPIRIT

Every day will I give thanks unto thee : and praise thy Name for ever and ever.
Psalm 145. 2

The Collect
From 'Christmas Day'

ALMIGHTY God, who hast given us thy only-begotten Son to take our nature upon him, and as at this time to be born of a pure Virgin: Grant that we being regenerate, and made thy children by adoption and grace, may daily be renewed by thy Holy Spirit; through the same our Lord Jesus Christ, who liveth and reigneth with thee and the same Spirit, ever one God, world without end. Amen.

The Proper Preface Upon Christmas Day
From 'Holy Communion'

IT is very meet, right, and our bounden duty, that we should at all times, and in all places, give thanks unto thee, O Lord, Holy Father, Almighty, Everlasting God.

Because thou didst give Jesus Christ thine only Son to be born as at this time for us; who, by the operation of the Holy Ghost, was made very man of the substance of the Virgin Mary his mother; and that without spot of sin, to make us clean from all sin.

ADOPTED INTO GOD'S FAMILY

*God sent forth his Son, made of a woman, made under the law, to redeem them
that were under the law, that we might receive the adoption of sons.*

Galatians 4. 4–5

The Gospel. *St. Matthew 1. 18*
From 'The Sunday After Christmas Day'

NOW the birth of Jesus Christ was on this wise: When as his mother
Mary was espoused to Joseph, before they came together she was
found with child of the Holy Ghost. Then Joseph her husband, being a just
man, and not willing to make her a publick example, was minded to put
her away privily. But while he thought on these things, behold, the angel
of the Lord appeared unto him in a dream, saying, Joseph thou son of
David, fear not to take unto thee Mary thy wife; for that which is conceived in her is of the Holy Ghost: and she shall bring forth a Son, and
thou shalt call his name JESUS; for he shall save his people from their sins.
(Now all this was done, that it might be fulfilled which was spoken of the
Lord by the prophet, saying, Behold, a Virgin shall be with child, and shall
bring forth a Son, and they shall call his name Emmanuel, which being interpreted is, God with us.) Then Joseph, being raised from sleep, did as the
angel of the Lord had bidden him, and took unto him his wife; and knew
her not till she had brought forth her first-born son : and he called his
name JESUS.